To:
Maurice
from Margaret.
August 27th 2000.

Events in the Womb of Time:
A Damfool Career

Events in the Womb of Time:
A Damfool Career

J. L. C. Strang

*To Maurice with many happy
birthdays to come. It is a great
pleasure for me to know that those
who read this book really enjoy it,
because it is true throughout.*

Jim Strang.

The Pentland Press Limited
Edinburgh • Cambridge • Durham • USA

First published in 2000 by
The Pentland Press Ltd.
1 Hutton Close
South Church
Bishop Auckland
Durham

British Library Cataloguing in Publication Data.
A Catalogue record for this book is available
from the British Library.

ISBN 1 85821 741 5

Typeset by CBS, Martlesham Heath, Ipswich, Suffolk
Printed and bound in Great Britain by Bookcraft (Bath) Ltd.

To my beloved wife,
without whose support and joy of living
the volumes of *Events in the Womb of Time*
would probably never have been written.

Preface

This book is a memoir which, because it begins in 1947, required a reconstruction of actual events, stories, descriptions of life in north-east India, with characters speaking in the way of those times in dialogues which evince much more atmosphere and interest than the author could create without them. There are fictitious characters who are accredited with collected stories to reduce the long list of names; there are actual characters with fictitious names who would recognise themselves with approval and amusement. Planters, tribal people on or off the estates, the wild life and the wonder of the Himalayan foothills are all the material of this book. The British planters continued working for three and a half decades or more after Independence, and the book will tell how they liked living in Assam.

Chapter I

Before explaining the origin of the term 'a Damfool Career' let me relate how a young man who had thought himself settled in a flying career with the RAF, made a sudden and unpredictable change of direction. Several of his friends, admirable and decorated ancients of twenty-five, twenty-six, had left the squadron for university, or to join their fathers' businesses. Some took the plunge without any clear idea of what they were going to do. It takes time for some of us to make new friends, and one of the Spitfire squadrons being disbanded made it difficult for the leftovers from one to make a sudden change of loyalty to the other; but at least there were good types, good pilots: Jag, a returned prisoner of war, keen on flying and excellent at aerobatics; Ted and Shag, good in the air and on the ground, both steady characters. In the post-war period there was no swift return to the golden days of peace: the whole nation's food continued to be strictly rationed, and wartime dreams of toast thickly spread with golden butter, apple pie with cream, and bananas, gave way to a kind of sour resentment that victory was turning out to be more of a punitive austerity than a return to the good old days. In the RAF there was an additional rationing which hit us hard. Except for survey photography, and high-altitude cruising to explore (as one later found out) the after-effects of the atomic bombs which had been dropped on Japan, flying exercises were rationed to four hours per month for each pilot. None of us would have admitted the truth, that for us peace had arrived too soon, frustrating our thirst for death or glory; and we hid this guilt. There was vague disillusion, and even the attitudes of ground crews were changing from the keen dedication of the War to the boredom of being in a backwater, without the stimulating urgency of the past six years.

In mid-1946 therefore, when the Air Ministry wanted a pilot from our squadron to take a Spitfire out to the Far East, I volunteered immediately. It meant plenty of flying hours, and I was to plan my route to suit the distance possible for this aircraft, using a belly tank with an extra 90 gallons of fuel, landing at any RAF airfield within reason, all the way to Bangkok. The prospect of revisiting old haunts along the North African coast and Palestine, perhaps to meet old friends, took me on a splendid trip in a beautiful aircraft, cruising at 28,500 feet all the way. This is not intended to be a romance about flying; the trip with all its landings and happy meetings in Mersa Matruh and Palestine went well. It was a thrill to land at Petah Tiqva, and find the officers' mess still being served by the same jovial Italian prisoners who were there in 1944. On the Spitfire squadron there I was delighted to find the inimitable Mike Castle, ex-medical student, with whom I had done my flying training in Southern Rhodesia. He described his frightful experience in the King David Hotel in Jerusalem when canoodling with the charming girl he later married. Just at a most passionate moment 'that bastorial terrorist bomb went off with such a helluva noise that we thought we were suddenly in the dock on the day of the last judgement!' It was the last time we met, and I have never been lucky enough to meet him again. Unless he was killed in action, or lives still in some quiet village in Devon and comes across this mention of his name, it might be another case of youth taking too much for granted, and realising it too late. From Palestine onwards it was for me all new territory. It was also strange new weather, with the monsoon due to arrive whilst I flew across India. After a marvellously explosive curry in Karachi, I took off for Allahabad sweating in my thick clothes and furry boots which I needed at height, bouncing in the turbulent haze even at high altitude, and hoping I would be able to see the famous great rivers of India to find my way to Allahabad. I knew it would be extremely hot there, and made up my mind to descend at fair speed, to be able to land and strip off my thick clothes quickly. At just above 20,000 feet I was horrified to miss a vulture by about fifty yards, and immediately checked my oxygen supply to see if I was suffering from the shortage known to simulate intoxication. I found my destination, and began to descend rapidly, but the lower air was extremely humid, and my cockpit canopy misted over inside and out, thus I was forced to circle at 10,000 feet, suffering the warming up of the aircraft to clear the condensation enough

2

for me to see what I was doing. The turbulence was violent, and I began to regret the large hot curry I had eaten. The radio reception was poor, but I hoped they had more or less understood that a Spitfire was approaching to land. Riding the bucking aircraft as carefully as I could I straightened out of the steeply curved approach to land, and luckily touched down without trouble, only to discover that my engine had stalled, and the five-bladed propeller stopped as I coasted off at the intersection. I told control of my trouble, and managed to reach the taxi track before coming to a halt. Later I learned the ambient temperature was 48 degrees Celsius, but at the time I simply leapt from the cockpit, burning my hands on the hot metal frame of the windscreen, and began disrobing at speed, trying to seek refuge in the shade of the outer wing.

It soon became clear I would have to wait until a new magneto arrived from Britain to replace the one which had been found faulty: a very unusual occurrence with a Rolls Royce engine. In the event I waited for about a week. The heat was worse than anything I had ever experienced even in Africa and the Middle East, and that must have been part of the effect on the very poor morale of the ground crews and officers of that place. The flight sergeant fitter was a regular, and told me his men were fed up to the teeth with having to stay in this godforsaken place whilst others were taking all the available jobs back in Britain. I had my old tropical kit with me, and enjoyed being back in shirt and shorts again. I spent most of the time in the swimming pool, wearing a sun helmet as soon as the sun was well up. I made friends with the officers there, and was invited one evening to join some of them attending a farewell party at an army officers' mess, for a colonel who was being demobbed. Things were rather tense in Allahabad at that time, with several outbreaks of Hindu-Muslim trouble, and we were told to wear revolvers when outside the air force station. The party went well. It was the first time I had come across an assembly of British and Indian officers in one officers' mess, and I found it quite fascinating. There was much happy drinking, and I spoke with many of the army types, Indian and British. It was very impressive to hear the same from all of them: they worshipped their commanding officer, and were very sorry to be losing him. Eventually, after a most amusing conversation with a hefty south Indian captain, who invited me to spend a holiday some time with him on a coffee plantation in the hills of the south, I turned and saw the CO, moving from

3

one group to a space on the crowded floor. He stood gazing around, chewing a pipe, with a white bull terrier at his feet, and I hinted I would like to meet him, whereupon the captain took me over and introduced me to his 'boss' with a huge smile. The CO was lean, brown, and had a faraway look in his eyes, with a very faint smile. He said he had heard I was the pilot of the Spitfire which had landed some days ago, and asked me odd questions about where I had come from, where I was bound. In time I said it must be a wrench for him to leave his unit, with so many officers giving him such praise whilst lamenting his departure. He surprised me by saying, 'Yes, they are a grand bunch, and so were the chaps we left buried in Burma; but I've had enough of the Army and I can't get out soon enough, back to civvy street.' This was a surprise to me, and I confess I thought the idea of civvy street was depressing. I asked him what he was going to do; which part of England would he work in; did he have a family?

He smiled and shook his head. 'I'm going back to my old job,' he said. 'In 1935 I came out to India to be a tea planter, in Assam. I've dreamed about it all the time, and can't wait to get back to it.'

This shook me. 'A tea planter! I've never met a tea planter before.' I remembered my father saying once that tea planters were a damned hard drinking crowd. 'Tell me about it, please. I haven't the vaguest idea about what it could be like.'

He obviously wasn't a hard drinker, as he refused all offers of drink by the various majors and captains who came to us every now and then, sometimes joking at me as a pilot who was a teetotaller; but he began to speak about the life he loved, often gazing into the distance, and although it was many, many years ago I remember the gist of it. It was not a life for the socially minded, not where he lived, in a rather wild district up in the north-east. One needed plenty of good books, good fishing tackle, a gun, a rifle, plenty of good gramophone records (before the days of electric players); and one should have no tendency to drink too much. The harvest season lasted about eight months, the middle five of which were hot, humid, with long hours of work and a lack of communications. The other four months were known as the cold weather, wood fires at night, cords and sweaters at morning office, but after breakfast into shorts in the splendid alpine summer weather. No harvesting, plenty of time for fishing, shooting, sometimes a game of polo or two, and beautiful scenery, birds of every kind, vast areas

4

of unpopulated country where wild duck and wild animals abounded. The work was, once one knew enough about it and could speak to people in their own languages, mostly out of doors with country people; many were tribal folk who knew more about the original world than oneself, and were a pleasure to work with. There was much more, but it was clear that for this man it was a rare thing: a full life. He began to switch the conversation back at me.

'You obviously like flying a lot, especially Spitfires; but how long are you going to be able to carry on just for the joy of flying Spitfires? You're twenty-two you say. Isn't it time you began to grow up, time to find a fuller and lasting kind of life?' His words burned into my very narrow mind: 'You can't expect to go on flying Spitfires all your life, can you? Even if you stay in the Air Force you won't enjoy being a uniformed clerk, to be posted sometimes where you don't want to go, until the time you either move up to exalted rank, or have to leave just when you are in your prime at forty something.' He was smiling as he spoke, but the directness was an unexpected criticism; I think I resented it at the time, although I admired him and what he described of his life in the wilderness. At school before the War I had vague ambitions of exploring wild places, and was influenced by people like Peter Fleming, Lawrence of Arabia, and the Everest climbers, and had often said I wanted to trek the whole way along the foothills of the Himalayas, turning south from Upper Assam down to the Shan States, Burma, and eventually to what was then called Siam. He left me in a state of mental disturbance, in which I found it so difficult to try myself for the crime of what I later christened as infantile paralysis of the personality, that my subconscious archivist put the meeting away for a period.

When the magneto arrived and was fitted, I flight-tested the aircraft and made plans to continue my journey: next stop Calcutta – Dum Dum airfield. The wing commander (flying) at Allahabad told me I was not to fly alone to Calcutta, and he was arranging for a Mosquito fighter to lead me there in formation. I tried to explain the Spitfire was a pressure cabin aircraft, and should not be flown too long in the heat of lower latitudes because of the pressure glands at the canopy joints, but he was adamant. I tried to explain my engine used fuel with more than the normal amount of lead, and could not cruise for long throttled back without a risk of spark plugs being too cool and 'leading up', but again he was adamant.

The following day I dutifully flew off in formation with the slim pinkish Mosquito, which levelled off at something like 9,000 feet, cruising at (memory fails) something like 240 m.p.h., which was a worrying combination for me, as apart from the other drawbacks my consumption at 86 gallons per hour would not leave me with much reserve. Within an hour we ran into tremendous vertical development of cumulus and cumulo-nimbus cloud, with vicious turbulence. This was the leading edge of the monsoon, arriving on time in June. The Mosquito climbed to 12,000 feet, but finding the cloud was beginning to close below us, he waved his wings and turned to head back to Allahabad, I turned with him, but opened formation so that I could look below at the Ganges through gaps in the cloud. I soon found enough to confirm a fairly good position, and with what I can in later life recognise as conceited foolhardiness, I did a quick appraisal of range and fuel, looked at the time, and set course, climbing for Calcutta. Levelling off at 28,500 feet I found myself cruising amongst the anvil tops of the massive thunder clouds. After a long time I tried calling Dum Dum, but the electrical interference amongst the lightning of these clouds made it impossible to hear any reply. I began to descend on course through thick, darkening cloud on my reckoned plan of approach to Calcutta, and tightened my safety harness as the aircraft bounced violently, hoping my directional gyro would behave in spite of the turbulence. The magnetic compass went mad in the continuous lightning in cloud, and I began to regret not having turned back, as my fuel situation began to look rather demanding of accurate navigation for which perfectly clear skies were generally desirable. At the estimated time of arrival over Calcutta I still had no radio contact, and had descended to 800 feet with no sign of a break or of cloud base. Knowing Calcutta to be at sea level was comforting, but I was warned there would be tall factory chimneys, and the Victoria Memorial! I decided quickly to fly south for fifteen minutes with superb conviction that I was on track, so that I would be able to descend further over the labyrinth of channels of the Ganges, find the ships in the Hooghly, and fly north to Calcutta. This is what I thought I was doing, and I lost height to 300 feet, to break cloud into lashing torrents of rain. Within seconds I had to take quick evasive action to avoid a factory chimney about fifty feet below my wingtip. I slowed down to about 200 m.p.h., at which speed it was still possible to see through the rain on the windscreen, and began to turn in a large circle, unable to look at my map at this height, when suddenly a black airstrip flashed under my port wing, looking as if it was a smoothly flowing river. There were several RAF Dakotas parked there, and an Avro Anson. There was no windsock to be identified, but the tee indicated the direction for landing. Having about twenty minutes fuel left I decided to land.

I was not well received. It took a long time before a jeep came out and showed me where to park, which was a long way from the control tower. I thanked the Lord it was cooler here, although I was sweating from a combination of the humidity and the tension of my self-induced problems. I apologised to my guardian spirits for having put them to the trouble of coming to the rescue of such an idiot, and wondered with great reverence why I was allowed to get away with it. I had landed at Alipore. After about three-quarters of an hour the rain abated, and I climbed out, closed the hood, and trudged through the puddles to the control tower. That I was made to feel so bitterly unwelcome had very little effect on my normally hypersensitive character.

'No! There's no such thing as your hundred plus octane fuel here. You'll have to get it from Dum Dum. That's your problem. You shouldn't have landed here.'

Once I discovered how close we were to Dum Dum I decided the best thing I could do was to take off and fly there within a few minutes. Visibility was good enough. When I said I was going to take off someone said the trolley accumulator for Spitfires wasn't working. I said it didn't matter, I would swing the prop myself, and trudged off again. I hoped the cartridge starter would work and get me out of this miserable but oh, so welcome place, and it did, shaking the hidden occupants of the monsoon-stricken field so much by the loud explosion that many heads appeared from hatches, doors and windows, to see who was attacking them.

Dum Dum was better, far better. I stayed the night and next morning took off after an early breakfast for Rangoon, the next stop. From there I flew next day to Bangkok, where I delivered the sweet aeroplane in excellent condition, warning them that the controls were very stiff compared with unpressurised Spitfires. There were several old chums of earlier days there, and we enjoyed ourselves hugely, reminiscing the vast store of memories stored during our tiny air force lives. When I told the story of my arrival in

Calcutta, the CO gave me a withering rocket, telling me the time to imagine just what the result would be if I had killed myself and destroyed an expensive aircraft, is always to think it out before attempting such a stupid exploit. That night I didn't sleep for a long time, sweating with embarrassment, flinching repeatedly at imagining a crash landing without fuel, either in the Hooghly or in Calcutta.

After two days, during which I saw something of Bangkok, in those days mostly unsophisticated and still with its network of canals, much impressed with the beauty of the girls and the excellence of the Chinese food, I found the Air Force had a place for me on an aircraft bound for England. It was a shock to find myself assigned as 'additional second pilot' on a four-engined Sunderland flying boat. I had never flown anything bigger than the sedate old Avro Anson, a twin-engined aircraft resembling a single-decker bus with wings. It didn't take long for my pride to deflate. We set course for Calcutta, and climbed laboriously to about 8,000 feet, at which height we trundled at about 140 knots for hours, bouncing ponderously in the turbulence of the summer sea air. The catch was that the automatic pilot was out of order, which was why the extra second pilot was required. It was a different kind of flying: the huge hull contained a kitchen – called a galley by the crew – and there were two bunks which were really very comfortable after several hours at the controls. Eventually we landed on the Hooghly not far from Calcutta, and were taken ashore in a launch in reasonably fine weather. As far as I can remember we then had to wait for three days for a brace of generals who were to be taken to England. We were given rooms at a transit mess in a flat over shops in Park Street. There too things seemed to be tense with Hindu-Muslim disturbances becoming more frequent, and we carried revolvers whilst walking around. Just below the flat was the Oxford Book and Stationery Company, where I browsed amongst the books and finished up buying Gandhi's *Story of My Experiment With Truth*, and Lord Wavell's *Other Mens' Flowers*, the latter an anthology of poetry which still lies to hand, rebound, as an old favourite. I enjoyed the luxury of excellent Darjeeling tea in the packed lounge of the Grand Hotel, where service officers and businessmen sat and glowered about them. On the last day before we left I carried on exploring Calcutta, and found myself in the commercial 'city' area, where huge offices abounded, with displays of brass plates on each side of the huge portals. The streets were packed with people

8

of all kinds, hurrying about their business. I saw two burly Britishers in linen suits and ties, with files in the crooks of their arms, turning across my track to mount the stairs which led to an entry bordered with brass plates. I was curious to know what their business was, and went closer to the brass plates, looking for a clue.

I had not thought of the colonel's farewell party since I left Allahabad, having been very fully occupied and preoccupied in retrospect with my journey and outrageous luck; but when I saw on one of the brass plates the name 'British India Tea Company Ltd.' some perverse imp in my disoriented brain seemed to hiss in my ear, telling me: just have a look! I went into reception and started the pretty young ladies giggling when I asked to see the Manager of that company. Eventually I went through various doors, repeating I wanted to see the top man, and was finally shown through the door bearing the title of Chairman. I went forward and saluted, removed my hat, and shook the hand he offered.

'Well young man, what do you want with me?'

Some part of my mind appeared to have provided me with a plan of action, as I heard my voice quite calmly say 'Are you looking for young men like me to train as tea planters?'

'Yes, in fact we are. I think you are a pilot, aren't you?'

'Yes, sir.' Responding to his questions I explained how I came to be in Calcutta.

'How soon could you start?' he said smiling. 'We haven't been able to recruit during the War; most of our planters went off to the Army, Navy and Air Force, and we desperately need people like you as soon as possible.'

I asked him to tell me something about the life of a planter, and he did; but it was quite different from what the colonel had described: there was very good social life, plenty of tennis, bridge, good clubs where one met everyone; cricket in the cold weather, rugby in the rains. Daughters and nieces came out in the cold weather, known as the 'fishing fleet', and most of them found husbands within a few months. I asked about shooting, polo, fishing, and when I learned the best fishing was on the North Bank, I said I would much prefer to be in a remote, wilder area than in what sounded like somewhere not far from London. He wagged a finger and told me that those places were for people who misbehaved, got into debt, meddled with other mens' wives, upset the daughters of the labour force and so on, and

9

had to be sent off to the wilderness to teach them a lesson. Seeing my unenthusiastic expression he laughed heartily, and said that the wilderness was all very well, but too much of it could be bad for a man. Medical facilities were difficult over there, and sometimes the nearest hospitals which could operate on amputations or difficult deliveries were over a hundred miles away, over terrible roads; and in the rains half a dozen bridges would be washed away. 'We've lost some nasty cases, you know. Maybe it'll be better with antibiotics, if we can get them, but don't think the wilderness is a paradise, especially in the rains. I never even try to visit them on the north bank in the rains; but in the cold weather it is absolutely marvellous.'

He gave me a letter to the head office in London, telling me they would have to arrange an interview, but that I would be welcomed. I was interviewed soon after arriving in the battered grey city by the crusty old chairman of the group of tea companies to which the brass plate company also belonged. He was furious when I told him it would take time for me to leave the Air Force, as I wanted to transfer to the reserve.

'I don't want to take on people who might suddenly be called up if trouble breaks out again. We've had a terrible time trying to cope without all our young planters, and many of whom were killed, using all the old sweats from the First World War and not so old chaps too old for the War. We have several who are beyond retiring age, waiting to be released, some of whom haven't had any home leave since 1940.'

When I said in that case I would have to withdraw my application, he threw a tantrum and said, 'All right, damn it! But for goodness sake get a move on. I want you on a ship as soon as possible. Understand?'

'Yessir. I've been reading about government ideas on giving India home rule. How does that affect the future of those working in Assam?'

He threw his hands in the air, shaking his head vigorously. 'I'm damned if I know, young man. And I'm sure nobody else knows. It might happen. It might not happen. If you have been in the War you'll know you don't sit down and contemplate what might go wrong; you get down to it and do everything to ensure that whatever the enemy – and by that I mean the Labour government – does to us, we have at least tried to do our best to minimise the damage. I have a lot of money tied up in India, so its a huge risk for me. If you're not prepared to take a risk, then it's not for you!' His voice was raised, but the look in his fierce eyes was somehow appealing.

10

'I'll join, if I may.'

'Right, that's settled. The company secretary will organise everything. I'll call him. You have to understand that when you arrive in Assam you won't be a glamorous young air force officer any more. You'll be an apprentice, an understudy, a learner, starting from scratch, and there's a hell of a lot for you to learn. Got it?'

That is how I entered the tea life. London wanted me on the next ship, and were furious when I delayed for several months in order to arrange to transfer to the air force reserve. In one of my visits to the company secretary in the City of London, I learned the chairman was one of the top twelve richest men in Britain, that he had a heart of gold, and that his overbearing brusqueness was probably due to having poor eyesight, which dashed his hopes of becoming a fighter pilot in the first war. I was mollified to hear from the very benign company secretary that the chairman had described me as very promising material.

Finally I was booked to travel a few days after the beginning of January 1947. I had two weeks to go through the rather traumatic experience of metamorphosis before boarding the ship. Jag was despondent, and could not understand how I chose to give up the flying I so much enjoyed. We had been doing formation aerobatics together, far from prying eyes, and were achieving such proficiency that Jag – an ex-Cranwell man – had great ideas about us making a name; but I really felt in a trance. I knew I still dearly loved flying, but somehow I felt drawn away from the drab austerity of a Britain which seemed to be overcrowded, and which in a surprisingly short time had lost the remarkable wartime friendliness and morale which had been so encouraging.

It seemed I would spend the three months of my demobilisation leave in Assam learning to be a tea planter. This didn't worry me at all, as that winter was so depressing I could not leave it soon enough. Stunned by the farewells to my flying friends, to their wives, to the widows who were terrified of leaving the warm comradeship of the airfield village to take their small infants into a cold, different world, I took the train to Southampton on a bleak, bleak day. I was leaving my total fortune in a bank in Whitehall: £65, and trying to concentrate on garbled principles garnered from a mixture of religious books I had read amongst the tattered novels of the corrugated iron arches of the pilots' crew rooms. I was compelling myself to believe I

11

had made a reasonable and interesting choice, and must concentrate on doing my best for the sake of doing it. I hardly remember the train journey, but remember mounting the gangway.

Having been a troopship throughout the war the ship was still wearing its drab wartime colour, and although it had not yet been brought back to its pre-war splendour as a P & O passenger liner, it had been rendered infinitely more comfortable in comparison with the troopships which had cruised in convoy on various long journeys, all beginning through the dangerous wastes of the Atlantic. The weather matched the leaden hue of the ship, and turned the bleak sky, the sea, and the very faces of the people on and around the ship to the same colourless shade. The sky was a total expanse of grey cloud. The dull camouflage of the docks with their webs of dark cables produced a vague sense of grim enclosure. The cloud base was high but the cloud had no shape, and there was a chill wind from the north-east. There were many in their early twenties like myself, clad in officers' greatcoats with badges of rank removed, collars up, and I could see those on the quay below trying hard to laugh and slap backs in efforts to cheer up the assortment of moist-eyed girls and pale elderly parents, as well as themselves, before mounting the gangway which would lead to several years of separation and uncertainty. I was glad I had already said my farewells to my people far away in Scotland, and then in the south at the old pub next to the airfield. That had been a good send-off, with sentimental strains one never expected, including the five minutes sitting on a parachute in the cockpit, shaken by the welling up of emotion. That was the night before boarding, and Jag, Shag, and Ted had, in their cups, promised they would give me a farewell flypast in Southampton. You would see my wry grin as I thought of it; they would certainly not be feeling up to flying after that very late night session.

Having stood at the rail, gazing down at the intermittent flow of reluctant passengers for over an hour, and feeling myself sink dangerously near to the regret I had resolved never to allow, I decided to explore the upper deck and climbed until I found myself on the open expanse of the upper deck forrard. I could see more from here of the land I was about to leave. There were no other people around, only faint noises from those on the quay, and a low buzzing from a ventilator nearby. The note of the buzzing seemed to change, and I went closer to the ventilator to listen intently, but my ears persuaded my head to swing round, and high against the pale grey sky I saw three Spitfires in close vee formation at about 3,000 feet. They swung in a wide circle around the ship thus identifying themselves as Jag, Shag, and Ted. The formation flew to seaward losing height, about a quarter of a mile away to port on a course parallel to the ship, moving eventually far enough ahead to begin a steep descending turn to starboard, lining up dead ahead of the ship in a shallow dive, approaching at high speed. They barely cleared the mast in close formation, tearing the muffled blanket of indistinct sounds with a crash of rich and arrogant noise. Rising steeply whilst diverging from each other, they climbed back to around 3,000 feet. From the quay and the lower decks there came a ragged chorus of cheers and jeers. I hoped no-one would report this low flying, and watched as they curved round in well-spaced single file before diving again. Each of them performed a beautiful climbing slow roll, one after the other. They joined formation again, and flew low along the starboard side, with Jag in the lead gently rocking his wings in the gesture of farewell. I stood with both arms waving above my head, and watched them climb away northwards, my vision clouding, staring at the blurred specks until the spell was broken by a quiet voice immediately behind me.

'Friends of yours, I think?'

I nodded, reluctant to turn with moist eyes, and felt a gentle hand squeeze my shoulder firmly before quiet footsteps receded towards the companionway. I would have been disappointed had they not come, because we had never taken chances; but I would never have known quite so much concentrated sadness at the decision to give up flying those beautiful aeroplanes, to give up flying, full-stop. 'You might think that this is the end . . . well, it IS!' I hummed the last, truncated line of the strangely funny but tragic song of many, many parties in the Air Force, and turned to face my new life.

The ship left harbour just about dusk, and it was not long before we were making good way down the channel, with various saloons open for drinks. There were all the drinks of pre-war peacetime available at duty-free prices, and the liquor flowed liberally. Most of the passengers were old sweats, returning after their first home leaves for many years, a few with their wives; they were planters, bankers, merchants, civil servants and army officers in uniform. My meagre experience with alcohol was that for me, if I was depressed it would make me even more depressed, and I had lemonade with a tot of ginger ale in order to stave off those boozers who regarded it as an insult for anyone to remain teetotal in drinking circles. Dinner was wonderful: plenty of everything the poor rationed population of Britain dreamed about, and most of us ate fairly early and copiously; there was wonderful fruit salad and ice cream of which I had two helpings. After dinner I wandered around the various saloons, not exactly seeking company or even acquaintance, and finished up eventually quite late where there were less people, but one or two loud voices arguing in robust but jovial tones with a hint of acerbity showing through. One tough-looking Scot, flushed and bright-eyed, well lubricated with his national tope, wagged a finger at a scrum of several happy younger men and lectured them in rasping tones.

'You lot don't seem to have heard what this *corry jukit* [left-handed] government of yours is hellbent on doing to India. We've heard talk of giving India its independence at some time in the future when they show signs of being able to do it themselves; plenty of talk! Queen Victoria was always on about it long before even I went out to Assam. (He looked about thirty-two.) But this bunch wants to hand over to them and let them get on with it without any more cafuffle, and it might be sooner than you think, my fine fellows; and when it does it'll mean they can't wait to see the last of those who have sat on their necks since the East India Company first began. So what the hell do you lot think you're up to? Where the hell did you get the idea of a new career, in India of all places? Damfools the lot of you! What a damfool career! You must all be mad, or stupid, or worse!'

There was a chorus of happy jeers, but I noticed there were many of us smiling without the smile reaching the eyes.

'Come off it, Alastair!' A young Scot who obviously knew him spoke in a like accent. 'Where d'ye think you are going if it isn't Assam, the land of your dreams? You must be the biggest damfool of us all, surely!'

Alastair grinned, and put up a beefy hand to quell the noise. 'Aye, ye may well be right, but it's different for those like me. Five years before the War I joined tea, then I joined the Army, went into Burma, and spent three years on Death Railway under the Japs. You might not be able to understand that the idea of settling in Britain after all that is ab-so-lute-ly impossible.' His face seemed to swell, and his jaw clenched in a frightening grimace for a few seconds before relaxing into an attractive smile. 'But you lot! What

14

you don't understand is that you will be in India for just long enough to let it get under your skin. The people will drive you mad, the climate in the rains is intolerable, the Calcutta agents irritate you beyond belief, playing at being proconsuls; but you will fall so much in love with it all that when you are told it's time to leave you will realise just what a terrible mistake you have made. Yes! I am the biggest damfool of all, but there's no other way out for me. You lot should get off this ship in Bombay, work your passage back to Britain, or Canada, and pay off the ticket for this crazy journey once you find a job.'

That was how the term 'damfool career' came into being, and Alastair imprinted it so heavily that many of us discussed it at several intervals during the voyage. We found that Alastair had won the Military Cross in Burma, and whilst a Jap prisoner of war had his toenails pulled out one by one because he refused to kowtow to the low-ranking prison guards. One of his contemporaries warned us to watch his normally wrinkled forehead, and if it became smooth to leave him alone straight away. 'He'll be all right in Assam,' he said, 'the people up there understand that kind of thing.'

The Bay of Biscay was very efficient in keeping people below decks until we swung round in warm sunshine aiming for Gibraltar. The sombre outfits of the cold north gave way to shirts and, for the planters and ex-service officers who had been in warmer climes, shorts. It became easy to identify other ex-air force characters who had served or trained in Rhodesia or South Africa, by the unusually short shorts they wore. Some of the older Indian civil service people looked down their noses at us, and the ex-Indian army people strutted around in what were variously known as 'Bombay bloomers' or starched 'divided skirts', which seemed to remain rigid whilst the wearer moved his legs in a stately walk along the decks. The sun was glorious. There was plenty of deck tennis, some deck golf, shuffleboard, and much sunbathing in the friendly sunshine. It was good to meet others bound for Assam, most of them very similar in expectations and interests regarding wild life, and the exploring of remote areas.

After about a week an acquaintance introduced me to a character who had heard there was someone bound for the company he worked for in Assam, and he introduced himself with a broad smile. His name was Guy, from a family of well-known London stage actors. He was a handsome chap, with a military moustache and the large mobile mouth of an actor, with the clear diction which was in those days considered essential. He had been a captain in the Army, and like most of the others was really looking forward to returning to Assam. He put his head on one side, and with eyes twinkling asked me; 'You're the chap who was waving farewell to those Spitfires, aren't you?' I began to learn a great deal from him about the shape of my new career in Assam.

Before we reached the Suez Canal the subject of our damfool career had been rising and falling almost like a tide, every few days, and the general effect was to diminish its effect on us. There was an interesting character who was in the Indian civil service who loved India, loved his job, and seemed to suffer continuous depression at the thought of having to give it all up. He told us of the dreadful Hindu-Muslim riots in Calcutta, which must have happened shortly after we had lifted the Sunderland flying boat off the Hooghly. It was recorded as the Great Calcutta Killings, and had been horrible beyond belief. This man had heard a first-hand account from a colleague recently arrived in London with papers and photographs for the India Office and the Secretary of State. It was incredible that such terrible murders and mutilations could take place, and there was fear in London that the British in India would be accused of fomenting this kind of thing in order to prove India incapable of ruling itself. The army was used to collect the corpses and dismembered pieces which were left in the affected areas where the stench of decomposition was vile beyond belief necessitating the use of masks to prevent the clearance teams from vomiting. Morale amongst British troops involved was undoubtedly bad, and troops had been heard complaining this was not what they considered the wartime service they had either volunteered for or been called up to do. It seemed the Muslim League was hell bent on the idea of preventing the British from handing power to an India in which a vast majority of Hindus would stifle the political aspirations of the Muslims, and probably lead to unacceptable impositions or even bloody massacres. The example of the very massacres they feared was being madly displayed, with terrible portent.

Whilst those who wished disembarked at Suez, a group of us who had seen enough of Egypt gathered round an interesting character who had been a forestry officer in Malaya, and had managed to escape the Japanese by walking north to reach Assam, along largely trackless routes through the forested hills and labyrinthine valleys, with many dying on the way. There were four of us for Assam and one for Sylhet, and his advice was that if things went wrong, and it became impossible to reach safe airstrips to be lifted out, or to reach controlled seaports, it would be best to march northwards for Bhutan, Nepal or Tibet. This would mean strict training as soon as we got to Assam: hardening of our bare feet by walking as much as possible without shoes, because those who walked out of Burma who couldn't cope when their shoes wore out were the first to fall by the wayside. Practise carrying loaded packs; collect tins of things like meat and cheese; have sealed packets of raisins, parched rice and flour. Have sealed bottles of salt. Obtain a tribal flint, striker and dry tow for lighting fires. Acquire a throwing net and remove all the leaden weights, and have little cotton bags in which to load stones instead, and learn the art of netting small fry, marvellous food in the forest rivers of these areas. Take friars balsam, Collis Brownes Chlorodyne, and any sulfanilomide you can lay hands on. Take a small bottle of gentian violet, and plenty of any anti-malarial prophylactic tablets. A sharp bush-knife and a sharp small knife were most important; but on no account any firearms. He told us how to cut a green bamboo in order to boil water in the nodal cup, and recommended either dew or rainwater in leaves as the best for drinking. I think we were tickled at the idea of making such a trek, but Guy told me afterwards this sort of thing would probably not come to pass. He thought the British government would surely organise a proper evacuation of all its nationals before withdrawing the Army. 'It might not even happen,' he said, 'if the Hindus and Muslims carry on hacking each other to death there will probably be an outcry against the idea of home rule. Not everyone wants it, you know.' I think most of us were at a loss to know how to form an opinion, from sheer lack of knowledge.

Guy was a delightful raconteur, and kept me amused with character sketches of the members of the company hierarchy whose names I could never have hoped to remember. He went so fast I found it difficult to insert my questions between his anecdotes. He used many terms in Hindustani, and told me not to try to note them down, as I would learn fairly quickly once I had to deal with the vast majority of estate people who had no English at all. I showed him a book on Hindustani which I had bought and he laughed, saying it would have been quite good for the Indian Army, but the Hindustani used in Assam was a mixture of so many languages, including bits of Assamese and Bengali, with many other dialects thrown in. The language varied from estate to estate, depending on the mix of tribes. Labour was recruited from many parts of India, mainly because Assam was a fertile land with a remarkably low population density, and labour was simply not available for tea estates. Three of us who were pilots gravitated to Guy, whose lectures were highly entertaining as well as informative, and as we were all going to be in the area Guy knew well we could be fairly sure of what to expect. From other old sweats we heard stories which were anything but encouraging, but slowly a picture emerged of many different tea districts over a huge area stretching about 700 miles eastward from Darjeeling, through northern Bengal, all the way to Upper Assam on both sides of the Brahmaputra. Every district was further divided into smaller districts almost like the wine-growing areas of Europe, each having different levels of rainfall and fertility, some being clustered into social or club groups, and others where neighbours were ten to twenty miles or more apart. The voyage passed quickly; and with sunshine, good food, and much learning about what the damfool career could entail, morale rose. The risks in the future became ridiculously small, especially to the earthbound intrepid birdmen.

Chapter II

In the heat of the Red Sea there were many like myself who felt perfectly matched to the environment, prowling the deck in the sun, and lying in the shade like lions replete, gazing into the distance. The warm nights kept us on deck in the cool breezes, scanning the brilliant sky with the feeling that with a raised arm one could stir the mists of stars. We lay watching the foremast sway gently against the midnight blue, revelling in the friendly presence of the bright navigational stars. The thrill of seeing the Southern Cross, the brilliance of Sirius and Venus, and the flickering figures in our wandering brains of light year distances to the stars in the square of Pegasus all combined to intoxicate, or hypnotise. We agreed there was something like reverence for the mystery and beauty of what we saw night after night, understanding it no more than great music or a wonderful sunset but being deeply grateful for the immense display. One night there was an incredibly brilliant green bow wave, brighter than any of the ship's officers had ever seen in long years at sea, a luminescence that reflected on the many silent faces that watched for several hours. It was too beautiful to be uncanny, but it inspired awe even in the ancient mariners on board.

When we were two days from Bombay, communications seemed to increase remarkably between passengers, cutting across the automatic clustering of those with like destinations, similar interests, same war services. The young man who slept in the bunk below me, ex-Navy and very debonair, suddenly asked me where I was bound, and when I said Assam, to become a tea planter, he showed surprise and told me surely I could find something better to do than become a 'coolie counter'. He told me he was joining a bank in Bombay, where there was an ideal social set-up for young ex-service officers: plenty of sailing, bridge, tennis and cricket. I laughed at him and explained I wanted to get away from that sort of thing, to see something of the primeval world before it disappeared, but he was not at all impressed. I remember two rugged Scots, returning from army service to their planting jobs in Darjeeling, complaining they wanted to be posted to the plains for a change. Having thought Darjeeling must be a wonderful place to live I asked why they wanted a change, and they told me once the monsoon arrived the estates at 7-8,000 feet were often in thick mist for several weeks at a time, which made everyone depressed. I happened on a group of ex-army officers drinking light beer before what we had all begun to call 'tiffin' (lunch), telling each other of their liking for different types of Indian, mainly developed whilst serving with regiments recruited from particular districts and regions. There were two ex-Gurkha officers who could not speak highly enough of their favourite infantrymen, and told stories of their exploits. One tall hawk-faced fellow praised the Pathans, and spoke with a light in his eye of these tough men, also from the mountains; he reminded me of Lawrence's affection for the Bedouin. Another was for the Dogras, one for the Sikhs, two for the Rajputs, and one for the Coorgis. There was a real enthusiasm for the quality of these various types of soldier, which impressed me, and gave me a useful perspective on the amazing diversity of different races, tribes, castes and communities of this vast country. I began to be aware of India as a country of vastly different peoples with different languages and customs, thanks to these 'pongo' officers, who infected me with a keenness to find out more about the inhabitants of the country where I had chosen to live. It was not everyone on the ship who showed that kind of enthusiasm; one heard endless criticisms of the people, the laziness, the corruption, the heat, snakes and insects; but there tended to be a pattern showing the complainers to be those living in towns, cities, crowded areas. India was surely not the only country in the world where the people in the remote rural areas were known as 'the salt of the earth'.

One began to hear more and more about 'old women' which was the name for live-in mistresses. It was said that in earlier days when tea estates were being created in a virtual wilderness, conditions were not considered suitable for European women, and it became common for planters to find suitably attractive companions, mainly from some of the hill tribes to the south of the Assam Valley. Guy pointed out that the Assam Valley was in many places over a hundred miles wide, from the Himalayas and their foothills, to the north to the Naga, Khasi and Mikir Hills to the south. His tales about 'old women' were very interesting, and he warned us never to be so ill-advised as to become involved with any of the immigrant tribes who worked on the estates. Some were very attractive, and as he said, 'You might be unimpressed when you first arrive, but after many months living on your own, working hard and feeding well, you will undoubtedly find – especially in the Indian spring – that nature with its perennial purpose sends all the scented blossoms, birdcalls and orchids, and girls' voices singing mischievously in the warm dusk; then, my dear chaps, you will find many look lovely, and you will have to be very much on your guard. Be warned! He described how many tyros found it too easy to organise an 'old woman', and went into it with little forethought or imagination, finishing up with squalid disputes that often cost them dear when they realised the girl of their choice was in fact an embarrassing nuisance. He was quite emphatic about his own intention to marry soon, but kept his plans to himself.

Our estimated time of arrival in Bombay was early enough in the day for Guy to surmise that the company's agents would put us straight onto the train for Calcutta, which meant I would not have time enough to see much of the city of Bombay. That is in fact what happened. We saw the monumental Gateway to India, a huge arch which some of the old sweats were calling the gateway from India. 'And never too soon for me,' one old sweat was saying as we neared the harbour. He was fifty, and said he had five more years to do before retiring, and would probably make it before 'the balloon went up', as he put it. As we drew closer there was an increase in noise from the harbour, where many figures seemed to be moving in preparation for our docking. Overhead the seagulls and crows added to the din, and kitehawks trilled and gyrated, watching for the intermittent discharging of food from lower portholes. The sea breeze was welcome, but it promised to be warm. Guy came up behind me and shouted over the noise, pointing to a well-dressed Mexican-looking gentleman, with moustache and sideburns like a cowboy film villain, who was scanning the ship from a vantage point near the customs entry. 'That's or chap! Beppi di Mello. Thank goodness! He'll look after us, don't worry. He'll come aboard soon, and I'll catch him outside the Purser's Office below. See me there once the gangway is down. He'll have some rupees for us. I don't think you'll have time enough to spend any, but the idea is to make sure you have fifty chips [rupees] to show your appreciation for his services. He's a company man, but he really is worth a good tip, and he is likely to remember those who either forget or deny such recognition so that even although it might be four years before one requires his services to see one safely on the ship returning home, one might find it difficult to raise his enthusiasm to its previous level.' With a sly grin Guy disappeared. Di Mello was a godsend. Guy was polite and jovial; our baggage seemed to come smoothly out of the scrums of quarrelling stevedores, mostly clad in turbans and loincloths, sweating and yelling and pushing each other furiously. We were taken by taxi to the railway station, and loaded into a compartment with bunks and seats, and our heavy baggage was stowed in the luggage truck where it would be securely locked all the way to Calcutta. We were two hours early, but felt this was the way to do it. It was warm and rather humid away from the sea breeze but Guy promised it would be cooler once we were on the move on what was to be nearly three days' journey: a thousand miles to Calcutta.

It was interesting to see many passengers from our ship arriving later in the increasing congregation of porters, officials, beggars and pedlars of various wares, edible (but not recommended), wearable, and 'presentable'. On Guy's advice I showed no interest. A strange entourage arrived to enter the compartment next to ours: an ill-looking Bengali with a slim, rather serious-faced woman who turned out to be German. The other Indians who had helped them along with their baggage made Nazi salutes with very stiff expressions before leaving them. The lady was dressed rather untidily in Indian clothes, and looked very lost and unsure, as if India was very new to her. The Bengali wore a long dhoti and a rough grey Western sports jacket; he never looked at us at all the whole way. We heard them speak German, but neither of us was able to understand, and in any case they seemed to avoid being overheard, just in case. We had several books to read, and when Guy saw I had Forster's *Passage to India* he said it was a good thing I had not read it on board ship, because many Britishers who lived in India, especially some of the 'heaven born' Indian Civil Service people, took a very dim view of the way they were portrayed. I read the book through on the journey, and found it quite fascinating, and decided to read it again after I had been a year in the country. We had collected mail from Mr di Mello, and I showed my letter from Calcutta to Guy who guffawed and promised he would give me descriptions of all those under whom I would work in the superintendency of George, laird of four estates which had factories, and another four smaller estates without factories. He was always warning me he had opinions of his own about people, and cautioned me never to be amazed at the incredible differences of opinion of different people in describing the same character. I told him I had learned something of this in the Air Force, and welcomed what I used to call different views.

The journey began with great commotion, the reason for which was difficult to understand. Before long we were clacking out of the built-up area into a vast area of virtual desert, with high flat-topped hills ahead, ruddy in the evening sun. There were very few signs of fertility, and the landscape was sparsely scattered with small farmsteads with herds of lanky cattle and flocks of long-legged goats. As darkness fell we put on sweaters, and Guy began to tell me what to expect when I arrived.

George was a veteran captain of cavalry who served mostly in Mesopotamia in the First World War, a Scot with an anglicised military accent and a gift of oratory which he exploited at every opportunity. Although he was known as a patriarch he was not very old, although people said he had cooked his age, reducing it by three or four years with remarkable foresight. His hair was silver, quiffed with horns over his ears, and his eyebrows were black and bushy, very useful for impressing people with the strength of his mood when bent on finding out the truth. He was a hard worker, and expected his teams to follow suit. His wife was a charming and talented person, very sad not to be blessed with children, but with a good and intelligent sense of humour. He was a bit of a dandy with his well-cut dark blue shorts, yellow stockings and brogues, and perfectly ironed white short-sleeved shirts, all of which contrasted well his bronzed head, arms and knees. He wore glasses all the time, and had a habit of focusing on one when he was displeased, so that the powerful lenses magnified his pupils, hypnotising the object of his displeasure like a rabbit. He was known as the Superintendent of the group, and because of a shortage of planters he managed the estate where he lived, and was a kind of general manager over the other estates in the group. There were six groups in this particular company spread over Assam. George had, as far as Guy could gather in London, several estate managers, all too old for service in the recent war, and one who had been a pilot in the first war. He gave me thumbnail sketches of them, and I shall describe them as the narrative takes me to them. The train stopped at many stations for our three meals each day. The tea was mostly awful, but the mutton curry (which Guy said was goat) was, in spite of being very hot, quite enjoyable, served with shot-hard peas, spinach and either rice or chupattis. Guy asked many questions about life in the Air Force, and I told him several stories in return for the many he told me, although I confess I was unable to make him laugh as much as I did at his. He described how before the War he worked in the Panitola district, and was picked to play rugby for Panitola Club against the Madden Club in Dibrugarh. There were few cars in those days, and no reliable buses, so the team went by train, wearing their rugby kit in the warm weather. The match was a great success; Panitola won, and much beer was drunk before the team boarded the train to return the twenty-five miles or so home. Guy later fell deeply asleep in the dimlit carriage on the unupholstered board seat, and when the train arrived at Panitola station the others woke him and leapt off the train with him following in a beery stupor. He managed to jump off just as the train pulled away, and found himself standing amongst the hooting team on the crowded platform without any shorts. Women screamed and hid their faces, whilst men clicked their tongues, and rascally boys bit their arms to stifle their laughter. His team mates had pulled them off whilst he slept and thrown them out of the window on the way. He had to take off his shirt and gird his loins with it, and they let him sit in the cab of the old Austin lorry until he could drop off at his bungalow. 'I was so new then, unused to the amount of beer the others could drink, and by Jove, I was furious at losing my old school rugger pants; but that's the sort of thing that used to happen if you were dim enough to let them trap you.'

On the endless drab plains we saw camels used at the farms to draw carts and harrows; several times we saw the beautiful black buck antelopes, dainty gazelle-like creatures which Guy said were very difficult to approach with a rifle. By the end of the second day we saw much more of greener foliage, more wooded hills, but nothing very lush. We seemed to sleep well in spite of little exercise and much creaking and clanking. We read a lot, and talked a lot, with Guy keeping me both amused and interested. I began to learn some Hindustani from him by asking what he was saying to the bearers who brought the food aboard. The time passed quickly without either of us becoming bored, and when we finally plunged through the last hundred miles or so of ricefields and shady trees to arrive in Howrah station, noise began again, the noise of people yelling at each other, the hooting of other trains, and of many lorries, some pre-war, others ex-wartime vehicles, all honking ceaselessly. I noticed soon that people shouting at each other were simply conversing. We were met by a chubby, cheerful Durgadas Babu, who wagged his head sideways and told us not to worry, all was in order. We identified our baggage which was taken on a hand cart by a team of porters, and eventually left the station for our hotel. Guy was furious that we were not being put into the Grand Hotel, but Durgadas explained they had been fully booked, also the Great Eastern Hotel, fully booked, and we were taken to another small hotel in the Chowringhee, but at the wrong end. It was not very impressive: the toilets were of the 'thunderbox' type; the servants were willing but rather clueless, and I saw Guy's meaner side. He said he would create hell at the office tomorrow. The food was disappointing, even after the railway food, and as the beer was warm Guy took me along to the Grand Hotel lounge, where we found it even more crowded than I had seen it last June. We finished up in Firpo's, sitting under whirling punkahs whilst Guy had his iced beer, and I had a very odd tasting fresh lemon.

Next day we dressed in jackets and ties to report to the head office, and there we split up for the day. I was taken upstairs and went through the huge offices with dozens of electric fans, and scores of clerks at desks all piled with an amazing amount of paper. This depressed me, as offices were not my favourite environment. I met several senior people who were: an accountant; an assistant 'writer' who gave me six hundred rupees and said he would take me out to lunch and help me with this allowance to buy things I would need to take up to Assam when I left by train next day. It was quite a shock to discover what I needed: bedding including mattress; clothes for personal wear; crockery, cutlery, and some cooking utensils; riding boots for polo and light breeches, and notebooks. I was told these were all things not easy to get in Assam. When I said I had plenty of my air force shirts and shorts, and needn't buy more, I was told that khaki was only worn on the North Bank, but where I was going I would be expected to wear white shirts shorts and slacks. When we visited the various shops I managed to forget the white shorts, as they showed me the army-navy type, with broad waistbands, double buckles, and they were long enough to touch the floor if one kneeled, as a kilt is supposed to do. The slacks were made from excellent rough linen, as white as snow; but although the waist fitted well, there were many pleats, transforming the slacks into voluminous long pantaloons such as seen in cartoons of French dancing masters. The fussy assistant officer helping me suggested perhaps I would find a tailor 'up there' who might be able to alter them to fit my needs. We lunched at Firpo's, where my helper helped himself to several glasses of beer, and melted remarkably, telling me just how awful life in Calcutta was these days. He had been in the Navy on minesweepers during the War, and had been stuck at Calcutta for a long time. I didn't see the 'Chairman' who had first interviewed me the previous June, and thought perhaps I must get used to the humble position described by the London Chairman.

As our previous night had been very much disturbed by the dreadful noise of shouted conversations and clattering crockery, Guy had told the manager, a very gloomy and apologetic man with a huge belly and large pouches under his sad eyes, to warn the staff to make less noise; but it made things worse, the manager arguing with his minions at regular intervals in addition to the shouting and hooting of traffic and people in the Chowringhee, below our window. The trip back to Howrah early next day was very interesting. Most people seemed very happy; many were bathing at hydrants gushing at pavements' edges; straining porters pushed large handcarts laden with huge loads; bullock carts and large cows got in the way of honking lorries, and many schoolchildren with uniforms seemed to be making their way to school. We were both glad to board the train for Assam, which appeared to be less booked than the Bombay-Calcutta 'express'. Guy was disconsolate, and assured me I would find Assam a different world after Calcutta.

'It's the same all over the world, you know. People in offices who never get out to see what the hell all the paper work is about: bank managers, council clerks, battalion orderly rooms, brigade staff; they're all the same. I'm sure it's something to do with constipation. You must have had that sort of thing in the Air Force.'

I had to agree with him. Once the train moved on its way I told him how I had asked for a job in Calcutta. He laughed when I mentioned not meeting the Calcutta Chairman, and said he was on the ship to England. 'A damned good type, old Geoff! One of the few ex-planters who rose to such a position in the hierarchy. Quite a lad in his day, my word!' I told him of the germinal incident in Allahabad, where I unsuspectingly absorbed all the colonel had told me, and described him to Guy, wondering if he knew him. 'My dear chap, when all positions are filled in Assam there must be over twelve hundred planters all told. By the sound of it he must have been on the North Bank down Mangaldai way. Its quite wild down there, lots of game, and lots of trouble from tigers.' When I asked if there were many tigers about he told me they were actually regarded as vermin. Most of the Assam tea estates were near to tall forest, either fuel reserves for the estates, or the government reserve forests, and such forests held tiger, a few bear, elephants galore, wild pig, muntjac – called barking deer – and sambar, a large deer with heavy antlers with few points. The tigers had over the years begun to help themselves to the cattle of the local villagers and the tea estates. He said it was a damned nuisance when the manager handed one a shotgun with heavy cartridges and a torch and sentenced one to sit all night in a tree in order to shoot the tiger which had killed too many cattle, including the one under the tree in which one had to sit. 'One helluva bore,' he said, 'being bitten to death by mosquitoes, trying not to fall asleep, and usually failing to raise a trace of the tiger. It's not my idea of fun.'

He then told me an extraordinary story which had been reported in the *Calcutta Statesman* newspaper well before the War, with a photograph of the two people involved. I can but give my recollection of the story, having heard several different versions of it over the years. In one of the North Bank districts, probably Mangaldai, a man-eating tiger had been killing more and more people. It was said to be an elderly male, wounded by someone who had tried to kill it many years before, which was unable to kill either its natural prey in the forest, or had been finding the village cattle too fast for his lame spring. The manager of the estate which was in the centre of the worst affected area was a good hunter himself, but found the old tiger too clever for him: it seemed to know too much, and never returned to a kill which had been found. It would certainly not touch the tethered bait of the buffalo calf over which he had sat frequently and long, under pressure from local petitioners who had lost cattle or beloved family members. He was losing too much sleep, and sent word to a forest officer who was known to be an experienced *shikari* (hunter), inviting him to spend a week, an invitation supported by the agonised Sub-Divisional Officer to whom several village headmen had complained. The forest officer was able to come, and had spent a day with trackers trying to work out how the old beast tended to move. He had chosen a period in the cold weather when there was no cloud, and in a week leading up to a full moon. There were no kills of any kind for the first few days, and it was decided to tie a buffalo calf to the outside of the bungalow garden fence, on a soft earthen path where the gardeners had noted tracks about once a week where the tiger had passed in the early hours when all was quiet. The forest officer asked for word to be sent to create plenty of noise on the edge of the forest at about eight-thirty, which was the normal time for people to turn in, leaving a gap in the forest leading into the estate. After an early supper the manager and the forest officer sat in the shadow of the bungalow verandah, well back so that they could not be seen in silhouette. The bungalow was typical for planters and civil servants: raised about nine feet from the ground on heavy timber pillars. The rooms were built on good wooden floors, the walls resembling the Tudor buildings of old England, with panels of white plaster contained in dark timber frames about three feet square. The verandah was large, protruding forward from the sitting room, surrounded by a stout wooden rail, and entry to this upper level was by wide wooden steps from below. From where they sat they could see the buffalo calf clearly in the moonlight. All lights on the verandah and in the rooms were switched off but the lights below, beside the servants stairs, were allowed to remain on, in order to display the semblance of a normal night. After sunset there was no movement of people; they were securely battened in their cottages, fearing where the man-eater would next strike.

The forest officer had a small cocker spaniel, and he assured the planter it was not only well trained, but had such acute senses of smell and hearing that he was considered indispensable on such operations. They had agreed neither to move nor to speak, and with the infinite patience of *shikaris* they settled at about nine p.m., knowing it would turn out to be a very long vigil, and possibly a fruitless one. Tigers lived by using their incredible powers of deception, their deep appreciation of the possible deception exploited by their prey, or their enemies, and those who would seek to kill a man-eater knew before all else that patience was the most powerful virtue of all.

It was somewhere between twelve-thirty and one that the forest officer became aware through his deep sleep that his spaniel was tugging at his sleeve, and came to his senses with disappointment that he had slept on the job. He looked slowly towards the planter and saw he was no longer in his seat, and beginning to think his friend had crept off to bed, he rose, annoyed it had all come to nothing too soon. He stretched himself, looking for the buffalo calf, and with a freezing shock saw, on the brightly moonlit lawn, the planter moving slowly away to the drive with his forearm in the mouth of a large, lanky tiger. Telling himself he must be dreaming, the forest officer pulled off his shoes, seized his rifle, and with all the craft he could muster he went down the stairs, followed by his spaniel, crept behind the tiger and its captive until he was sure, either that the tiger would let his victim free, and turn or flee, or that he might come close enough to shoot the beast safely without injuring the planter. He could see the tiger's ears twisted back, and on an inspiration signalled to the spaniel to go forward and distract the tiger's attention, which it did. The tiger stopped and uttered a deep moan, and the forest officer moved rapidly forward and fired from close behind the planter, into the centre of the animal's ribcage, dropping it inert on the drive. The planter's arm was hardly marked; the teeth of the old tiger were anything but sharp, but they found its rear left femur had been broken by a single lead ball, and had healed so badly that the muscles of that limb were wasted. The planter explained that he had slumbered, and when the great beast had taken his arm in a firm grip he had thought himself to be dreaming a nightmare, but then the frightful truth dawned and having seen the spaniel move furtively decided his only hope, being too soon drawn away from his rifle, was to go quietly, believing the spaniel would do what it actually did, bless it.

This story gave me such a thrill, and such an insight, that I asked for more, but Guy said we should swap yarns. I had mentioned about the sad business of disbanding one of the Spitfire squadrons, and told him of a nightmarish experience I had in that connection. In the early autumn of 1945 we began flying the other squadron's Spitfires away to an airfield where to our horror we found over a hundred of these elegant aeroplanes parked in row after row, mostly fighters, with some of the beautiful pale blue high-level reconnaissance aircraft, polished for extra speed (against Air Ministry recommendations): and no-one could tell us what would happen to them all, although one engineering officer said it was likely they'd be used as scrap for making the frying pans from which they were made. We took it in turn, two at a time, after the aircraft had the cameras and radios removed, and each pair, at intervals of one or two days, would take off and give a display of aerobatics in the evening sun before taking them away to be discarded. A Humber Snipe shooting brake (nowadays called a station wagon) would collect us and bring us back in a very down-to-earth fashion.

There came the evening which I do not forget, when Tommy and I took off and did our best to show our mettle by going through the book of aerobatics for the benefit of colleagues and their ladies sitting in the warm evening sun. Late that evening when we arrived back approval was expressed, and one lady spoke of being enraptured with one of us 'who zoomed in a vertical roll, and rolled and rolled and rolled, and actually went so low that he disappeared behind the trees beyond the county boundary. A magnificent display, and thank goodness you are both back!' Indeed. Tommy pointed sardonically at me and told them to listen. In the vertical upward roll I aimed to finish by doing a stall turn – more like a half cartwheel – but to my horror I could not return the control column (joystick) from the roll position, even using two hands. With the speed dropping alarmingly I panicked that if I didn't do something about it I would fall into a stall and begin to spin, which with a locked aileron was a recipe for disaster. I kicked the rudder, and jabbed the stick forward, and managed to increase speed, rolling below the horizontal. I then did more rolls than I had ever done, one after the other, pushing the nose when upside down to avoid losing height. There was a little slack, but I couldn't get the stick across. It was a fairly new aircraft, and I was aghast at what was happening. Becoming exhausted at the strenuous efforts to break free, and fighting a losing battle to stop losing height, I became worried at the protests of the engine with frequent inverted loading. I managed to raise the nose when I must have been about 500 feet, grabbed the hood jettison knob, and released my safety harness at the same time. To my horror the hood stayed put, my body without the harness lurched out of the seat, and I instinctively grabbed the control column with both hands, telling myself this had to be the end. The stick broke free, and the aircraft miraculously righted itself like the good Spitfire it was, I with one foot lodged over the undercarriage gear, the other under the parachute on the edge of the bucket seat. At about 160 m.p.h. I climbed like a roaring crab to 1,000 feet saying prayers of gratitude, watching the instruments and not daring to move the stick for fear of a repeat of the trouble. At that relatively safe height I gingerly rearranged myself into the seat, refixed my safety harness, and used the rudder to prevent the undignified skidding to port. I carefully pressed the hood jettison knob, to ensure the canopy would keep to its rails, and realised how slim my chances were if it had come off, as everyone on the squadron rated the possibility of an easy 'bale out' without the usual flap cockpit door very poor indeed. After a while I tried the tiniest angle of bank. There was a funny scraping feel, but I was able to turn on to course for the 'graveyard', realising I could not dare to make a normal Spitfire approach to land, which involved a steep curved approach to keep the runway in view up to the last moment, when one then had to level the wings, and line up with the runway, unable to see ahead past the huge nose containing the fuel tanks and the thirty-two litre Gryphon engine. I found my destination easily enough on that beautiful golden evening, but being without a radio I ruled out the idea of circling and waggling wings in order to convey I wanted to make an emergency landing. I began to make a straight approach, swinging the nose gently with rudder to see that the runway was clear. Then to my serious concern I saw much activity on the grass area to one side of the runway, where gliders and their multi-engined tugs were taking off. Within seconds there appeared a barrage of red Very lights fired from the control tower, intended to frighten the insolent Spitfire coming on the approach like a played-out salmon. I did not have enough fuel to divert, either back home or to another quiet airfield, and continued on what I was sure was a clear runway, satisfied if anyone was coming in behind me he would be better equipped to 'go round again' albeit cursing me roundly. There was no-one behind or below, thank goodness; I landed safely and smoothly, and turned off, to be led by an irate load of wide-moustached aviators in a jeep to the control tower. I parked but did not switch off, and when one purple-faced, highly decorated squadron leader mounted the wing belligerently, I waited for his first burst of fire to subside and then explained my problem with an aileron lock, plus no radio. He swore, with large eyes, and pointed to where I should taxi for the Spitfire park.

Tommy was waiting there, wondering what had happened. When I had switched the engine off, and climbed out onto the wing, I remember feeling quite exhilarated.

'What the hell were you doing, coming in like a Flying Fortress?' I smiled with the smugness of sweet survival; and I felt quite cool, quite unaffected.

31

Pride goeth before a fall. I jumped from the wing to the ground, hardly three feet, and felt my knees give way. I had to sit on the wing, amazed to feel my knees tremble so much. I told Tommy what had happened, and swearing soft oaths he climbed onto the wing to move the stick, and felt the scraping of 'something damned odd'. The squadron leader arrived with an engineering officer and a very businesslike look. I described what had happened, and after a search we found one of the screwbolts in the leading edge of the aileron had been loose, the nut inside having fallen off, and by some strange stroke of fate the screw had somehow drifted forward when the aileron was fully lifted near the completion of the vertical roll, and protruded far enough under the wing skin to prevent its return to neutral. The bolt was bent, and the engineering officer said I shouldn't have kept trying to pull the stick across; I should have waggled it so that it would have come free. Tommy gave him a withering look of pity, and pointed out the inability of pilots to have the foresight – or perhaps hindsight – of expert engineers. The squadron leader laughed boisterously, and thumping me on the back asked if I would like to change my underpants in the officers' mess, or have a drink to celebrate survival. We declined, blaming the long drive back, and after making a full report on the strange affair of the loose screwbolt, we drove away. Tommy was a very experienced aviator with much operational flying experience, and wore a Distinguished Flying Cross from the RAF, and another from the United States Air Corps. He also wore what many pilots wore who had survived many 'near things': a facial twitch. It was not always there, but as we drove back in the dusk I noticed it as we talked, and wondered when the weak feeling in my knees would disappear. That fascinated Guy, to whom I clarified the technicalities, and eventually I told him hopefully it was his turn.

We left the long landscapes of ricefields and mango trees eventually, and saw hills in the west which Guy told me were the Khasi Hills, a favourite spot for planters who took local leave in Shillong. He explained that home leave came every four years, when one had six months from leaving the estate until returning to the estate with ship's passages paid each way, plus railway tickets to and from one's home. The ship journey was between two and three weeks each way, and the passage included free meals but no free drinks, and was often the best part of one's home leave. In the years between we would have to leave the estate for a fortnight each year, usually after pruning was finished, any time from January to the end of March, and many would take their two weeks' holiday in Shillong where the altitude of around 5,000 feet was cool by comparison with the plains in March. Guy described the Khasi womenfolk as very attractive. Many of the nursemaids (ayahs) of planters' children were Khasi girls. Young bachelors often went to Shillong to meet suitable Khasi girlfriends with a view to arranging a residential liaison down in Assam. Most of the Khasis were Christians, but not all. Although marriage with the Khasi girls was one of the few 'native' marriages not severely frowned upon by, for instance, the Indian Civil Service, not many planters kept mistresses 'in purdah' (behind the curtain), but to marry a tribal – or for that matter any oriental woman – was a recipe for career paralysis and ostracism. In later years things changed. Guy described how the Khasi people were matrilinear and virtually matriarchal. It was the youngest daughter who inherited all from her mother. They had the attitudes of the South Sea Islands to children born out of wedlock; those who were mistresses wanted children, and if they eventually left their planter partners for whatever reason, their maternal families would welcome the children as part of the family. The Khasi men who were well educated managed their marriages in a way similar to Europeans, and many did well in the civil service. Many girls went in for nursing, and won praise for their services in many of the estate and local hospitals. Guy pointed to the eastern slope of the hills in the midday sun, rising over the undulating forest country now appearing, and said the wettest place known in the world (at that time) was a place called Cherrapunji, lying at the top of the steep rise of the first hills encountered by the south-west wind which had left Australia to cross the equator, bringing the warm moisture-laden air of the monsoon to India. It often had over 300 inches of rainfall, mostly in the monsoon season.

Before sunset we were travelling through country where there was much forest, and we went to sleep with Guy promising the country would become better and better as we went. Next morning there was a sparkle to the scene. The air was clear, the colours bright, and there was a freshness in the air, but this was not caused by altitude. Apparently the Assam valley, further away yet than we had already travelled, was barely 300 feet above sea level. The Brahmaputra river rose in Tibet as the Tsang Po, and flowed out of the Himalayas into the part of Assam we were aiming for. From the area in which we would be living to Calcutta was 800 river miles. In earlier days, said Guy, we would have spent about five or six weeks travelling up to Assam by river steamer. He had never done it, but nowadays it occasionally happened that planters would travel from Upper Assam by steamer, mostly to Gauhati, the capital of Assam, or even to Calcutta, travelling much faster with the current. The old cabins were comfortable, the food was good Indian fare, and the water of the huge river was cool enough to make life on board very pleasant. The captains were Muslims, called *sarangs*, and they were very strict about preventing unmarried girl companions aboard. I saw much of the pleasant rural scenes where rice fields lay in large glades with huge primeval forest covering most of the land. Guy showed me several coveys of wild jungle fowl, feeding and taking the morning sun in quiet corners of the ricefields, where they scratched for grain in the stubble. These birds were the wild ancestors of the European farm chickens. They were shy and sly, not taking to wing unless they were forced, and flew like supercharged pheasants. They abounded in Assam, and were splendid eating. Planters mostly took a serious interest in preserving them from out-of-season poaching and snaring, keen to keep them flourishing. We saw several barking deer in the sun some way from the train, dainty animals which were very shy, and not often seen in the open.

We saw elephants working, and Guy explained the Assamese system of catching and breaking in wild elephants. Shikaris would explore the forest foothills at times of the year when they knew what the elephants would be feeding on. Sometimes it would be the tender shoots of hill bamboos, sometimes wild bananas. On the North Bank it would occasionally be cultivated bamboos and bananas, and from October to December it would be cultivated rice in the fields; but that is another story. Once the elephant herds were located, the '*mela*' (gathering) of hunting elephants would drift into the area. This would mostly be in late spring, when many young elephants would be born, and the elephant catchers preferred them as young as possible; they always had plenty of tame mothers who would suckle those stolen from their own parents. The point was that the younger they were, the easier they were to train as working elephants. It was also the time that families of tigers, somehow programmed naturally to recognise an elephant about to give birth, would stalk the cow, wait for the delivery, and create terror, isolating the new calf and killing it. The herd would surround the bereaved the cow and the dead calf, but the tigers would wait until they abandoned the body, and then enjoy a family feast. The elephant catchers had older experienced animals called '*khoonkies*', who were adept at isolating young elephants of one to four years old, and they would form up on either side of the beast they had headed off from the herd, squeezing it between them and forcing it away eventually to a place where other men would have their heavy ropes ready to tether their captive. If they were more than a year old they would be tied so that the right forefoot and the left hindfoot were secured to trees fore and aft, leaving them with only two feet on the ground. Thus they kept them, bellowing and trumpeting in fear and pain until they became so exhausted that the tethered feet were allowed to take their weight. They were given fodder, but as soon as they began to rebel their feet would be hoisted again, and they would struggle so frantically that the ropes would cut into their flesh, and only when they were exhausted again would they be allowed to stand naturally. It sounded appalling, and I expressed horror at the cruelty used, but Guy said there was a lot of money in it for the catchers. Tea estates used elephants for heavy uprooting of jungle clearings, and stacking timber, as did the forest department. They were well cared for and well fed. When I said the tribals who did the catching must be very callous, Guy said quite a few of them were said to be opium addicts, as were most of the 'mahouts' or riders who worked the elephants. He told me it wasn't only the tribals who were callous. On the North Bank before the War there was an ex-planter who lived in Britain during the Indian hot season, and came out to catch elephants in the cold weather. He had permission from the forest department to build a temporary house with bamboos, plastered reeds and a thatched roof. It was big enough for a bedroom, dining room, drawing room and kitchen, which he furnished with cane furniture and unpolished timber tables. It was situated near a good river on high land. The man used to bathe in the river and change into his dinner jacket every evening, using vapour lamps with incandescent mantles for reading in the evening. He employed an expert team of mahouts and elephants, paid them well, and would manage to capture and sell enough elephants to enable him to continue doing this until the early 1930s. He would use an elephant to creep up on sambar stags at salt licks up some of the small rivers, and fed well on venison. He was disinclined to accept invitations from planters, and not having a vehicle never attended the nearest club, which was about twenty miles away.

Guy became quite preoccupied as we trundled on in the train, saying he was having to make sure he readjusted to the tea life. He said he was hoping for a management soon, as there would be many people ready to retire, including those who had stayed beyond retiring age because of the War. He told me I was very lucky in that respect, as this factor, which included the five years or more without recruiting, would help to accelerate our promotion to the rank of manager, which meant having responsibility for a whole estate and factory, with a population of 1,500 people or more, providing all the services which in civilisation were provided by municipalities, councils, governments and the like. That meant water, limited electricity, housing, roads, medical care and responsibility, as the Air Force used to call it, for 'good order and air force discipline'. It sounded a lot. Guy asked me what the company was going to pay me, and having had to look up my contract on the ship in order to be able to compare terms with other beginners, I was able to tell him 350 rupees, about £27 a month, which seemed to me plenty to live on with free house and servants, and what I was told was cheap food. He said it was not bad, but it would take me quite a long time to acquire things like curtains, bedding for a guest room, and so on. He advised me to keep my ears open and remember that people retiring would be selling all kinds of things: furniture, glasses and crockery, shotguns and carpets. This advice was well taken, but it made me dizzy, after having lived with batmen and officers' mess facilities, to contemplate establishing a home of my own, never having had to do anything of that kind except learning camping lore with the boy scouts.

Guy explained we would arrive at his destination in Upper Assam, a station called Tinsukia, somewhere around one-thirty in the morning. I would continue until about two a.m., and dismount at a station called Lahoal, the nearest to where I was going to live. 'We can hardly expect any reception committees to greet us,' he said, 'but it will be so good to be home again.' This second day was perfect, with a clear blue sky and golden sunshine all the way. He gave me a tremendous amount of information about procedures used in dealing with labour and staff on the company's estates, but warned me these differed from group to group as well as estate to estate. The names of planters were legion, and although there were pungent appraisals of many, there were only two that I would remember. One was George, the Superintendent, and the other Nicky, the Assistant Manager I was initially to stay with on arrival. He did warn me it had been more than five years since he had seen any of the people he described in such detail, and said if they had changed as much as he had in that time they would scarcely be recognisable. I noted he seldom gave strong opinions on anyone, recounting incidents which if true would illustrate their character; but often he would say when stories, albeit amusing, shocking or impressive, were actually hearsay. He said one had to realise this part of the world was fertile ground for legends, and as time went on they were adorned and altered quite outrageously purely because people loved stories about characters and incidents; and if they added to them, either to increase the fame of a hunter or to increase the ill repute of a trickster or a Don Juan, it was accepted as a good story. He confirmed this applied to everyone, the Assamese, the Bengalis, the tribals of all kinds, as well as the planters.

'You will probably hear stories about me to send you into hysterics,' Guy said wryly, 'and when you hear stories about yourself they have been mangled beyond belief and carried so far that you simply cannot find any guilty person to seize by the throat for slander or worse. The best way, my dear chap, is to ignore it. If you believe every story you hear you might enjoy many delightful tales, but you might also begin to suffer from insomnia if the tales are mischievous as so often they are.'

By the time the sun was setting we began to catch glimpses of tea estates from time to time, some of which Guy was able to name. I asked him what some of the planters on the ship had meant when they described estates or districts as having 'too much labour trouble'. He told me how there were indeed some districts which had a bad reputation for labour trouble. It was usually where there were many estates close to each other, mostly with a small town in the vicinity. Some of it was caused by political agitators: some was caused by bad managers who became headstrong and believed the only way to maintain discipline was to frighten people, and went too far by frightening them so much that they rebelled, sometimes with violence. Over the years there were cases, fortunately few, where managers or assistants were beaten, sometimes to death, often because of wild rumours spread by disgruntled people who had been sacked for some crime or causing trouble by continuous quarrelling with neighbours. Guy said five years in the Army had taught him a lot about handling people, principally that there is no truer saying that power corrupts, and absolute power corrupts absolutely. He said that Indian people generally were to our minds very litigious. They would spend all they had in an action to secure justice in disputes involving land, inheritance, stolen property, seduction of a daughter, failure to fulfil dowry payments, and many, many other quarrels; but they had a great desire for justice, which led them into these costly actions; unfortunately when it seemed they had little hope of succeeding because, it was rumoured, bribes had been given, either to witnesses or court clerks, or even to the police. This would lead to an increase in the outpouring of hard-earned savings in desperate attempts to fight bribes with bribes, and end in miserable indebtedness. Most of the people who worked on the estates, if they could not settle their differences with each other, would petition the manager to hear the complaints and defence, and give a judgment which everyone could accept. Guy said he had stood by as his managers had settled cases, and remembers one who would swiftly arrive at a conclusion, saying in an aside to him that the man complaining was an out and out bad hat, and deliver judgment without taking the trouble to cross examine or hear witnesses. The effect of this kind of so-called justice was to plant grudges in the people who sometimes were obviously wronged. No-one would dispute what the 'sahib' had ruled: he was thought to be wise, and known to be the most powerful person on the estate. Guy was sure that was the way to start trouble. Most of the other managers were either Solomons or Pilates, one of the latter telling him the best way to deal with sticky cases was to keep remanding pending appearances of further witnesses, so that they became tired of the whole thing, and often patched it up themselves.

I could have listened all night long, because this was the kind of thing I needed to hear, at least to prepare me for the real first encounter with my new career. I said to Guy we had travelled a long way since leaving the ship, but there had been virtually nothing said about our 'damfool career'. He said he was aware there had been great uncertainty on the ship, but for many it had always been a difficult time, especially for people leaving children or wives behind, and for wives who really didn't like living in India. 'You should bear it in mind if you are sensible enough to want to marry happily, that the best thing to do is to have a good look at girls who actually want to live in Assam: planters' daughters or sisters who have seen enough of it to want to come back. It is one helluva risk to bring some fresh young thing out here who will find India in general quite a shock, and the Assam rainy season is a dreadful period in which by mid-September everyone, white or black, is either quarrelling or resigning or wanting to go home to Mummy. Remember what I'm telling you: you never can tell.' Guy went to sleep with a quiet smile. We were awakened by the staggering stop of the train at his destination. There was a cold, thick mist, visibility about fifteen yards. Guy bustled to get off and see his baggage unloaded, and dashed to shake my hand and wish me luck. 'I'll be seeing you, sometime!'

Chapter III

We had both been sleeping when the train had wakened us by jolting to a stop. After seeing Guy disappear into the mist with dim figures carrying his luggage, I sat back, surprised at the thick mist, feeling now very much on my own in the cold wooden confines of the ancient carriage. The train began to move again, but there was no attempt to accelerate, and I realised the visibility for the driver must be very poor. Guy had mentioned they had to keep watching in case cattle or buffaloes had decided to lie on the track. Wondering how long we had been chugging along so slowly I looked at my watch, and was amazed to find it was just after two-thirty a.m. It was well after three when the train hooted, and dim lights appeared ahead. There was no platform, but I could see four men in turbans and blankets coming forward from what I took to be the tail light of a vehicle. When the train jolted to a stop I jumped down to the earthen ground. Another figure loomed out of the mist, with a broad-brimmed Gurkha hat, broad shoulders in a heavy army greatcoat, under which I could see he was wearing shorts with thick socks and sturdy shoes. He was speaking to the huddled men in blankets who went to work collecting my luggage and came forward, his face shaded by his broad brim under the dim lamp.

'You all right?' A quiet, husky voice.

'Yes thanks! I'm very late, I think.'

'It's always late with these mists.'

We shook hands and exchanged surnames, then he said 'Come on,' and took me to an old Austin lorry where the men were fixing the tailboard after loading my luggage. He called out to the driver who started the lorry, then he opened the door, telling me to get in. When I was in he shut the door, stood up on the running board with his elbow through the open window to hold him secure, and called '*Chelao*!', a word I was to remember, thinking I knew what it must mean. I protested there was room for him inside with me, but he said 'No, no! I'm all right,' and we drove off. I thought it was going to be very cold for him outside like that, and pushed my hands into my coat pockets, settling down for the last leg of my long journey to a new career. We had hardly travelled quarter of a mile when the lorry turned left over the railway hump and headed south. This was it! I was speculating how long a journey it was going to be when after about fifty yards the lorry stopped, and in the dim headlights I saw another blanket-muffled figure with a *pagri* (turban) opening a double gate, through which we drove, round the edge of a lawn, up to a pillared building.

'Here we are!' said the man Guy had called Nicky. 'They'll bring your gear up. Would you like a cup of tea?'

'No thanks! I think perhaps bed would be best.'

'Right, look! I get up at six-thirty and go to the office. Breakfast about seven-thirty, OK? We've got to be ready for George's car to pick us up and take us down to his office. It's only about two miles back along the road. I'll tell them to wake you about seven. Just about time for forty winks.' He laughed a husky laugh and I followed him upstairs. There was someone holding a hurricane lamp at the top of the verandah stairs, a man wearing a white *pagri* with a dark green band and a badge on it, and a blanket round him; he was shivering from the cold. Nicky took the lamp and led me into a huge room in which there were two beds, one made up, the other without anything, not even a mattress. Our footsteps echoed on the dark wooden floor. He showed me the jug and basin on the black table behind the bed. 'They'll bring up some hot water at seven for shaving. Look, there are only two blankets on the bed. I would spread your greatcoat over it; it's cold, you know, down to forty-two (Fahrenheit). Sleep well!' He disappeared into the dark, leaving the hurricane lamp on a small table.

I unpacked my pyjamas, sorry I had left my thick flannel ones in Scotland, and climbed, shivering, tired, and deeply disappointed into the cold sheets. I turned to put the lamp out just as a noiseless figure materialised like a ghost. He was draped in a blanket, with a mop of grey hair and a large grey moustache. He picked up the lamp saluted gravely, and disappeared as silently as he had come, on legs and feet like a moorhen. I lay on my back, unable to accept that my dream of living in a wild place looked like being shattered: fifty yards from a railway line, quarter of a mile from a station. Lying there in the large, cold room I began to wonder how I was going to get myself out of this hopelessly unsuitable place: I would tell this George I had been misled, given false impressions. It seemed my brain was beginning to fulminate, and I feared no sleep would come, but I slept deeply until two hours later I was awakened by the sound of a railway engine hooting about a hundred yards from the bungalow. In the dim light of the mist-bound dawn I could see it was six a.m., but the confounded train continued intermittent hooting on a lugubrious note which plunged me back into my depressed state of disillusion. I slept no more, and kept telling myself I had of my own volition walked into this with no-one else to blame, and I must be steady, watch for escape routes, hope for changes, not start upsetting people. After all, this chap Nicky was a Colonel with the Gurkhas, and got a Military Cross in the Burma campaign. Wait and see what happens next.

He came in to breakfast, without his hat, wearing a thick sweater and rubbing his hands, saying again it was dam' cold. He looked like a tall, hefty young Winston Churchill, with sandy hair and the pink complexion of a baby. He was in shorts, and his strong legs were covered with a blonde fuzz; I thought it must help to keep him warm. He had the sort of wrinkled forehead that indicated concern, but even when he smiled the wrinkles remained as if he was apologising for his sense of humour. He told me office was easy this time of the year, people being reluctant to get up early in the cold. He explained how the 'line *chowkidars*', vaguely translatable as the village watchmen, came to hear the plan of work for the day, after which they would go off and amble through their housing area, calling out which teams were to go to which place for a particular kind of work, taking the necessary tools with them, men, women and children. He told me most of the pruning of the tea bushes had been finished, and he was sending the women and girls to cut thatch for house roofing; and the men were divided up into gangs who were to clean out the drains in the fields, start repairing roads, and various other things which meant very little to me. Breakfast was spartan and no doubt very healthy: two small tangerine-type oranges from the Khasi hills, a boiled egg, and toast, followed by thick dark tea, the only virtue of which was its scalding heat. I asked if the smoky flavour had a special name, and he told me a name in Hindustani, which he translated as 'wet firewood'. Good coal was difficult to obtain, and the only other source of fuel was from old shade trees being removed from the tea areas: good wood, but any firewood stacked to dry out was prone to disappear magically, and was therefore burned in the kitchen before it had been dried out, with plenty of smoke from the sap.

'On the North Bank we would get tons and tons of the most wonderful firewood from the riverbeds. Enough firewood for everyone and plenty to spare: dry dead wood; in the cold weather we'd collect enough of it for the bungalows and Indian staff to last all year.'

This led me to tell him I was must taken aback to find myself in such a place as this, virtually on the railway line, having been attracted to Assam by the stories of wilderness. I asked if he was ever on the North Bank.

'Do you know, MacStorm, I dream of the North Bank. This place gives me the creeps. It's too near the town; the labour lose their tribal discipline, booze too much; and the planters are all in each other's hair: bridge, tennis, boozy curry lunches every Sunday. George will tell you you must mix a bit, not grow jungly.' He grinned. 'There's George's car. We'll have to make a move.' I warmed to him. 'Put shorts on, the mist will clear by ten, and when we come back we can go straight out and I'll show you what goes on.' I changed into shorts with knee stockings, put on a thick pullover and silk scarf. When he saw me he wheezed. 'You're ex-air force all right. You all loved your fancy scarfs, didn't you!' I told him the ideal of the silk scarf was to avoid chafing the neck from constant 'rubber-necking', watching for specks in the distance. As we were driven along the road parallel to the railway line he gave me some hints. 'George is all right, you know. Bit of a showman, but damn' good at his job. Ex-cavalry officer. Being ex-air force you'll be all right with him. He was a real old bastard when I joined, all the senior men were: all ex-service officers from the first war. Kept on telling us we needed a spell of service discipline. Since we came back from the War they keep telling us: you see! Made a man of you, didn't it? And you've shown what you were made of; gives you a different attitude to life, eh!' He wheezed happily. We drove over the railway track again and entered a fenced compound of large buildings, which Nicky told me was THE factory. We parked outside a small block of offices, single storey on a high plinth with a small lawn outside. As we mounted the steps a large figure emerged from one of the doors, over six feet, with bright blue eyes sparkling in a pink-bronze face topped by rich mahogany hair. He was wearing brown slacks and a jacket made from white towelling, buttoned tightly over his ample belly. He had a topi under one arm, and came forward with a huge brown hand extended, smiling broadly.

'You must be MacStorm. Hamish MacStorm!' His grip was warm and firm. 'Hallo MacFortune! What do you think of him?'His voice was deep, and rich with the slow Highland brogue. I thought Guy must have told me about this man. 'I hope to meet you later, once you've found your feet, MacStorm. I think the Laird is expecting you.'

As we moved along the plinth verandah I heard a voice speaking what I thought was Hindustani, loudly and insistently, and as we turned into the open door of the last office I saw a perfect fit of Guy's description of George, sitting behind his large desk, stabbing his pipestem at an Indian who stood holding a large pile of files, swinging his chin from side to side in a gesture I was to find commonplace in future: his head rocked a little, but was neither a nod nor a shake of the head. Seeing us arrive George rose suddenly. He laughed at the man holding the files. 'All right, Chakravorty. See what you can do.' He came forward to greet us, and shook hands firmly. 'Welcome MacStorm! Very welcome! Eh, MacFortune? Sit down gentlemen, please.' He wore his immaculate dark blue shorts, white shirt, and a thick yellow pullover. These people didn't seem to feel the cold.

He spoke for about ten minutes, telling me of the great shortage of assistants, and the shortage of labour, with so many of the tea estate labour having been taken to build the roads into Burma, along with planters to manage the operations. He said there was going to be a great demand for tea in Britain, and the British government had made it clear they wanted as much tea as possible in order to lift rationing restrictions soon. He was telling me I'd never regret joining such an enterprise as tea: producing something that was good for raising people's spirits without any hangover, and so on. He was full of enthusiasm, and imparted it expertly. He asked me what I flew, and was rapturous when I said Hurricanes and Spitfires, with a very short time on Meteors. He asked if I had any questions about anything at all, saying he realised I had just arrived and probably not had time to think about anything. I said I was questioning myself about having got the impression Assam would be wild, the estates remote, and far from the madding crowd, only to find myself living next to the railway line, not far from a town. How long would I be staying in such a place?

He leaned forward fidgeting with his pipe in both hands, and looked at me earnestly, beginning to speak quietly but very distinctly. 'One has to look at it this way, MacStorm, and I think MacFortune will agree, that this is a way of life beyond compare for those who decide to stick with it once they have seen enough of it to balance the good with the bad, the joys with the frustrations, the successes with the failures. I tell you it was a dreadful comedown for me to come out here in 1919. It puts me in the position of being able to understand a little of what you must feel. Let me tell you what will be happening for the next year. You will stay with MacFortune for six weeks to learn an awful lot about how to organise yourself in order to live on your own; the rudiments of estate organisation; the way to start learning the language; how to deal with all the different people you will be involved with; the systems of books, accounts and inventories; the general protocol of planting society – which this last war has already changed, by Jove, eh! MacFortune? After six weeks you will move out to a large estate about twelve miles the other side of town, not far from the Brahmaputra, where we are hoping to send one of our returning ex-army chaps to release the permanent manager who will then have his first home leave in the UK for six years. You'll like it better out there: much more rural than this. There's no doubt that where you are now is one of the least desirable billets in the company; but out there you will really be out in the country, as we say at home. They have a good stable; there's plenty of good shooting; good local bazaars for buying food; and good fishing this time of the year in the river lagoons on the Brahmaputra. Now, MacFortune, I want you to collect some papers for this young man: application to open his bank account in town. Take him in to see the club and meet people.' Turning to me he asked, 'Do you play bridge, tennis, rugby, polo?' I said the last two, and he gave a broad grin. 'I used to love my polo,' he said, 'not that I was ever much good; but once I came to wearing glasses they kept falling off, and I was so blind without them I was a dreadful danger to everyone else, so I had to give it up. Good! MacFortune will teach you well about everything, get you off to a good start. He'll propose you for the club, and I'll second you. I'll get Arthur Claude to second you as well; he's ex-Royal Flying Corps, used to be an instructor. You'll like him. Now is there anything else? MacFortune?' We stood up, and I said people on the ship had been very depressed by the latest newspaper reports and rumours about the Labour government's intention to give India home rule. What did he think of our chances?

George stood tall and gave one of his wide, rather stern smiles, his bushy black eyebrows coming down together over his distinguished nose. 'I can talk to you chaps as if we were still fighting a war for our survival: you will understand how I feel, how I believe we should feel who care for this job, for the people we employ, for India!' He leaned forward, both fists on his desk, and with his jaw forward said, 'Britain has been talking about Indian independence since Victoria's time. It is something that some day will be a magnificent achievement both for Britain and for India; but I cannot see it happening for many, many years to come. India has a long way to go, you see. Did you hear of the Great Calcutta Killings, hardly six months ago? If you think that was terrible you must remember that is what happens even when the British are still here, with great numbers of troops, not to subdue India, but to keep them from killing each other. You see, MacStorm, there are more than three hundred million people in this country. If they all wanted to be independent under their own government, they could get rid of the British in a long weekend, just-like-that!' He uttered the last phrase like a machine-gun, snapping his fingers. 'This last war was fought in the cause of freedom from oppression by Nazi and Japanese hordes. India, oppressed by the Mughals for many centuries, was slowly absorbed by the British, said by the Indian Congress now to be oppressing India. I cannot believe we shall hand India over to a turmoil of ambitious politicians until we are sure we have done our best to help them succeed. The downtrodden peasantry of India is crippled by debt to rapacious moneylenders and landlords. Many of the people who have come a thousand miles to work on the tea estates for what to you will seem like a pittance have done so to escape their debts which have multiplied through generations. There is too much corruption, MacStorm, and the peasantry, the tribals, law-abiding stalwarts virtually without police protection, want to flee to the wilderness to run their own lives on their own little patches, God help them! We have to put all that in order before we can hand over a system that will really work, under a keen but inexperienced government.'

He was very eloquent, and I could easily accept he believed what he was saying. I knew I had a lot to learn about this country. I thanked him, and he nodded with his broad smile, but turned to Nicky, asking him if he didn't agree, to which Nicky diffidently replied that he thought the government now in power back home meant well, but seemed to be very romantic, thinking with their hearts instead of their brains; but he thought one had to live with rumour, and hope for luck as in the War, and if we lost our jobs too soon we'd have to move on somewhere else.

We left the office with George talking to Nicky about arranging for someone to return the Dumpy level, so that he could check the levels of the drainage in the 'northern outfall area', whatever that was. 'You'll be able to teach MacStorm a bit about using it, and explain the principles of drainage.'

As we drove back Nicky said, 'Wasn't he magnificent? He really does it well, doesn't he?' I had to agree. He made everything sound fine, fixed, and all clear to take-off.

'Who was the chap we met outside the office, the big Highlander?'

'Oh! That was big Mac. MacDonuill. I'll tell you about him.' As he said this he pointed with the hand on his knee at the driver and with the other hand touched his ear. 'It's amazing what can be deciphered by members of the proletariat, you know.' I saw the driver's eyes flicker at us through the rear-view mirror, and nodded.

When we arrived at his bungalow he looked at his watch and said we would take a look at the '*malibari*', which meant vegetable/fruit garden, as the people would only now be drifting out to work. It was a large patch where cabbages, cauliflowers, carrots and other what he called 'blighty' (*vilayati* – meaning foreign) vegetables were growing in large numbers. There were Cape gooseberries, tomatoes, spinach, beans of several kinds, and many papaya trees heavy with fruit. He explained the foreign vegetables would only grow well in the cold season, but spinach and some of the indigenous beans would grow all the time. He paid a lot of attention to everything, chatting to the *malis* (gardeners), showing me the various pests one had to watch for, explaining the benefits of doing this sort of thing mainly to save money, and also to send surplus stuff to the group hospital for the resident patients.

Returning to the bungalow he led me under the verandah to show me my bicycle. It was not a new one, as they were hard to come by, but I could have it second hand at fifty rupees, about £4, which seemed a good bargain. He told me it had belonged to a chap who had left the company to settle in

New Zealand. We then set off to cycle a fair distance through the several parts of the estate, which spread from end to end about three miles. The mist thinned very slowly. We stopped when he had to speak to the field staff, mostly in English, and to the *sirdars* (foremen) in Hindustani, who were all wearing *pagris* and old European-style jackets over their other clothes. Those who were working amongst the tea bushes wore shorts, and I understood straight away that shorts were clearly the only wear suitable, as the bushes were planted at various patterns four to four-and-a-half or five feet apart, and as they were trained to cover the ground as much as possible to suppress weed, walking in the rows between meant the sharp branches would tear anything but tough drill shorts to shreds. Nicky said nothing about my short Rhodesian shorts, but I found it hard going, following him through stretches to look at the men cleaning drains. I looked at the scratches on my thighs when we reached our cycles, and looked at him. All he said was that within the year my thighs would grow more hair and become tough enough to resist the scratches. The people at work were very curious about me, but kept their heads down on their work until I looked away from them, when I could feel their eyes focusing on me. The *sirdars* saluted with a combination of a vaguely military salute and a slight bow, with some of the older ones making a real old-fashioned traditional 'salaam', leaning forward with the back of the hand downwards, sweeping it up to the front of the head, saying '*salaam Sahib*', or '*salaam Hazoor*'. Nicky explained '*salaam*' meant peace, and that the Hindus and Christians would rather not copy the Muslim '*salaam aleikum*', although it actually meant 'peace be with you'. He gave me a very good tip: when returning the greeting it was always best to say '*salaam Ragubir*'. The same applied to anyone who salaamed, but it would take time to learn people's names. Girls seemed to like making salaams, and the older women, but those between would only salaam if they were about to make a complaint.

When we came to the thatch-cutting in a scrub area alongside the tea, the sun was beginning to shine through, and the mist began to clear more quickly. We tied our sweaters on the handlebars, enjoying the warmth, and the world began to appear more cheerful. The women and girls were very vocal, chatting gaily as they carried on with their work, rather like old-fashioned wheat harvesting, making large bundles which girls carried off to be measured for girth before they were added to a stack by the lorry track.

Nicky told me what they were saying: who was the new '*chokra*' *sahib*? (Boy sahib). Was he straight out of school? He told them I was a *hawa jahaz ka shikari* pilot (literally an aeroplane hunter pilot) which drew undulating soft moans of amazement, and bright stares. He pointed out the different tribes with their individual style of dress, beads, and hair styles, but I couldn't keep pace with the names. Some of the younger unmarried women of particular tribes were quite impressive in appearance and bearing, with bright beads in many coils round their necks, one tribe with white, orange and blue, another with yellow and green. Some tribes were dark, with their hair in a kind of chignon behind one ear, others were paler, with small chignons high on the back of their heads. The men of the different tribes also had similar hair arrangements, their long hair in a knot behind the ear, as well as plenty of the same colours of beads. Nicky told me when they were speaking their own languages, which seemed to be many, and said they were probably saying things they didn't want us to understand; when I asked what kind of things he smiled sideways at me and said there was an awful lot to learn.

We went back to the bungalow for 'tiffin', as lunch was henceforth to be called, and had some kind of a mutton curry, greenish-yellow and very hot, with rice and beans, and some poppadom, here called *papur*. Nicky told me mutton out here was mostly goat, and was always best curried. I told him how I had enjoyed good curries, different from this, in Karachi and Allahabad, and he explained that the best curries came from central and western India, where the use of spices was much more sophisticated than in the areas from which the planters' cooks came. He told me the curry spices he was using came from south India, in a bottle, but he would very much like to find a good cook who would make the real savory curries of people like the Punjabis and the Dogras. The curry was followed by several Khasi oranges.

Within the hour we were back on our bicycles, and rode out to the furthest sections of the estate, checking the work in reverse order this time. Nicky showed me work which was called a 'clean out' prune, being carried out by about forty handsome, dark young women, of good build and proud demeanour. They were well dressed, and all wore scarlet plugs in their earlobes, with small circular mirrors set in them. Nicky said they were Mundas from Chota Nagpur, Christian Mundas who were good workers

49

and saved money, which I found amazing considering the wages they received. He said all Mundas, Christian or animist, were very strict about following their religious or tribal morals. They did not approve of any union except marriage, and he had only heard of one affair between a Munda girl and a British planter. It seemed like a real love affair, and the girl moved in with him. A few days later they were found in the man's bedroom, tied together with a spear through both of them. He told me some of the other tribes were the opposite, but it was best to beware getting involved, and to stick to one's own customs and morals. I had to agree, thinking nature intended one should survive, after all.

We cycled back along the northern boundary, beyond which we could see a neighbouring tea estate. There was a large stretch of rice fields stretching out to groves of trees, and within fifteen yards there were four adjutant storks which paid no attention to us, preening their slate grey plumage and looking very preoccupied with private matters. Nicky pointed out three different kinds of mynahs in chattering flocks. We saw and heard several tree pies, heavier than the European magpie, with rusty plumage and a call like a muted guitar. Two blue rollers did aerobatics for us, flashing their contrasting blues as if they were flying for the love of it. As we moved through the work and around all the paths and fences of the estate Nicky kept up a fascinating flow of information and explanations which was never boring. It seemed to me there was so much to learn about everything one saw or touched, as well as what people said. I remember feeling somehow grateful that whatever the disillusions brought on by being over romantic, it was not going to be a case of firm resolve to pursue a new way of life however boring it turned out to be. It showed all the signs of being packed full of interest not only in growing things for a living, but in developing the art of understanding and motivating so many people of different kinds in such an undertaking. This was not what I had expected from the Allahabad Colonel's description: it was a reassuring discovery.

We got back to tea at just after four, and I found the thick dark liquid, with condensed milk and less smoke, very welcome. Nicky told me that next day two hundred bamboos would be delivered from George's place, where they had huge plantations of them, and it would be a good idea for me to learn to count in Hindustani by counting them into stacks of twenty, with four men, who would only stack as I ordered, so that I would have to

50

repeat the numerals up to twenty – ten times. He said that was good enough for a beginning; in fact many of the planters he knew never got much beyond that, because the labour used what was once the ancient medieval system in England: one score and ten, three score and ten, two score and four etc., and the people who kept the books were mostly keen to speak English and improve their fluency. I took down the numerals on a piece of paper, and he told me we would be going into town on Saturday afternoon, and would first do some shopping, when I could buy a notebook for writing down phrases, colours, words and names etc., until I could commit it all to memory. We went down to the office, where he began showing me all the books, records and maps used in the running of the estate. I was surprised there was so much involved, and stood by as he made some checks of various figures, beginning to see that as in the Air Force and any other undertaking, one could not escape paperwork. It soon became dark, very quickly, and Nicky took me behind the office to another low building. As he unlocked the door a servant materialised out of the gloom as if expecting he was needed. There was an oily smell, but too dark for me to make out what was happening. Nicky gently eased me back against the wall, and I vaguely saw the servant bowing rapidly, gasping as if with exertion until after a few seconds there was a click, and the sudden clattering noise of a diesel engine starting up. As it settled down there was suddenly light, dim to start with, but I saw Nicky at a switchboard turning a wheel which brought brightness, and the engine settled to a healthy beat. I felt a warm glow of satisfaction, now being fairly sure I would not have to read and write with a hurricane lamp on the small table in my room. I was then shown the battery room next door, and gathered that most of the battery plates which hung in the large glass jars were no longer any use, and as new plates were in short supply until cargo ships got back to normal, we had to run direct with the 110-volt direct current generator from sunset to about nine p.m. We then went along the path to the kitchen, which was about fifteen yards from the bungalow, where I saw a large wood fire with four 4-gallon tins of water standing on iron rails over the fire. Nicky said this was our bathwater: eight gallons for him, eight for me. In about ten minutes time the '*pani walla*' (waterman or kitchen helper) would carry the water to our baths in the enclosures under the bungalow, and pour it for us. He warned me not to turn the cold tap on too much, as the old enamelled iron baths soon cooled the water down.

Eventually, much refreshed and warmly dressed in sweater and corduroys, I went into the living room and saw it properly for the first time. It was a large room, and at one end on a broad raised fireplace a large wood fire burned cheerfully, radiating welcome heat. On each of the tudor walls there hung a black wooden shield, mounted with crossed Gurkha kukris, points upwards, with a regimental crest and number above them. On the black timber floor there were several large rugs, woven and tufted, of white cotton. Within minutes my host appeared, clad in a thick grey army shirt, and a long grey and purple Burmese '*lungi*', a cloth wound and tucked at the waist, reaching to the feet, which were clad in grey army socks and '*chappals*' (stout sandals). He was followed by his uniformed servant bearing a tray with two glasses of mandarin juice, which he lifted, giving one to me.

'To the Air Force,' he said with a broad grin, and I replied:

'To the Gurkhas!'

We sat near the fire, and as if he had discarded the discipline and concentration of the day's work with his working clothes he began asking questions. What aircraft did I fly? Where had I been, and what did I do? How on earth were you able to charge around the sky in those terribly fast aeroplanes without losing your nerve? Didn't it make you feel sick? He was so keen to know about flying, but said it was not something he had ever wanted to do. He spoke wistfully, of watching the Hurricanes, the Dakotas, flying back home after whatever they had been doing over the front, envious that they would be safe, and dry, and having a half decent meal back at base, without the grating whine of the giant cicadas, without the biting ants, the mosquitoes, the leeches. This put me in a position to ask him to tell me something of his time campaigning with the Gurkhas, to tell me how he had won his Military Cross. He frowned, looking at his watch, and said tomorrow was pay day, and the day after being Saturday we would go into town, see the shop where they sold some imported food and drink, drop my application in at the bank, and then go to the club to see the polo, meet some people. 'When we come back we'll have a drink and I'll tell you about the Gurkhas.' He called for dinner as it was nearly seven-thirty, and we went in to a welcome dal (lentil) soup with onion and some croutons like small hard cubes of dark mahogany wood, followed by half a small roasted chicken each, with hard peas, boiled potatoes, and cabbage. Dessert was what he called 'Subaltern's Soufflé': an egg caramel custard.

We returned to the easy chairs by the warm fire, and I realised we were both very tired, partly because of the disturbed previous night, and for me because of the impact of so much that was new and strange, and the new experience of cycling a long way over rough tracks. I said to him it was wonderful to be able to see the blue ranges of the Himalayas, forty miles or more to the north of the estate, and he told me that was nothing compared with living on the North Bank. One was so close to the foothills that one couldn't see any of the snows, but in the cold weather when the wind came from the north-east, there were no thick mists as on the South Bank, because the air coming from Tibet and the Gobi desert was so dry that for about fifteen miles south of the hills it stayed clear. I reminded him of what he had said in the car that morning about MacDonuill, that he would tell me about him later, but added I didn't want him to keep us up too late. He looked at his watch again, then put his elbows on his knees and stared into the fire, which had been well stoked whilst we dined. 'It doesn't take long,' he said. 'It's a very short but sad story. He's a splendid chap, you know. I always felt he was like an angel who lost his wings and got mixed up with this world by mistake.'

MacDonuill came out when he was in his mid-twenties not long after the great Depression had destroyed the family business which had once promised a long and happy career. He was tall and well built, remarkably good looking with bright blue eyes and splendid teeth, which he still had. He spoke the slow lilting brogue of the Gaelic speaker, with a diction made perfect by the dominie education of his early years. The ladies were greatly taken by him, and the young ladies of the 'fishing fleets' were all competing for his attention; but although he would dance beautifully with most of them, he never seemed to fall for their charms, in spite of the high quality of looks and intelligence some of them displayed. He would have a bottle of beer after a fine game of rugby in which he invariably excelled as one of those full-backs who now and then used his speed to drive through a chaotic field to score an unexpected and urgently needed try. He had boxed as an amateur and never allowed anyone to spoil his happy good looks. After his beer in the club he would often sing Gaelic songs in a deep, rich baritone, pleasing his listeners and enjoying the occasion. He went on his first long leave after four and a half years in Assam, and met a beautiful dark-eyed English girl who was spending a holiday with her parents in the Scottish Highlands. They fell deeply in love with each other. In those days one had to ask the company's permission to marry, it was said because accommodation had to be arranged by employers, who provided it free. He was due to return that October to Assam within a few weeks of having met this girl, and arranged, with the company's permission, that she would travel out by sea the following October. He would meet her in Bombay and travel by train with her to Calcutta where they would be married, and a reception and wedding party would be arranged at the club in Assam. The people who saw the photographs he brought were sure he had made a fine choice, and they congratulated him, looking forward to seeing the handsome couple flourish among them.

Mac was a man who not only was imbued with the traditional Scottish thrift, but having seen his own family reduced to severe financial stringency by the Depression he set himself the most difficult limits of expenditure so that he would save as much as possible, in order to have money enough to make his bungalow suitable for his future wife. One bottle of beer a week, eggs and chickens from his own keeping, and all the food he could grow in his own compound. Nicky wrinkled his brow and tapped his right index finger repeatedly into the palm of his left hand to stress the virtue of Mac's economy. Love letters were exchanged, and showed their love to be growing stronger through their separation. The time came when Mac made the journey to Bombay, and went to meet his fiancée, feeling a mixture of nerves and joyous anticipation vibrate throughout his body. She eventually appeared when most passengers were leaving the customs hall, her hand on the arm of a young ship's officer. Mac thought she looked pale and must have been nervous, and told himself this was why she couldn't produce the radiant smile he had dreamed of for nearly a year. As she came forward he felt a flicker of fear in his chest: she was not looking into his eyes, and as he raised his arms towards her she raised one arm forward, her hand clenched with fingers downwards. 'I've broken it off,' she said. 'I'm giving your ring back. I'm going to marry someone else.' Mac was shaken, and felt his heart thud with perhaps a mixture of disappointment and anger.

'Were you wearing this ring on the boat?'

She nodded. The ship's officer, some fifteen feet away, adjusted his peaked cap and frowned with his chin forward; a tall dark man with a film star moustache. Mac moved round the girl and walked slowly toward him, holding the ring before him in the palm of his hand.

'Was she wearing this when you first met her?'

'I believe she was.' The officer's eyes dilated with a sense of threatening danger, before narrowing with suspicion.

'How will she ever be able to trust you after you scorned an engagement ring. I think you will have to carry something to remind you never to break faith in your life again.' With that, as swift as a striking cobra he leapt forward and swung a mighty punch, hitting the officer on the side of the head, sending his white-capped hat rolling in the dust. The girl fainted; Mac picked her up and placed her on a customs bench, and walked away as several ship's officers ran to the writhing figure of their colleague. Others told the story describing the way the punch knocked the officer into the dock, but he didn't tell me that.

Mac travelled back to Calcutta where he delivered a letter to the office before opening time, giving his apologies for the cancellation of his wedding 'due to unforeseen circumstances', asking them kindly to forward his enclosed letter to Padre MacLean, who was to have married them. He returned to Assam, told his friends to tell everyone the wedding was off, and became reclusive, never attending the club and never visiting his friends. Some of the young bachelors kept visiting with the idea of convincing him he should look at it as a very lucky thing to have been saved from what would never have been a successful, faithful marriage, and the only way to wipe it all out was to have a jolly good party with the boys and let the whole dreadful episode sink into the mud where it belonged. He resisted this for nearly a year; then one weekend he invited about a dozen of his friends to a bachelor party which lasted from Saturday night until Sunday evening. From that day onwards he drank hard, mainly the whisky, but never showed its effects. His work was faultless, he worked long hours. After two years, through the mistress of an older planter, he acquired a Khasi wife, and through the years they had three children. When he went on home leave he always went alone. He rose to the rank of senior assistant manager, and sometimes did acting manager whilst permanent managers went on home leave, but was never promoted as his experience and capability deserved.

'You see, MacStorm, there are several sad lessons to learn from old Mac. Be as sure as any man can be that you pick the right woman to marry and to love. If you want to carry on living in your own forefathers' tribal tradition, bound by your own desires to follow the way you were raised, never let your ideas of nature cheat you into thinking you should mate with the most attractive girl in the world. If she belongs to another age, another culture, another tribe, beware, beware! You won't understand it yet, but you will be terribly tempted as I was, as I often am, by the force of nature in this incredibly fecund part of the world. Here the heat dictates the thinnest of wear for women, for nubile girls, who are by their ancestry and their closeness to primeval nature, impelled with amazing force, uninhibited by our so-called puritanical restraints, encouraged by a tribal society still desperate to multiply and survive. You will soon recognise the way these girls look at you. They know by the age of six far more about human fertilisation, reproduction, and the bearing of children than we know. They look at you as a male, bigger and better fed than most of their tribal males. They don't think of sex the way we do. Most of them think without words; their vocabularies are tiny. They think with the large part of the brain which was in men's skulls thousands of years before language was developed, before writing was invented. There is a powerful logic in their thinking, more powerful than ours on the matter of how nature originally made us think.' His serious face with wrinkled brow turned from the fire, to which he had been addressing this fascinating homily, and suddenly broke into an outraged, husky laugh. He looked at me, slapped his knees, and said it was time to stop all this nonsense and go to bed. I thanked him for his tale, and he turned. 'You know, when you live on your own your only defence is to try to make sense of the things that strike you, that affect you more than other people. It won't be long before you start talking like me. You'll turn into quite a jungly philosopher if you stay long enough. Sleep well!'

The next day went well. The same train woke me early in the morning, and because I treated it like a village church bell telling me the time, and had learned there were only three trains a day, the demeaning situation of living almost on a railway line seemed to diminish, a little. I spent the time until rising in thinking what was to be done that day. At breakfast I said I supposed bacon was not easily available, and received a slightly frosty reply that they sold it in town, imported stuff, but it was very expensive. Talking of frost, I had started making a list of all the things for which I should need to save money to buy, on Nicky's advice. Most of it, like a refrigerator, wireless set, curtains and kitchen gear, should be second-hand, from more senior planters who could afford the new stuff beginning to arrive since the end of the War.

I spent the first few hours after breakfast counting bamboos and learning numbers. Nicky had told me to meet him at ten-thirty at the dispensary, which I had not yet seen. It was another building on a plinth, with a large open waiting room where sick people attended morning and evening. The compounder was a Bengali, a very talkative and repetitive man who seemed very nervous, whose job it was to examine all new cases, take temperatures, examine tongues, feel spleens, and to ask for transport to take any cases needing attention by the doctor in George's hospital. From the sick register we saw one of the commonest afflictions was worms: intestinal parasites, which led to other problems like anaemia, increased susceptibility to things like flu and measles, and seemed to affect young children badly. Nicky said this was mainly caused by poor sanitation, and jungly habits of defaecation, and it was something being talked about as requiring action in the near future. After lunch George's car rolled up, and Nicky confessed sheepishly he was going to buy it from George, who was taking delivery of a new car at last. His old Crossley was a handsome car with an aluminium body, which Nicky said was a godsend with so much cattle manure on the roads and tracks. The cow droppings contained so much sulphuric acid that steel mudguards (or wings) would rust through in a very short time. Lorries and cars had to be painted with several coats of red lead underneath, and covered with several more coats of bitumen, to prevent rust from ruining the metal. It all had to be seen in the context not just of cost, but the huge distance involved in shipping things from Europe or America.

After lunch I went with Nicky to the office, and helped to count the piles of notes and coins for paying the labour. Most of the notes were in bundles with string around them, but they were all dirty, and Nicky warned we would have to wash our hands after counting, and later again after paying. At about three-thirty we followed the pay money, which was carried in wooden trays by several men and escorted by the *chowkidars*, to a large shed on the edge of a clearing which today, instead of carrying a few cattle and goats, had dozens of shops with wares spread on cloths on the ground, selling everything. There was much paddy (unhusked rice), lentils, papayas, Khasi mandarins, small potatoes and tomatoes, kohl rabi, horseradish, cauliflower and dried fish from the rivers. The air was full of noise: shopkeepers calling their prices, children screeching with delight at the hope of receiving sticky 'sweetmeats' from parents with money to spend. There were chickens, ducks, all alive and struggling to escape the cane thongs holding their feet together. There were eggs galore; Nicky told me the fresh ones were excellent, small but with deep orange-red yolks and a good flavour.

Nicky paid every worker on the estate himself. First the men, then the women, followed by the 'youths and maidens'. Their names were called from the alphabetically ordered paybooks, and Nicky would count the cash and hand it to the person, who saluted on receipt, the men with the right hand raised, the women with both hands together. Whilst the men were being paid the women sat and stared at me, the new '*chota sahib*' small or junior sahib, whispering to each other. Eventually their place was taken by the younger ones, who stared as much; and if I returned an interested stare, a hand would come up to hide a mouth daring to smile, and sideways looks would be exchanged, as well as elbow digs. It was interesting to see so many distinctly different types, and I thought I felt the stirrings of artistic leanings, long stifled by the coming of the War, now roused by the colours both of skin and clothes, richly lit by the golden afternoon sun. It was a fascinating picture, all the more enjoyable as it was new. I greatly admired Nicky's dedication and patience in seeing the payment finished, written up, with a list of non-attenders appended for further attention. It all took more than two hours, and when we arrived back for a wash and tea, Nicky started the generator so that we could lift the bonnet of his car and look at the engine. After dinner we talked about tea nutrition. Nicky had a diploma in agriculture, and knew what it was all about, and it became more and more interesting as we progressed. We went to bed at nine, and I was off to sleep before I could sum up the day.

Chapter IV

On this, my first Saturday in Assam, Nicky took me in his newly acquired car into the town of Dibrugarh, a few miles away from where he lived. He drove through the main street and bazaar area, past the Anglican church, and out to the north of the town where we could see the Brahmaputra river, nearly a mile away across a patchwork of flat, sandy scrub areas. Beyond the river lay the distant North Bank, with a dark blanket of forest extending beyond to the Himalayan foothills, blue in the clear sunlight, rising in ridge after ridge into the distance, with a few snow peaks showing faintly to the north-east. I asked him where the North Bank estates lay, and he pointed west-south-west, about fifty miles or more away. The area to the north was sparsely populated, and there were few motor roads; there was a sawmill about twenty-five miles away which operated not far from the edge of the Brahmaputra, able to send its timber in large rafts all the way down to Calcutta. In the hills there were tribes known to the Assamese as Abors, who were described as Sino-Tibetan, and according to anthropological books were leading a bronze age style of life. Nicky said they came sometimes to the local bazaars in the cold weather, and when we drove back into town he pointed out a party of them, the women carrying large back packs made from woven reeds. They were short, sturdy folk who wore their own spun and woven textiles, decorated with their own distinctive designs. The men were recognisable by the way they cut their hair in a kind of inverted bowl, over which they wore hats woven from strong fine cane, with a flat brim, and the crown vaguely like a Norman helmet. The women and men wore their homespun black embroidered clothes, the women's wraps to below their knees, but the men wore short tabards about their shoulders, and brief cloths fastened to a cane belt, like a weight-lifter's truss, exposing fully the

59

well-developed thighs and calves of mountain people. Both sexes wore necklaces of turquoise and other semi-precious stones, mixed with some silver ornaments and charms. Salt was precious to them, and they would always buy a lot to take back to their villages. Their territory spread from the Subansiri in the west to the Dihang in the east. Beyond their boundaries there were other Sino-Tibetan tribes of various kinds, speaking their own distinct languages, with only vestigial similarities. There were British 'political officers', mostly ex-army officers who used to tour the tribal areas and administer justice. Nicky said the Abors had many years ago murdered their political officer, it was said through initially testing his divinity by ham-stringing, to prove whether he was divine or not, and when they found he succumbed like a normal human they killed him. A British punitive expedition was sent, which burned many villages, since when there hadn't been any more trouble.

There was so much I found fascinating. The lure of the distant wilderness resurged strongly. Although I regarded our proximity to a town as a serious disappointment I saw that it was virtually a frontier town. Not only were there tribals from the hills, but I was learning there were so many different communities living all around us: we were in a rich field of diverse communities, with different languages and cultures, and it captured my interest strongly.

We went to the bank to put my application to open an account through its brass letterbox. We went to the Planters Stores where Nicky ordered things like light bulbs, a wire cutter, disinfectant for the dispensary and so on. He said except for food and clothes one would find whatever else one needed in this general store. Then we came to the Doom Dooma Stores, which widened my eyes with its stocks of pre-war luxuries in abundance. There was New Zealand butter, French and Italian wine (which Nicky told me never travelled well), whisky of many kinds, Amstel and Allsops beer. There were English biscuits, French cheese, Australian cheese in tins, and round sealed tins of Liptons' tea. In addition to food and drink they had all kinds of household stores. It was inconvenient for me to convert thirteen rupees to the pound, and Nicky said one and six to the rupee was the best way. However, as he had told me on the second day, he would treat me as a paying guest, do all the purchasing, and settle at the end of each week, therefore I confined myself to the delights of gloating on what was available:

tinned peaches, tinned cream, tinned sardines, fruit pastilles. I wondered if one could send food parcels to Britain, but Nicky explained how long it would take, how much it would cost, and how uncertain it would be that it would reach its destination, and I dropped the idea. There were several planters, some with their wives, buying food, lace-edged muslin netting to keep flies off plates of food, biscuits, butter etc. Nicky exchanged greetings with some, and eventually took me to buy some ruled notebooks for my language and management notes. At about four-fifteen we drove to the planters' club, parked the car, and Nicky took me in to see what it looked like. There were people in tennis kit coming and going, with tennis being played on the courts outside. A few men were drinking at the bar as we passed, and I noted the way Nicky waved happily to them without responding to their taunts or invitations to join them. We kept moving and left by the front door. From the front steps we could see the polo ground, about a quarter of a mile down sun.

Several riders cantered lazily around, hitting balls to each other, and we walked over the large expanse of grass to where there were about twenty horses tethered under a row of huge trees, with their *syces* (stable lads) tightening girth straps and brushing them down. There was a long trestle table placed between this row of trees and the edge of the polo field, where several ladies either sat on chairs facing the field across the table or busied about with teapots and plates of sandwiches, most of them wearing or carrying broad-brimmed hats. Nicky took me to where the players stood in various knots: most of them lean, brown men in riding kit, some wearing their polo topis, all turning to watch us approach with the kind of fixed, dispassionate stare I had always associated with mariners and aviators. I was introduced to the first knot by Nicky as 'ex-air force – Spitfire pilot', and shook some firm hands. One short, pleasant-faced man with a dark moustache said: 'Spitfires! No damned good. I've flown Hurricanes; excellent aeroplanes.' The others laughed, and one told him to stoop shooting lines. He told me during the War the commanding officer of a Hurricane squadron at Dinjan airfield took him up in a Hurricane, letting him sit on his lap, and actually let him use the controls! He was Charlie Crewe-Read, Nicky told me, a brilliant shot; he was a horseman who looked as if he was going to fall off any moment, but could score goals by hitting from the halfway line with fantastic force and accuracy. There were also many new faces that I couldn't remember names or locations, but several faces seemed to register, I think because of the character they portrayed. A team had come up from Jorhat, a place about sixty miles south-west on the South Bank. I remembered Nicky introducing me to a good-looking, well-built chap in a blue polo vest, ex-army. Afterwards he told me this chap had been two and a half years on Death Railway, a prisoner of the Japs. He had certainly recovered physically, but there was something in his face which showed a different kind of look from the others.

One of the ladies came forward and asked if we would like some tea and sandwiches. I was introduced, and when she heard my name she said, 'Ah! We've been hearing about you. Come and meet the others.' When I asked Nicky how on earth she had been hearing about me, he smiled indulgently and gave the answer I was to hear so often: 'Jungle telegraph. George. Calcutta. Cooks meeting in the bazaar. One of the ladies seeing us in the Doom Dooma Stores. That kind of thing.' The sandwiches were good, and I ate hungrily. The tea was at last excellent, and when I said so one of the ladies gave a tinkling laugh and said her husband would be very pleased to hear what I had said. Apparently the polo players took it in turn to provide the tea leaf for polo days, and I learned there was fierce competition to earn praise, and it often led to much rough criticism and caustic humour. Eventually polo started, and although the horses – all called ponies – were very diverse in weight, height and speed, the game was full of action. It was astonishing to hear the torrent of abuse hurled between sides during the charging gallops, most of it being the sort of thing we would never have dreamed of using except in circumstances of mutual baccalorean fury, far from the sensitive ears of ladies; but the ladies showed no sign of outrage or disapproval, and followed the chukkas with enthusiasm. I laughed at Nicky having blushed when introducing me to the ladies, who were, one must admit, a remarkably good-looking collection, but he pointed at me as having blushed so much that he could not but keep me company. The ladies ranged from the age of about twenty-four to fifty-odd, and seemed a happy lot.

I was introduced to a large, tough-looking Major who rode up later on a fine, large charger, dressed for polo. He was known as Monty, and was the permanent Indian Army officer who was Adjutant of the local battalion of the Assam Valley Light Horse, a territorial unit. He asked me if I would join the battalion, saying it would be a great help if I wanted to play polo as I would be issued with a horse, saddlery, and receive a monthly cash allowance for feeding and caring for the horse. He said I would be expected to attend periodic parades and exercises, of course, which gave me a slight feeling of distaste; but I signified assent, and he said he would send me the papers to fill in. Nicky took me aside eventually and suggested I wait until I was posted to my 'next billet', as he called it, explaining one should always clear such things with one's manager. He said that my future manager was in fact there, and he ought to introduce me to him. 'That's him,' he said, pointing to a chukka in progress, 'Jack Telford; a most unusual person. He'll look at you like a police detective, and he'll cross-examine you, but don't worry, he's always like that, with everybody. He's one of those very clever people who become so obsessed with their ideas that others think he is too eccentric. He's a highly competent planter, and is always racing ahead with his ideas on everything. You'll learn a lot from him; but just in case you are taken in by his sometimes very relaxed comments or remarks, you should look out for the very vaguest suggestions of what will, if you don't detect it, turn out to be orders which you either forgot or didn't agree with. It can be rather exasperating.' This gave me a feeling of uncertainty, and as I watched the polo I saw Telford ride his beautiful pony – one of the few horses one could call a polo pony – as an expert in the saddle and at the game.

'I believe there's a bit of animosity going on in the polo crowd,' said Nicky. 'Telford is leading what he calls the young Turks, all of them older than me, to dislodge the old fogeys who select themselves for the tournament teams. Old Philip there: portly gent, who sits his horse well and hits a straight ball, but according to Jack hasn't got the drive and fury needed to beat Jorhat, Moran, Nazira, and Cinnamara. You know, MacStorm, there's backbiting in all club activities out here. You have to watch it; be careful you don't agree with anyone. If you do you will reap a crop of enemies you haven't even met before you've been here a couple of months.'

When the chukka ended we strolled to the lists where Telford was holding forth in a gentle but insistent way to the others of his team, and we stood listening as he told one of them only to try a long shot at goal if the opposition was following at speed; but if the field was waltzing in circles trying to claw the ball from you, concentrate on knocking it out to someone well placed for a run and a shot. I could see cold grins from the others who were clearly interested in enjoying their game even if they lost. Nicky winked at me, drifting to a spot halfway to the tea table where he eventually intercepted Telford, and managed my introduction to him.

'Oh! MacStorm. Yes, you're coming to me, aren't you?'

'Yessir,' I said, shaking hands.

He looked at Nicky with a wry grin. 'You surely haven't taught him that, have you?' He looked at me, head tilted forward and to one side. 'We don't sir each other in tea, you know. We have a kind of relaxed discipline, don't we, MacFortune?'

'MacStorm was a pilot in the Air Force.' Nicky smiled apologetically. 'It'll take him time to forget his service discipline.'

Telford laughed slowly down the scale. 'But he was in the Air Force you said. I know for a fact there isn't much discipline in the Air Force. I met them all at Chabua and Dinjan; Americans and British: all Christian names and private personal uniforms.'

Remembering Nicky's valuable forewarning I smiled. 'There were times for Christian names, times for formality. If you hear me say sir it would probably mean I was reverting to formality, rather like . . .' I groped for a simile, 'like coming down to the speed limit when seeing a policeman.' The reaction was barely noticeable, but I thought his amber eyes glowed for a second. He changed the subject, and told me he hoped I would learn as much as possible from MacFortune who was a trained agriculturist, before coming to work for a man whose ideas were thought by most people to be wrong. I told him MacFortune had not only taught me a lot already in my first few days, but had transformed my initial disappointment at finding I was to live virtually on a railway line into a really keen fascination to become involved with planting and its people. He was quick to ask how I came to choose a career in tea, and I said it had something to do with being fond of wild places, where there weren't too many people. He was surprised to learn I had not been based in India with the Air Force, and amused at the tales of the colonel-tea planter having captured my imagination. I said I was interested in taking up polo, and wondered if it was a wise thing to wait until I move over. He seemed to find it a good idea, and said there would be room in the stables for another horse or two. Mrs Telford appeared from nowhere, shook hands with Nicky and me, and said she had guessed I was the ex-air force person coming to 'our estate'. She was a very good-looking, dark-haired woman with remarkably smooth skin showing the pleasant tone of very light sunburn. Her voice was pleasant, slightly nasal, with a studied King's English pronunciation. She asked us to have more tea and sandwiches which we did, I with gusto, being quite hungry ever since my arrival in Assam. More people approached, introducing themselves and pleasantries were exchanged. One man, after introducing himself partially – wearing dark glasses so that I could not round him off, as it were, by looking him in the eye – asked me why on earth I had come out to this godforsaken country to start a career in tea just as it was becoming likely it was all going to fold up, with the British government deciding to accelerate India's independence. Telford broke in to tell me independence for India was out of the question until the day India was able to provide people who were able to run this large country of theirs, and that day was a long way ahead. They need us to show them how to do it – after all look how long it took Britain to arrive at a state capable of governing itself properly. Dark Glasses suggested Britain was not a very good example, after two world wars in which millions of people were killed, and I noted how Telford's eyes really did fix Dark Glasses with the blazing stare of a predator. I was waiting with breath held for what Telford's eyes promised would be a swift and sharp delivery, when Nicky suddenly said it was time we moved back to the club, and asked the others to excuse us.

As we walked back across the huge cropped field Nicky asked if I had seen Telford's eyes focus on Stapleford, and laughed his husky laugh. 'You have to get to know people. Telford's all right once you get to know a bit about him. He's always obsessed about something, or somebody. Helluva tough disciplinarian with his assistants, Indian staff, and labour; but he's basically good to them all; he gives them what he thinks is good for them, and he is mostly right. Stapleford is an odd sort of chap: always going around deliberately upsetting people. It doesn't pay to go too far with that sort of thing. Managers don't want people like him who upset their staff and labour. His wife always seems scared of him, that lovely dark-haired girl with big, dark eyes. I'll point her out to you. Doesn't it make you angry when you see a lovely girl married to a scruffy tyrant, or a bore, or a dead beat?' I grinned and nodded. The sun was just over the trees around the club, and hearing the thunder of hooves on the turf and the hoarse yelling of the riders, I turned to see what was happening in the last chukka. The late afternoon sun lit the scene with rich gold: the horses and riders looked splendid, one team in scarlet waistcoats, the other in bright blue, with the sun catching the gleaming sweat of the ponies, the floral dresses of the ladies, and the white clothes, coloured blankets and shawls of the local people lined up on the side of the polo field. The green grass and the huge trees made the scene similar to any rural area in Britain in late summer, and I reminded myself how ridiculous the idea would be to aspire to play polo there.

I asked Nicky what he thought of my idea to take up polo, from the financial point of view, wondering why he had neither taken it up nor commented why. He said he was not a keen horseman, never had been; but he said as long as the A.V.L.H. more or less subsidised it at government expense it shouldn't cost too much, but one had to look at the logistics involved. He asked if I had ever heard the word logistics before: 'A Yankee word, you know. We had a lot to do with the Yanks in Burma, and they used the word for what we would call transport of supplies and all that for an operation. Good word! What I mean is if you haven't a car you will be dependent on someone else to take you to and from polo, not just to this place but all over Upper Assam. I think Telford would help you, especially if you turned out to be good and keen. He's off on home leave in April for six months. I've heard the jungle drums suggest his acting manager will be Louis Foyle; he joined tea about the same time as I did. He's a real country Irishman, good rider, and he used to play polo before the War. Apparently he's married, so I don't know what that might mean as far as polo and horses go; but he's one of those really pleasant characters, good mixer but not a compulsive socialiser, with a marvellous sense of humour. He was always keen on the prettiest girls, and I am interested to see the wife he has brought out.'

By this time we had arrived at the club, and from the number of cars parked outside I saw a lot of people had arrived. We entered the main room where the bar was already crowded with men. There were fewer ladies, all sitting well away from the bar in circles round cane tables, mostly with what looked like gin and lemon. They had a good look at us as we went in. Nicky wrinkled his forehead and murmured in my ear that we needn't get involved in drinking unless I was desperate, and would have a drink when we got back. I nodded, and we began to meet people. I remember one large elderly Yorkshireman nearly crushing my hand in his huge fist, who introduced another Yorkshireman: a new ex-air force assistant coming to learn how to grow tea, with whom I chatted for a few minutes. He was ex-Bomber Command and had been on Lancasters, but because of the noise of conversations I found it difficult to understand what he was saying. We decided all the conversations we heard around us were difficult to understand, mostly being about tea, using a vocabulary of botanical and agricultural words mixed with Hindustani. I met several friends of MacFortune, and within half an hour he suggested we quietly disappeared, which we did. It became dark very quickly after sunset, and as we drove through the town we passed several of the polo ponies, well covered against the chill of the evening, being led by their syces. Nicky told me some of them would have to walk fifteen miles home; no such thing as horse boxes out here. It actually felt good to arrive chez MacFortune; the gaunt dark bungalow was becoming more familiar, and we took off our blazers, put on thick pullovers, and settled before the fire of blazing logs.

My host rose and stood with his back to the fire, legs wide apart. 'Now!' he said, 'I have a bottle of Scotch. Join me. Let us drink toasts in the real stuff!'

I begged to be forgiven, as I was not a spirits drinker. I would be happy with a double orange juice, truly. I explained I never drank during the War, and afterwards had tried cider and beer without becoming keen on either. After pressing me further without shaking my desire for the delightful juice, he took his large bunch of keys from his pocket, lifted a glass from the tray on the table near the door, and went to the far end of the room where the old leather chest lay. He went down on one knee, opened the chest, took out the bottle of whisky and unscrewed the top.

'Are you sure, MacStorm? To celebrate your arrival, your first weekend in Assam?'

I declined again with thanks, and he poured his measure, screwed the top on, replaced the bottle in the chest, locked it, and came back to the tray. He called the bearer and told him to bring my orange juice and some water. Whilst we waited he asked me if I had lost any really good friends in the Air Force, seen them 'bite the dust' so to speak. I thought for a while, and when I nodded he asked me to tell him about it, and I chose to tell of how

Johnny died. We raised our glasses and drank to the Gurkhas and the Air Force, and I reminded him after this tale was his turn, to tell about his MC, which he had promised.

Johnny and I were on the same flying school in Rhodesia, and after a spell in the Middle East finished up together in England on our favourite Spitfires. We were both airborne on that fateful day, climbing out on separate courses, through several layers of steamy cloud, and when I had reached about 20,000 feet I heard him making a distress call. His engine was on fire and he wanted instructions. I scanned the direction in which I thought him to be and soon saw about eight miles away a thick trail of black smoke. Someone was asking Johnny to transmit for bearings to be taken, and I called to say I could see him, and had altered course and increased speed to approach him. I also called Johnny and told him for God's sake to bale out, bale out, bale out! I came to within a mile and a half of the burning Spitfire and saw it go into a dive, showing orange flame as it went. At about 10,000 feet some tanks exploded, and the aircraft continued down until about a mile from the coast it hit the ground in another bigger explosion. I called to report what I had seen, circling at about 12,000 feet, and as I spoke I saw him just below me in his parachute, and said so jubilantly. I approached carefully to within about 200 yards, rocking my wings in salute, but after another closer fly-past I came to the chilling conclusion that his head was hanging forward, and his arms were inert, showing no sign of acknowledgement. I didn't think it could have been unconsciousness caused by oxygen lack, as he must have been well below 20,000 feet when he jumped. I reported this to the rescue frequency, and said I was keeping him in sight meanwhile. Within ten minutes I called again to report Johnny as descending into a big stack of developing cumulus, about 2,000 feet deep, and suggested they send a slower aircraft to patrol well below the cloud. I gave a position, which was just over the coast. There was an off-shore breeze. I descended a few miles away through a gap in the cloud, and found visibility very poor in the haze. At last I was told to abandon patrol and return to base, and without seeing the parachute again I turned and flew back, very depressed about Johnny hanging inert, wondering if he had been overcome by fumes, or burns, or perhaps he had been hit by the tail plane when abandoning the aircraft. Later the commanding officer had news that an Avro Anson had seen the parachute, and stayed by it, seeing no movement

68

from the pilot. An air-sea rescue launch saw the parachute come down about three miles away. The sea was very choppy, and although the launch and the Anson searched until dark there was no sign of the parachute or the inflatable dinghy. About ten days later his body was washed up on the coast, and an examination showed he had died from fumes and burns long before he went into the sea. We had been very close friends, both mad keen on flying as well as having the same taste in books and music.

The day before his death Johnny was very depressed that the War was going to be over soon, before we had a chance to win the glory of the small purple and white striped ribbon. He had snapped at one of our colleagues who had said he couldn't wait to get back home and out of uniform, to knock down a few pheasants and partridges, catch a few trout, and get back to real life on his father's farm; it was very unlike Johnny. Although he was game and intrepid as any of us, he could in absent-minded moments be seen with an expression of what one of his girlfriends once called 'sweet sadness'. I remembered sitting outside the officers' mess in Palestine late at night, gazing at the glorious scintillation of stars and planets, listening to the nostalgic singing of the Italian prisoners who served in the officers' mess. We talked about how human beings over the ages observed the stars, and wondered at the mystery of man's ability to foresee death, and his difference from animals, and why. He mentioned having an aunt who was a spiritualist, and heard his parents say how she had spoken with spirits of deceased relatives, learning things from them which nobody would believe until something was found to prove indisputably she was right. When I told him I preferred not to have anything to do with the occult, he told me I was a bigoted Presbyterian who didn't want to see what we were probably meant to see; and I remember thinking him oddly petulant. For about a month after his death I kept dreaming of seeing him, hanging on his parachute, head forward, but he was always looking sideways at me with a bright-eyed smile. After seeing another friend of ours burst into flames on take-off, then explode, the dreams of Johnny stopped, and I had never dreamed of him since, although I had often thought sadly what a waste of a good man it was. I often wondered if there had been some kind of premonition which had made him unusually intolerant. 'It was always the best who bought it,' I said, 'and Johnny was a thoroughly good chap. It was very sad that when we met two girls at a dance, the one Johnny fell for actually fell for me: a slim blonde with beautiful green eyes. I admired her looks a lot, but didn't feel any tendency to fall in love with her. Her friend was a happy dark-haired girl, who fell hopelessly in love with Johnny, who spurned my advice to go for the blonde as a very unfair way to behave, and stood by the curvaceous brunette as if it was the honourable thing to do. He was scathing that I wouldn't give the blonde girl a chance, and for the first time told me he was disappointed in my attitude towards women. I had to tell him I was sure total honesty was best, but he refused to discuss the matter any more.' I described the awful breaking of the news of Johnny's death to the two girls, wondering if Johnny had after all been too good for this world; and since I was so deeply convinced he was wrong I might be hopelessly out of touch with the meaning of good and evil.

Nicky listened to this with rapt attention, and when I had finished he stared into the red depths of the large wood fire for a few minutes without speaking. He finished his whisky, stood again back to the fire and asked, as before, if I would join him. I declined, draining my orange juice and held it up tapping it with my finger, smiling in request. He called the bearer, told him to bring another juice, then went to the old leather chest, knelt, and went through the whole ritual again, offering me a whisky once more. After locking the chest he paced slowly back to the fire.

'Look, MacStorm! I'll tell you my story, but be patient. I have to tell it in a particular way so that you understand it fully. OK?' He raised his glass and said, 'To the best ones, who bought it!' He chuckled hoarsely, and we drank our toast. Then he put down his glass, and strode away to his bedroom, returning within minutes with an armful of thick cloth which he put down on the middle of the floor well away from the fire. He unwrapped it briskly, and I saw it was a huge tiger skin, with a great mounted head showing large fangs and a splendid ruff. Nicky went to his chair, and I rose to have a close look. My hands are not big, but when I gripped one of the large canines, forefinger against the small teeth, the tip of it showed beyond the crook of my small finger. Its claws were terrifying: large, sharp and black. I settled back in my chair, fascinated with the idea that such creatures abounded here in Assam, and stared from it to Nicky and back again. He pointed to it. 'You know, I shot this thing not five miles away from here when I had hardly been three weeks in Assam, when I first came out. Would you believe it?' I found it difficult to adjust my expectations of a tale to do with the

Gurkhas in Burma, to something about shooting a tiger, but managed to swivel my head slowly, incredulously, looking at the remarkably well-contrived snarl on the face of the tiger. 'I'll tell you about it,' Nicky said, and I settled to listen.

'I remember going down to this out-garden with my manager, following him around and asking questions. When we had been all round he had a long talk with the staff and the *sirdars*, and the line *chowkidars*. I couldn't understand what it was all about, but saw it was something serious. He told me the people on the estate, and the local villagers, were losing cattle at the rate of three or four per month, and were seriously upset at this depletion of their meagre wealth. They had no money in the bank, only cattle; some of them having only two which they used for ploughing their small rice fields. The whole area down there is thickly forested: lots of wild pig, deer, and tigers. There had always been plenty of tigers, and plenty of game for them to feed on; but something had gone wrong, either a shortage of game, or a tiger not able to kill the game. Sometimes it could be a wounded tiger, sometimes a female with cubs having lost its mate. Something had to be done. The manager was frank: he did not want to have to "sit up" for a cattle killer again. He had been in the artillery in the First World War, and his hearing was so bad it was useless trying to detect the forest noises any more. He asked if I was interested in trying it out, and being young and romantic I volunteered to try. He organised two men who would construct a platform hide in a tree over the next kill, and he would give me a talk on the whole business of dress, patience, sounds to listen for, and show me his heavy rifle with its torch clamped so that the forward left hand could press the torchlight on, and grip hard at the same time to aim a shot. Within the week there was a kill, a large white bullock was killed in mid-afternoon under a very convenient tree with a smooth trunk up to fifteen feet, and good branches in which to build the hide. My manager's advice was detailed and clear. There was room for me alone in the hide, which I reached by the primitive ladder made from two long branches tied together. The two men saw me into position just before sunset, and carried the branches away along the narrow, overgrown game track, talking loudly as they increased their distance until I could hear them no more. I was really excited, especially as the tremendous chorus of birdsong gradually died after sunset, and then I was completely baffled by all the weird noises which came at furtive intervals as it grew darker. Mosquitoes began to whine and bite, but I demonstrated my steadiness and remained still. The leaves around my hide had been trimmed enabling me to see the only way a tiger could enter and leave the kill area, but it was so dark I couldn't hope to see any movement. My manager had said it would probably be like that, and I must wait until I heard the unmistakable noise of the tiger either beginning to feed, or seizing the kill to drag it away. He had also said even the most experienced shots would sometimes spend long nights over kills without any sign of the tiger; he had once spent five nights one after the other on different kills before having any luck. Remembering this, and feeling tired, bitten, and suffering from foundering hope, I was shaken suddenly by a loud blowing sound below, followed by a crackling crunch. I switched on, and there he was, that one, and I aimed into the bulk of his shoulder, not quite vertically down, and he dropped like a sack of sand. There was one gurgling cough, and blood showed on the white body of the bullock. I watched carefully until I saw no more movement, and then shouted three times. This was easy! The men eventually called from about a hundred yards away, and I called them in. When I clambered down, feeling as proud as hell, I was amazed at the size of him. One of the men, the owner of the bullock, cursed and swung his *dao* (bush knife) as if to cleave the magnificent skull, and I thrust the rifle barrel forward to prevent the blow from falling. The men said they would have to bring four more men to carry the body out to the office shed, from where it could be transported to my bungalow next morning. I waited for about half an hour until the arrival of about ten men, who saluted me and cursed the tiger. Whilst I waited for them I began by gloating over the magnificence of this great beast, but slowly began to think there was something wrong with killing such a beautiful creature, and felt uneasy about it. He didn't have a chance; but as the locals say: they can't be warned off, so "*kya karega*", what shall one do? I was a hero overnight, and it got me off to a good start with the staff and labour and, amazingly, with the other planters, who had tended to look down their noses at new boys like myself.

'Surprisingly, after about three weeks the cattle-killing began again, and after the second kill my manager said I should try my luck again, with his rifle; how did I feel about it? I had sent the skin off, salted and rubbed with alum, to be done like this; but the cost was frightening, and I was quite sure

72

I wouldn't be able to afford to do it again for a long time. My manager said he would give me a bottle of whisky for the next skin, and the deal was done. The kill was again in quite a good place. All was arranged, and this time I took a small automatic pistol with me, and told the men I would fire two shots to call them when necessary. I mounted the tree feeling like a real veteran, and actually enjoyed the first five hours of my vigil. It was warmer than last time, and the mosquitoes were thirstier, making complete immobility impossible. You can't use things like citronella oil to keep them away: it's like sending a telegram to the tiger about what is in store if he approaches. At about two in the morning I thought I had suffered enough, and decided to fire two small shots with the automatic to call the men in. It was one of those "handbag" firearms which had to be cocked by sliding the top backwards, and as I tried to cock it holding the gun between my knees, it went off. It fired downwards, and so I fired a second shot for the men. When they arrived and I prepared to descend using the torch, I found the copper bullet lying on the bamboo platform, and thought to myself this pistol wouldn't kill a mouse; the ammunition must be old. I put it in my pocket and climbed carefully down. About a quarter of a mile along the path out of the jungle I felt my boot squelching, and shone the torch on it to see what I had trodden in. Blood was oozing from the lace holes, and the men laughed, saying by signs it was a leech I picked up on the way out to the kill in the evening. The thing is, MacStorm, these beastly little things first anaesthetise you, and then inject you with anti-coagulant so that they can suck away without the blood in the wound solidifying. Anyway, after another half mile I began to feel pain. By the time we reached my bungalow the two men were jolly nearly carrying me, the pain was so severe. When I took my boot and stocking off I could see I had shot myself through the thick inner phalange of my big toe. The bullet I had in my pocket had gone through my foot and through the thick leather sole of my boot, its energy spent before coming to rest on the bamboo platform. Look! I hadn't felt a thing, not the slightest pain or even shock of impact when it happened. I can't describe the awful indignity of it. The story flew round that I had seen something move below and taken a shot at it, hitting myself in the foot. Imagine, trying to drop a brute like that with a .25 automatic. Crikey! They had some good laughs about it, for quite a long time. I made things worse by trying to explain what actually happened, which made them laugh even more. Some of these humorous boozers give me the pip, you know. Listen, you must be hungry; how about some dinner?' I looked surprised and said I thought he was going to tell me about what he got up to with the Gurkhas in Burma, saying he had me all keyed up with anticipation. He went through the ceremony of putting a peg of whisky into his glass, and filling it with water, and continued. It was a long time ago, and I might get some of the details wrong, but it is a story deserving to be told, more than fifty years after it happened, and over forty-eight years since he told me.

'Look, I promise you I'll give you no bullshit or false modesty. I was a lieutenant with the Gurkhas, and we hadn't been very long in Burma, worming our way through dense forest somewhere not far from Myitkyina. The Japs were on the retreat, but in our area things had ground to a bit of a halt. In that terrain vehicles were impossible, and supply drops were hopelessly impracticable except in riverbeds, where they were wide enough. Fighters were not much use with ground attack in a situation where units were on the move constantly, either forwards or back, depending on close-quarter lunging by one side or the other. Maps were hopeless. There was this Jap strongpoint on the inside of a bend in a river. Attempts to flush them ran into trouble, and apparently without shifting them our forces couldn't find a way to encircle them – or something of that sort. I was told to take a platoon and make a reconnaissance of the strongpoint, something the Gurkhas are known to be very good at. You know, they move through jungle, undergrowth, grass, like leopards. It took me time to learn the strength of their patience; they would lie still long enough to delude anyone into believing there was no-one there. It took us a long time to find a way to crawl near enough to the crucial strongpoint to see it as clearly as possible. It was an old fisherman's hut, surrounded by thickets of terrible thorns. There were several machine-guns in the hut, and I had been warned of rifles on the high ground on the other side of the river. I sent two good men to investigate the high ground, and after a long time they came back grinning, showing me some empty Jap cartridges, signing they had gone days ago. With me I had a Subadar Major, a kind of senior NCO, who suggested we crawl closer in the low, thorny scrub, and we did this until we guessed we were about sixty yards from the hut. The Subadar Major pointed out the way the sun was sinking behind us, shining straight at the hut, with our ground in shadow. We could hear the Japs talking, laughing, and saw smoke rising. The SM indicated they would soon be eating, and showed me fifteen minutes on his watch. I asked him, whispering in his ear, what was he thinking of. He smiled, and said: "The chaps say fixed bayonets and charge, sahib." The only way. I told him of the machine-guns thinking of my revolver and their rifles, and – yes – grenades. He asked me to let him pick three men to sprint far enough to throw two grenades each, and said I should give the order to charge after the explosion. I went cold with fear, thinking I would be leading them into the jaws of death; but looking him in the eye I saw he was twinkling with sheer delight at the prospect. He said bayonets were all fixed, and pointed to where I could see one of the men with the grenades creeping like a cat, slowly, head down. This, I thought, is where I die a glorious death. I can't let these men down. If I took them away they would never look at me again, they would think I was yellow. Then I thought: I know it won't hurt, not unless I'm winged; then it will hurt later, but I might survive. All of this, MacStorm, spun through my head at a helluva speed, and I felt it was a dream in which nothing serious was going to happen: just a dream. I told the SM "ready". He nudged a man near him, all of us lying on our sides, and the man made a croaking cry like some jungle bird. The three men rose and sprinted at speed, dodging through the thickets of thorn, and from about twenty yards threw their six grenades into the hut without the Japs having seen or heard them. The men hit the ground, heads down as the grenades went off, and I leapt to my feet and yelled "charge", dashing like a wing forward, stocky little men alongside in a furious and outrageously ambitious charge. At about thirty yards machine-guns opened up. The sound of machine-gun bullets rasping past my ears made me shout louder. The Japs were yelling, some were screaming, maybe some from pain. I fired my revolver into the window I saw in front of me, and all the time I was saying to myself, "It's not going to hurt." The Gurkhas crashed in with kukris drawn and within less than five minutes the Japs were all dead, and minus their ears. I could have screamed with glorious relief, and went round slapping them on the back. I looked for the SM, and saw him walking slowly back the way we came. He heard me coming, turned and saluted smartly. "Counting for report, sir," he said. When we arrived at the figure of our losses, when I saw them lying there, I felt a terrible weight come down on me. The SM had a bullet graze on his neck, and one of the riflemen had a gashed shoulder from one of the grenades. There were no other injuries, only deaths. This would be called a successful operation. If it had gone just a little wrong, if a Jap had seen us start to run or heard a noise too soon, we'd have been wiped out, and they would have said, "That bloody fool MacFortune! He led them all to certain death; not a hope in hell. What a waste of good troops." But you know, MacStorm, these Gurkhas aren't dim; they wouldn't have tried it unless they thought we could beat the Japs, maybe losing some of us. I know I did it because I was more afraid of what they would have thought of me than I was of dying. I have to live with that, you know. I have to live with the loss of all those fine, happy, marvellous soldiers.'

We sat for a long time, watching the great pile of flickering embers. I thanked him for telling me his story, saying I would never forget it. I have forgotten details, I know, but not the essence; and nearly two decades later, when Nicky was our group scientific officer, paying us visits on the North Bank to give advice, we were invited to take him with us to dinner in the officers' mess of a unit of the Assam Rifles. They were camped in the foothills forest, and their officers were Indian Army men. The troops were mainly Gurkhas, with a mixture of other hill tribals. They had a Scottish-type pipe band, and after dinner they played pipes and drums in honour of Nicky. We stood by the huge campfire as the stocky Gurkhas played the wild music; and when they played the Gurkhas march past we saw Nicky, holding his watered rum like the rest of us, his face contorted in a scowling smile, with tears running down his cheeks, and I remembered that evening by another fire, in my first week in Assam.

At the end of the second week in Assam we drove in to the Doom Dooma Stores. I made a few purchases whilst Nicky made his. When we arrived back for tea at the bungalow I told the bearer to bring several things up on the tea tray. There were cream crackers, a tin of Australian cheddar cheese, and a packet of New Zealand butter, things we did not have as a matter of course. When the tray arrived Nicky reached for the teapot and halted his hand over it, looking at the things which had arrived. He asked the bearer, who was hovering in the background with a nervous smile on his mouth and an expression of concern on his brow, where these things had come from. I told him I wanted to show my appreciation for his hospitality, and hoped he would join in a little celebration. He looked very seriously at me, hands on knees.

'Look, MacStorm, you're paying for your keep, you know. You shouldn't do this kind of thing. I mean: thank you very much, but you shouldn't! You can't afford it, you know. If you want to save money for whatever emergencies might arise out here or anywhere else in this world these days, you really have to save like the dickens. Nobody likes to talk about it, but there is plenty of rumour pointing strongly to India being given home rule; it could mean the end of jobs in tea for all of us, and what will you do then? You will need money whatever else you want to do. Don't be taken in by all those chaps drinking merrily at the bar. Even if the British government doesn't give India home rule, and you manage to finish your career in tea, jolly well remember that you have to retire from this job when you are fifty-five, and you'd better save as much as you can all the way there. You'll want to marry some time, and it costs money to do that, and to have children, educate them, and have enough to live on when you're too old to work. You can't afford this sort of thing, you know. He waved his hand over the biscuits, cheese and butter, making me feel very guilty and spendthrift, but it didn't stop my mouth from watering.

'MacFortune,' I said, 'you are absolutely right. I won't do it again, but let us enjoy this well-meaning indiscretion of mine together, even if only to celebrate my coming of financially sensible age; please?' We enjoyed our tea, and Nicky continued to impress me with the virtues of thrift. Later that same evening he brought out his book of expenditure, and went through it with me, dividing the cost of everything exactly, even to the extent of counting the remaining matches in the box in use so that the division was as nearly perfect as it could be. I was impressed, and began to see I had to take a very sober view of managing my own finances with a much longer-term outlook than ever before. He told me I was not in the Air Force any more, and just because the company had paid my fare out and would give me free accommodation, servants, and fuel, I mustn't think it's like being in the services. He said I shouldn't listen to some types who kept saying: you'll never save any money until the last seven or eight years of your service, when you are promoted to superintendent and get good salaries and big commissions. Everyone can't be a superintendent, and many leave with a pittance, regretting all they foolishly spent on parties, booze, and on impressing their families at home when they went on home leave, living it up like Burlington Bertie.

At the time I took all he had said seriously, but it was a long time before I realised what marvellous luck it was to have spent the crucial first six weeks with that admirable man, from whom I received the significant and lasting impressions at the birth of my new life: the beginning of the Damfool Career.

Chapter V

I had not been long with MacFortune when the news broke that the British government had announced its intention to grant independence to India in June 1948. We were called to George's bungalow along with his other British staff to listen to the news on his wireless set. His Bengali head clerk had in an ecstasy of excitement told him his son had heard from a friend who had a good short-wave radio, that the BBC had very early in the morning broadcast the prime minister's statement; it was not very clear, but the Bengali programme from Calcutta had since confirmed it. We drove down and listened to the news in George's sitting room at seven in the morning, all of us standing staring at the wireless set in a state of what can only be called bemusement. George turned the wireless off once the item had finished and stood facing us, pipe clenched in his teeth, feet apart and hands behind his back.

'Gentlemen! It is quite clear His Majesty's Government has paid not the slightest attention to any of its officers or advisers who know India and its problems, and doesn't care what is bound to happen to the people of India when law and order give way. Never mind what is going to happen to us: hold fast, and let us wait to hear what Calcutta will have to tell us about our future. Let us carry on doing our best at our work, no mistake about that.' He gazed around the room. 'My Chakravorty said to me India would be very grateful for its freedom. "But sir," he said, "we are afraid of the Muslims. Our family is in Calcutta, and the killings last August cut down thousands of our people. You should not leave so soon."' George smiled. 'Whatever your people say to you, tell them we know as little about what is going to happen as they do; let us carry on as usual. Don't let it depress you until you know what the programme is. Any questions?'

'I hope Calcutta is going to arrange for all women and children to be sent back to Britain as soon as possible.' The speaker was Gerald Delapere, another pipe smoker, a small man with a face almost like a boxer, covered with freckles. He spoke with curt emphasis, jutting his jaw and looking at all the others in the room as if expecting support. George smiled down his nose at him.

'I have an idea that Calcutta is going to be in a bigger flap than Assam with this news,' he said, 'and I think one should wait before charging the situation with more emergency than it demands. It's a long time until next June, Delapere, and long before then we shall learn more about what the British government has up its sleeve, if it remembers or cares that there are many of us working in India apart from the Army and the Civil Service. Very well, gentlemen! It's a bit of a nasty punch, sooner than anyone would have judged wise who see the problems ahead. Let's get back to work! Let's show we are not collapsing into dementia as we hear the death-knell of our careers in the tea industry! We have always given of our best: let us continue to do so with absolute steadiness until the terms of our fate become known. Thank you, gentlemen! On with the job.'

I must confess to being very impressed with George's speech. There was a touch of Churchill 1940, but instead of the dreadful threat to Britain by the Nazi conquerors of Europe, there was the less dreadful but rather mournful threat of careers crashing prematurely to a sorry end, worse perhaps for those who had spent most of their working lives in India than for people like me. When I said this to MacFortune he gave a husky hoot, and said we didn't exactly have any beaches to fight on here, and it was winning that war that led to the Labour government giving itself a romantic thrill by doing this to India: 'It's magnificent, but they won't be here when the balloon goes up!' As we drove back to Nicky's bungalow he said I would be all right: anyone who can fly an aeroplane will be sure of a job anywhere in the world. I told him there were so many pilots looking for jobs all over the world that it was highly unlikely I would find a flying job, unless war broke out again. I asked him what he thought of doing, and he surprised me by saying he thought there was a possibility of at least another three or four years for us – that means those with experience – who might be asked by the Indian government to teach Indians to grow tea, administer estates and all that. I said he had been telling me it took many years to learn all the arts and crafts one needed to run a tea estate, certainly more than three or four years. He said the Indians would have their own ideas about that; they would probably want to take everything over as quickly as possible, run it themselves.

'You see, MacStorm, we've taught them to be good soldiers; they'll fix their army on our lines and do it well, provided their politicians don't mess them around. The same with their judiciary: very high-quality stuff there again, provided the politicians don't abuse the integrity of those who administer the law. One of India's biggest problems is going to be the sort of corruption in business and politics which is in their blood since Mughal days. They spent all their time and ingenuity in circumventing the government, and they've been doing it all the time under the British. They deceive each other in business, and will go on doing it. The Army is the real legacy they will have; that's where they would find the right kind of chap to become tea estate managers, with a sense of discipline, good handling of people, cleanliness, honesty.'

I asked if he didn't think Indian service officers would prefer their chances of rapid promotion in the forces when the British left; it would probably be much more attractive then the remote country life of tea. I said surely they would expand their army and air force greatly if they were to become responsible for their own defence, to which with a husky chuckle Nicky suggested I might in that case find it easy to join the Indian Air Force, which made me think.

That day was a mid-week club day, and Nicky decided we should go in after tea to hear what people were saying about the news. As he said, there must be people on their way from Calcutta offices to communicate with their companies' estates and perhaps give the staff some guidelines to follow pending further developments. The club was crowded, and the noise increased as time went on. George greeted us and introduced his wife. They had no children, and his wife Poppy was a handsome, well-built lady with perfect diction and a bubbling laugh, who kept a very straight and serious face between her frequent laughs, and talked much refreshing good sense. She said she was hoping to organise a drinks party soon, inviting people from other groups in our own company, and a few from other companies. She said I must find it rather disappointing to hear what the British government was aiming to do, just as I had begun to settle down to life in tea. I said I had been conditioned to the possibilities of such an early conclusion by the 'old sweats' on board ship on the way out from England. They seemed to be convinced the end was in sight, but not quite so soon, and that was what had shaken me most: June 1948. George said it was going to be very interesting to see just what the Indian Congress party was going to make of it all, as this sudden announcement must have shaken them to the core. 'There are many hotheads among them you know, but there are people like Nehru, and Vallabhai Patel who have been fighting most of their lives, waiting for the day India would be free, and they will be hard put to organise how they take over government in time for June 1948. Take the tea industry for instance: it is huge, with great amounts of British money invested in Assam, Bengal and south India; it is an industry involving agricultural and horticultural experience which it takes a long time to learn. I doubt very much if they are silly enough to sweep all British management away and replace it with their own people who haven't the first idea of growing anything except rice, mangoes and bananas. Tea makes good profits over the years, and India will want the tax, the foreign exchange, and will still want to sell its tea to the biggest consumer, which is Britain. There's a lot pointing that way, you know.' Poppy broke in with her bubbling laugh.

'My dear George,' she said primly, 'do you expect the Indian Congress to allow such practical considerations to stand in the way of getting rid of the British, who have put most of the Congress into jail time and time again for struggling to achieve their freedom? I'm afraid I find it quite appalling the way the British spent all their time extolling the British way of life and education, and when many of the Indians followed the British style, like Nehru's father, who sent his son to Harrow and Cambridge, they refused to allow him to join any British club in India. How could we possibly be so unsporting to such willing conformers?'

George regarded her with an affectionate smile. 'You are right, Poppet, absolutely right. The mutiny was far too long ago.' At this point a tall grey-haired man came and bowed to Poppy, placed his hand on George's shoulder, and whispered in his ear. George excused himself with a confident grin so wide it showed a need to cover any expression of concern. His wife smiled as he went.

'George is so sweet, you know. He is never really happy unless he has some sort of emergency. He says it reminds him of the War, the First World

War of course. He loves situations like this that seem to promise doom and despair. He has a gift for describing the utter desperation facing us all, and summoning up the blood, sort of thing, so that everyone feels almost heroic, resolving never to give way. You know I think he was actually speaking quite sensibly about a tiny hope that all will not be lost. It depends on how it is all handled. Perhaps this sudden short-term plan to grant freedom will take a lot of fire out of the Indian politicians' attitudes; they might even themselves be inclined to say "not so fast", when they realise there is so much they will need to do in order to run this huge country with something like three hundred and fifty million people. It must be frightening, don't you think?' She turned to face me squarely, with a quizzical smile.

I had to think for a few seconds before admitting I knew so little about India it was difficult for me to form any meaningful opinion. 'All I can say is how disappointed I am at the prospect of leaving a country, and people, for whom I have in a very short time developed a sympathy, a liking, enough to make me depressed at the prospect of having to leave it all and start again.' She bubbled with laughter, and looked sideways at me. I told her I had been warned on the ship about being hooked by India, and was surprised that the magic had worked so quickly.

'Yes, there is certainly magic out here at this time of the year. They'll soon be celebrating their fertility festival: they know all about nature's magic. The other time for magic is a little less fraught with fertility and all that sort of thing: it's the sudden arrival of the cold weather, the end of the sweaty, mouldy monsoon months. It is usually in mid-October, and even the least sensitive of us forgives and forgets all the tensions, hates, jealousies, and sense of exile, and falls in love with India all over again.' She gave another chuckle and another sideways look. 'Although you have obviously begun to fall in love with the country I don't think you have been long enough here to begin falling in love with the girls.'

To this I replied I had seen one or two I certainly admired, and I said how disappointed I was to have had no time in Bombay to see the beauties by whom Bernard Shaw was greatly impressed when he visited India.

'Ah! Yes, you are young enough to be a socialist. Are you?'

'I am politically nothing, really, but I certainly enjoy Shaw's plays, and some of his prefaces.'

'I wouldn't talk about Shaw except to people you know well. Socialism is not at all popular around here since the election after the War; and now they are all blaming the socialists for their crazy idea of giving India over to a bunch of political socialists who won't be able to control the place.' It seemed she was quoting rather than propagating, and I asked what her political feelings were. 'Mr MacStorm, I think the trouble with socialists is that they feel rather than think. In practical politics we need people who don't just have feelings, but are intelligent enough to help people to provide for themselves in a world where their natural lives are disappearing. The irony is that in India most people look after themselves; they don't need politicians unless the politicians can get rid of the landlords without finishing up with something like Russia. It's all very difficult.'

The rest of the evening was a vast mixture of comment and expression of discontent, and I can but retrieve various snippets which remain dimly in my memory. There were many voices, many accents, mostly incredulous, some sceptical, some verging on the hysterical at the totally unexpected news of such a precipitant transfer of power to an Indian government.

'Churchill would never have done anything so damned silly; but he was in the Army in India, wasn't he?'

'They're putting out tea in Africa, you know. That's where I'm aiming for. We'll emigrate to Rhodesia, or Kenya. The government must surely give us resettlement grants.'

'New Zealand for me, chum. It's a country with no problems except the one I like: it's a bloody long way from everywhere. You can live off the land, and I can take my old woman with me; no colour problems there.'

'We have to be careful. If we try to resign now the company won't pay our passage home, will they? They'll keep us here until it's too late to get out safely. They'll have to lay on the RAF to fly us out if Bengal blows up. That means we'll lose all our bloody stuff; it only needs one or two to start looting and the whole lot will charge in and help themselves.'

'I'm certainly sending the wife off as soon as we can make a booking on a ship. We're not due another home leave for three years, and I hope they'll make an advance payment on her fare.'

'We've nowhere to live if we have to leave. On home leaves we've been staying a few weeks each with my brothers and sister, and the rest in a seaside bed-and-breakfast. We've put all our savings into insurances for our retirement, and I doubt if I'll be able to get a job at my age with all the unemployment at home. We'll be properly jiggered by the look of it. It's all right for you younger chaps, you can work your passage anywhere in the world and get any kind of a job to keep you going.'

'I don't give a damn! I'm staying as long as the booze lasts. I'm dam' well going to take on four old women as soon as I can, and they'll look after me if you all have to push off.'

For a while I found myself caught up with a happy crowd of fellow 'damfools', all of whom were boozing away with careless abandon, and expressed their intentions of carrying on thus until the next shake-out took place. One of them was called Joe, an ex-armoured corps lieutenant, tall, well built and handsome, with a scar on one cheek and jaw, who kept his five or six companions in fits of laughter with his views on what was to be done to remedy the situation for all young ex-service people like ourselves. He pretended to be quite convinced India would revert to the way it was when the British first set foot there. They would start fighting again, and we should offer ourselves as soldiers of fortune. He personally would seek to join the Sikhs, the Marattas or the Rajputs. Others interrupted him claiming it better to join with the Coorgis, the Rajputs or the Dogras. Joe declared he would set up an agency, offering experienced officers to all comers, and cautioned everyone to remember there were other attractions in addition to the fighting qualities of the various countries; as in pre-vice-regal days there was also the matter of mistresses, and he for one would choose . . . but he was drowned by the loud protestations of the others, each claiming the superior virtues of one or the other states, districts or provinces. I tried to move on, being incompetent to pass opinions on the charms of the ladies of India, but Joe intercepted me, and with some rather loud charm had me confess to having been a pilot in the Air Force. Raising his hand solemnly he declared no help would be given to expatriate Brylcreem boys who, whilst the poor bloody Army and Navy slogged away in the squalor and danger of the desert, the Burma jungles, and the Russian convoys, took outrageous advantage of all the fair maidens (loud boos), temporarily abandoned wives of officers and gentlemen of the Navy and the Army (more loud boos), and since the War are mostly to be found hiding away somewhere remote from people like us, the senior services, who wander miserably taking refuge in booze after all the forced celibacy of miserable campaigns. I could see that Joe was enjoying his ham homily, and to the chorus of bibulous demands for a response I decided to reply in kind, and announced I was so horrified at the loose behaviour of the females of old England, who had picked up shocking habits from the Yanks, I sought to escape the frightful dangers of disease, or worse: of enforced marriage, which is why I found my way to this remote corner which, as we all seem to agree, is worth staying in by whatever means. This led to cheers and back-slapping, and seeing the apologetic grin of Nicky appear through the blue haze of unlimited cigarettes, I excused myself, and left Joe and his colleagues singing merrily, the only small focus of carefree merriment in the otherwise despondent club.

That marked the effect of the announcement of the date of June 1948. For people like Nicky and me it was bad enough, but being used to the unassailable dictates of high command which wrenched one repeatedly from a position which was becoming familiar and therefore more enjoyable than before, and sent one for reasons beyond the limits of imagination to some other area, theatre or unit, we could take this kind of thing in our stride, with but a questioning glance at one's age. The familiar unease returned, vague but ever present, having been thrust into the background after being implanted by the pessimism of fellow passengers on the ship. It seemed nothing could be done except to 'carry on as usual' as one had learned to do in wartime when there were mysterious threats, and no enlightenment likely from the equally uncertain companies who employed us. For me there was nothing usual about whatever continued to happen to me. I can look back with pleasure on many things, but the ensuing period at that time was remarkable. After my six weeks with Nicky, which I count as one of the crucially fortunate periods of my damfool career, I moved from the almost suburban environment of Baorijan to work under Telford at Medeloabam, a change as dramatic in environment as in many other ways.

Medeloabam was about seven miles from the one tarmacadam road which ran from the town of Dibrugarh south-westwards to Jorhat, a sizeable town not far from the Brahmaputra, about seventy miles from my new home. After Baorijan the estate was a delight to see. It was three times the size of Baorijan, had a factory of its own, its own doctor, and a small hospital. There were three bungalows, one for the manager which was large, built mainly from ancient timber with a thick thatched roof, standing in a large garden with beautiful flower beds, shrubs, and blossoming trees. The other two bungalows were empty for lack of managerial staff, one old, small and thatched, the other a few hundred yards from that of the manager, with a modern steel frame, beautiful timber floors, and an asbestos roof, which was the one I was to live in. There were two bedrooms, one on each side of the main sitting room, and a dining room behind the sitting room. All this was upstairs in the fashion of most of the old Assam and Bengal bungalows used by the British since their earliest days, the best feature being the verandah, which was under the same roof, but without walls on three sides. I was given six servants: one ancient cook called Sitaram, pressed to come out of retirement to work for me; one bearer, a handsome youth of about seventeen called Maniklal, and his helper called Nunoo, a gangling and nervous boy. Mangal was the sweeper, who was the only one who would by his caste be allowed to clean shoes, and clean lavatories. Maniklal and Nunoo had never been trained as servants, but I learned most people once settled in tea eventually kept their servants with them when they moved, therefore good servants were in short supply, and the drastic reduction of managerial staff in the War had led to the only good ones left being snapped up by those first back from the Army. In addition to these I had two gardeners, who seemed to know their jobs; but now I was to live on my own, and although I was making progress with the language it became apparent I needed to accelerate my means of communication. Telford kindly instructed his head bearer, a very dignified man, to visit my bungalow morning and evening to guide and teach my servants in their duties of looking after me, my possessions, my feeding, laundry and general comfort. He was taller than average for a tribal man, and seemed always to be wearing his white uniform with a wide-skirted coat, broad belt of green, and a *pagri* with a similar green band in it. He had a silver military moustache, and dark eyes which gave the impression of connivance in some mysterious agreement by which he would never be expected to say what he knew about doubtful affairs unless pressed in discreet surroundings to do so.

It was like entering another country to find the people at all levels so different. There were many different tribes and castes, and what impressed me most was the amazingly high number of good-looking people, especially the girls and women. Lest it appear in later times as if my descriptions of that life and its effects show an almost affected moral tone, I have to record what many of my contemporaries must already have done, that we all belonged to a social system which covered most of the civilised and uncivilised world. We learned, and firmly believed, that promiscuity was evil for the strongest of reasons: first of all it was unacceptable to make a girl pregnant, as it would almost certainly mean either marriage to the girl, whether or not one was financially able to found a family; and secondly it could mean suffering the shame and indignity of some filthy disease which, if ever it became known in the small and close communities of those days could spell ruin, escapable only by emigration. This fear was reinforced when as new young pilot officers we arrived in Egypt and underwent a few days of education on life in the Middle East before we were posted to our units. There were lectures on local customs, Arabic, Islam, and general health. The feature that impressed us with awful impact was a session of several films, some American, on the subject of venereal disease. They were brilliantly done, and Johnny and I were so deeply affected that we decided the risks of something like syphilis were not only physically degrading, but could ruin one's career, one's own health into the long future, and that of one's own wife and children. Promiscuity, the fuel of such diseases, was clearly out, and we evolved our own plans on the subject of ultimate marriage. It is less funny than touching to remember how we admitted we were not so much afraid of dying in action as we were of being burnt, blinded, or hopelessly maimed; but we had a burning and wistful hope that we might not be killed before we had been able to enjoy the beauty of what nature continuously thrust us towards: the consummation of the great desire. Trying to explain so often that one's celibacy was not an affected moral priggery, but the result of how ancient human societies developed measures to prevent suffering, especially for women and children, working on natural instinct and striving for healthy survival. I eventually arrived at an understanding of what had to be the origin of sexual morals; but that came much later.

Telford took me under his wing, and I rode with him in his ex-army jeep around the estate, through the delightfully wild locality, down to the edge of a huge forest reserve. He showed me tiger tracks galore, backwater pools on the vast Brahmaputra where large fish lurked in the pale jade depths, and he lectured all the time on what was going on in the field, soon giving me various tasks which gave me the chance to talk with people and make language notes. The weather was delightful, the days became warmer, and blossoms appeared on the many, many trees in and around the estate, some of them scenting the air with a fragrance seeming to activate what Tennyson had called 'a young man's fancy'. There was much laughter, and I began to enjoy talking with the people working in the estate all the more as I became more able to speak, albeit haltingly. In the second week Telford told me he had been talking to someone called Bobby Constable, whom he described as a 'speed merchant' kind of a chap, manager of an estate in another company. He had bought himself a Piper Cub, second-hand war surplus, and although he had flown solo after instruction in a flying club, he needed to learn a lot more before he could feel safe flying on his own. He wanted to meet me, having heard I was ex-Air Force, and wondered if I could advise Telford on marking a suitable landing strip where he could land safely having flown from about twenty-two miles away. Telford showed me on my copy of the estate map several areas where he thought there would be good possibilities of a landing strip without too much having to be done. He said it would always be better to remove ridges and bumps than to fill in ditches and drains. There had been about an inch of rain at Christmas, but otherwise there had been no rain since mid-October. Eventually we agreed on using a strip of 150 yards in the rice fields only a few hundred yards from Telford's bungalow, where four transverse water-retaining ridges were removed, providing a level, hard surface, with no trees in line with landing and take-off stretches. There were no telephones, and messages were sent by cycle messengers, who started off very early in the morning, had a meal with tea at their destination, and returned before sunset. Constable was thus informed of the suitable strip which I marked with lime dashes on sides and ends. He replied hoping it would be in order to land on Thursday afternoon about three-thirty, and have a cup of tea with Telford. Telford demonstrated how he briefed three chosen men to act as safety wardens, who would keep the cattle away from the strip area, and see that the crowds who would undoubtedly turn up remained well away from the strip and from the aeroplane once it was on the ground, especially when it was parked during teatime. He explained to me how none of the local people would have seen an aeroplane nearer than miles away at 2,000 feet, and would naturally want to come and touch it. He had himself worked on drainage surveys for several of the airstrips built during the War, had seen mainly supply Dakotas, Hurricanes, and Tomahawks, and had met the pilots and engineers, many of whom were Americans.

I had just finished having a wash and putting on a clean sports shirt, when I heard, then saw, the welcome figure of a silver Piper Cub approaching from the east in a cloudless blue sky. I jumped onto my bicycle and pedalled fast round the Manager's bungalow compound, seeing Telford wave me on to see the landing. The Cub circled the landing strip at about 600 feet before making an approach to land with the sun behind it. At about ten feet he opened the throttle, climbed away and made a copybook circuit, turning on to the final approach at 300 feet, gliding with closed throttle. I saw he would have to use engine to stretch his approach, and this he did a little late, coming in to land with a lot of engine, and touching down well up the strip. With a wheelless tailskid he pulled up with room to spare, and with a burst of throttle turned and taxied back to where I stood at the landing end of the strip, then turned, switched off the engine and got out. People had begun to appear from nowhere, almost as if they were popping up out of the ground, but the three stalwarts kept them well away, and Constable and I strode towards each other over the rough rice field grass. He was a strongly built man, in white shirt and shorts, wearing a white sun helmet. His face was that of a bird of prey: keen eyes with a fierce stare, and a high-bridged nose above a firm mouth and strong jaw. He put out his hand to shake mine with a hard grip.

'You must be MacStorm. Ex-RAF. What aircraft did you fly?' There was no nonsense about this man. 'When did you last fly?' I told him nine weeks ago, in a Spitfire, and he threw his hand towards the Piper Cub, where the three guards danced desperately around it keeping the gathering crowds from approaching too closely. 'Ever flown one of these before?' I said I had flown Tiger Moths and Austers, and he asked me to come and have a look at the Cub. 'You have a flying licence?' I explained I was an officer on the air force reserve, which seemed to satisfy him. 'Let me see you fly this then. I'll swing the prop.' I asked him first to show me the cockpit and tell me the appropriate engine speeds and airspeed for approach, cruise and landing, whereupon he stood with hands on hips and said, 'I thought you said you were a pilot! Surely you know enough to be able to take this round without having to do a special course on it?' I laughed, got into the cockpit, and asked him to show me the petrol cock, brakes, ignition switch, and had him tell me the speeds for climb, cruise, and approach for landing. I said I was ready, and he turned to the three guards and rattled some quickfire Hindustani at them, after which they yelled at the crowds, and ran along the sides of the strip warning people off, and chasing happy dogs which were having a game all over the strip. Constable swung the propeller, and as the engine started I felt the vibrations penetrate to my heart, and automatically said my pre-take-off vital actions, pretending all the other sophisticated items were there in the cockpit, scarcely able to believe my luck that I was about to fly again, despite having taken an almost religious vow never to think voluptuously of flying for the foreseeable future.

Little did I realise the portents of that day when I opened the throttle and swung the nose to point straight down the strip. There was little wind, and with the sweet-sounding engine at full throttle the Cub rose from the ground, taking to the still air smoothly, climbing steadily to show me where I now lived: the whole estate visible at a glance. The thrill of reverting to the concept of places as areas seen from the air, with all the character, size and shape of visible entities, warmed my thoughts with the familiarity of an aviator arriving over his home airfield after having wandered perplexed through bad visibility or storm. I flew a standard rectangular circuit at 600 feet, turning on to the final approach at 300 feet, throttled back, and somehow everything fitted perfectly. Even the most experienced pilots can never guarantee a perfect three-point landing every time, and without having to open the throttle I touched down about ten yards after the beginning of the strip, enjoying the gradual increase of noise as the weight of the small aircraft settled on the wheels. Without using the brakes I stopped and turned back to taxi to where Constable stood, hands on hips where I had left him. I swung round to face along the strip again, and found him coming in close behind the wing, holding his topi with one hand.

'Don't switch off!' he shouted. 'Take off and do that again. I want to see you do that again!'

I remember the bliss of receiving this privilege to fly again, even in this small aircraft for which, as if fate had shown mercy for my self-imposed abstinence from flying, I had been granted, for that day at least, perfect harmony with its tendencies and controls. The second circuit and landing turned out the same as the first, and when I taxied back to Constable as he ran round and shouted in my ear he was climbing into the back seat and wanted me to go round yet again with him to see what happened. It is no

91

secret that aviators treat their aircraft as persons, as mariners their ships, and I communed with this Cub, complimenting it on its excellent characteristics, asking it the favour of another good landing. Constable was a heftily built person, and this was a significant effect on the power and weight of our Cub, but all went well as if the magic of the encounter was indeed promised for the day. When we switched off and climbed out Constable removed his topi, and shook my hand with vigour. 'You are a real pilot,' he said. 'I have never seen any pilot, RAF or USAF do successive smooth landings like that in a Piper Cub. I used to cadge lifts from them up at Chabua, and they would drop them in, bounce, swing and blame it on the fact they were used to Hurricanes or Dakotas or Tomahawks; and here you are: never flown a Piper Cub before, not flown a Spitfire for two months, and you showed me something really impressive. I want you to teach me how to fly properly. I hope you will agree.' I began to tell him one couldn't always be sure of making perfect landings, but he looked at his watch and said, 'Come on! Let's go and have tea with Telford.' He had another few staccato words with the guards, and said something to the crowd which started the people laughing, and we walked off briskly, being saluted by the people who were still coming to see an actual aeroplane. We met Telford standing under a tree on the higher land above the strip, and he took us across his smooth lawns and beautiful garden to where his wife was sitting in the sun where wicker chairs and tables had been set for tea.

Telford must have been about forty-three, and when Constable told him he too should learn to fly, he said he was too old, surely, for that kind of thing. Between them they agreed on an arrangement whereby Constable would send his car to pick me up at about five-thirty on Sunday mornings, to take me up to his estate for the day, so that we could fly together until dusk, when he would send me back again after dinner in his car. Telford seemed deeply preoccupied during that conversation, and just before we finished tea he told Constable he would be going with his wife to their fishing camp on the North Bank for the weekend, and bringing a map showed us the river Simen running out of the foothills in thickly forested country. He said if we were going to fly next Sunday perhaps we should have a look to see if it was possible to make a landing strip on the fairly hard compacted sandy islands on the riverbed. He said to cross the Brahmaputra in a dugout boat with a 20 h.p. outboard motor, walk with porters carrying their camping gear and food along game tracks through the forest to the river campsite, took more than five hours. It would be interesting to see if we thought it was possible to fly there, and send men with the boat and supplies separately. It soon dawned on me, and it was confirmed by Constable, that flying in that part of the world was rather like the twenties and early thirties in Britain, when aeroplanes would land in any suitable field with the permission of the owner.

Life was becoming full of wonderful experiences again. Telford had been taking me out riding on several of the seven horses he had in his large stable. He showed me how to hit a polo ball, and gave me his riding master, a Pathan once in the Indian cavalry, to join me in practising to hit, and to handle the ponies when manoeuvring at various paces. I attended my first polo day on Saturday, and took delivery of my pony, a twelve-year-old army-trained chestnut gelding who turned out to work best on a loose rain, following the game of polo with excellent instinct and perfect discipline, without fear of other horses or the hoarsely yelled oaths of the riders. I ran into difficulties with enrolment in the Assam Valley Light Horse, because when I entered on the enrolment form the fact I was an officer on the Reserve of Air Force Officers, Montgomery the Adjutant threw his hands up in despair, saying I could not enrol, unless I managed to obtain Air Ministry permission to be seconded to the AVLH. That would probably take so long that Indian Independence would arrive, and possibly the AVLH would evaporate. He said he would have a word with the Colonel and see what might be done, and within a very short time I was told how I should follow advice to become a temporary trooper, never to appear on parade or in uniform, pending permission from the Air Ministry etc. Meanwhile I was to draw one horse, saddlery, stable boy allowance, and agree to exercise the pony by such activities as long rides, polo, and an occasional swim in clean river water. To begin with I was allowed to join chukkas without a polo stick, joining either side and learning to ride off and be ridden off, all of which was exciting and enjoyable. Sadly, no other people of my age joined the polo. On that first day I spoke with three ex-army types who seemed to be interested, but they said they needed to buy second-hand cars, or motorcycles, and lived too far away from any of the clubs to be able to play polo regularly.

On the Sunday I was collected by Constable's car and whisked to his estate twenty odd miles away, had breakfast on arrival at breakneck speed, with him swallowing his tea fast at what seemed to me to be ninety-nine degrees Celsius. He had a landing strip of minimal size, and said he often took several attempts to touch down accurately on the end of it so as to pull up in good time. We did a daily inspection of the Cub engine, and refuelled it through a chamois filter to take the water out of the petrol. I did a solo take-off and landing before saying we would take off together with about twenty yards to spare, and soon we were airborne, climbing to a thousand feet in the golden sunlight under a deep blue sky. We flew over the Brahmaputra, which was somehow Chinese, being a huge wandering strip of panels like carved ivory, which were islands of sand and silt from the Himalayas, intersected by the long, curving streams of jade water, paler where it was shallow, and darker where deep, a beautiful great sweep which wandered in graceful curves through the vast patchwork of dark green forest, pale golden rice fields, and sylvan countryside. Later we reached 2,000 feet and saw the snow peaks beyond the foothills, the foothills themselves being covered up to about 7,000 feet with thick primeval forests, some of the slopes being surprisingly steep. There were thick forests on the flat lands of the North Bank, amongst which there were occasional marshes and smaller rivers. It was remarkable to see such huge sweeps of country where there was no sign of human habitation. The map we used showed large areas of the mountain territory as 'unsurveyed', which gave me an exhilarating thrill. We found Telford's remote fishing camp, and circled, slowly losing height, surveying the sandy and stony islands, all of which appeared to be on the many bends of the river. The river itself and its surroundings took my breath away. It left the foothills through a steep gorge of solid rock, and descended in successive rapids of white foam into deep, green pools of beautifully clear water. Except for narrow beaches of pale-coloured boulders, the banks were covered with tall forest, some trees growing to nearly 200 feet. It was a paradise, and my heart went out to the Telfords, who waved as we flew over the camp. Downstream was one of the largest islands on a gradual bend, with a good width and no high trees too close to a curving approach and take-off path. The surface was fairly level, but there were many small boulders about the size of dinner rolls and cooking apples, which would have to be moved before landing could be made safely. Not knowing the meaning of the different colours of the sand and silt I was unsure of what

94

the surface would be like. The Piper Cub wheel tyres were sensibly large, and would not sink into slightly soft surfaces; but if the sand was too soft, and the aircraft nosed over, breaking the propeller, it would mean much difficulty in getting a new propeller to the aircraft, even provided one could be found in time to fly the aircraft out before the heavy rains arrived and brought violent torrential floods to fill the river and sweep the aircraft away. When I reported to Telford it would be possible to clear a strip for use only if the surface were approved as firm enough to bear the aircraft's weight without the wheels sinking in, he decided to send me the following week on what he called a 'familiarisation tour of Assam river and forest terrain'. My brief was to test the surface, and then begin clearing boulders and driftwood for a landing strip.

I set off on the following Thursday with one Gerella Shikari, an experienced Assamese hunter with some English, and experience of outboard canoe operations. We took two other men who would pitch our camp, and Gerella would contact an Abor village to invite men to come and help clear the strip if necessary. The weather was glorious, and the trip across the Brahmaputra fascinating. There were wild birds galore: ruddy sheldrake in mournful calling pairs; greenshanks, sandpipers, red wattled lapwings, golden plover, and a huge collection of various flocks of bar-headed geese; and I am sure I saw some greylags. The river was vast, each of the streams which had from the air looked about 200 yards wide turned out to be more than twice that width. The man steering the 24-foot dugout boat knew the shoals, and went to the outside of all curves, where the considerable current ran deep. The sun was strong, and the air over the river was cooled by water still giving hints it had come as the Tsang Po from the Himalayan snows many miles away. We stopped for a meal on a backwater, where the water was less cold, and I swam whilst tea was brewed, finding this the best lonely swimming place since the coast between Mersa Matruh and Ras el Kanayis, four years earlier. We left the Brahmaputra and proceeded carefully up the river where miles away the fishing camp lay. It was slow and careful going, and often we had to manhandle the heavy dugout against the current in several shallow, bouldery places. Eventually we came to the end of the navigable river, and by a small collection of huts on stilts we tied up the boat and met four Miri tribal men. Their women remained shyly in the background whilst Gerella talked to the men in

Assamese. He told me their language was similar to that of the mountain tribes, which I learned later was a Sino-Tibetan tonal language. The men were distinctly Mongolian, bare to the waist and without a trace of fat on their sturdy frames.

We began our walk of just under two hours through primeval forest on fairly level ground. Gerella showed me the tracks of tiger, bear, elephant, otter, wild pig, the scratching of jungle fowl and pheasants, the slots of barking deer, sambar and gaur. We heard the melodious fluting of green pigeon, caught glimpses of them in rapid flight through the trees, and saw the sober little form of an emerald dove, whose call was deep and mournful. I began to pick up Assamese words and phrases from Gerella, who told me not many people on the North Bank would understand Hindustani very well. The path we followed often broke away from the river, and whilst we were near to it we saw various duck rising from backwaters, and frequently saw smew and goosander flying at high speed in close formation down the river between the high trees on both sides. We came across fresh elephant droppings and tracks, and found a place where the herd had crossed the sixty yards or so of crystal clear water. There were plenty of small fish to be seen, and one of the boatmen grinned and showed his net, indicating we would have fresh fish at the camp. That first entry to the primeval forest was like discovering the delights of something new in a wonderful life. Gerella showed me a huge tree where tigers had recently sharpened their claws, another where elephants had rubbed their backs after a mud bath. It felt then as if I was being bewitched, and refused to care about being hopelessly vulnerable to the lure of such wilderness. There was a strange feeling of déjà vu; but I knew by letting myself be captured by all this it would lead to the ultimate pain of giving it up. My desire to find a place like this had been tinged with romance, but I had not realised the wilderness I wanted could be even more fascinating than I had dreamed.

We had not been long at the campsite when two Abor men appeared, wearing cane helmets and dark homespun tabards, with bush knives (*dao*) hanging in wooden scabbards on their chests. The muscles of their naked, copper-coloured thighs and calves were highly developed, their faces almost Japanese. They pointed at me with mystified expressions, and Gerella explained I had been in the aeroplane which flew over the camp last Sunday, which made them stare and moan softly. Whilst the men set up the bamboo frame over which our tarpaulin tent was to be hung, I went with Gerella downstream to survey the possibilities, and before long I had staked a possible strip fifteen yards wide and 130 yards long. It took a long time to clear the stones away, and some of the bigger ones had to be dug out and the cavities filled with sand trampled progressively in. By eleven next morning the mountain slopes had heated enough for a fair breeze to blow up the river, suggesting departures to be made between then and mid-afternoon. The first night we heard barking deer call. There was a pleasant noise from the night breeze in the treetops, and the sound of the rapids came and went with the wind. The second night we heard elephants feeding: branches cracking at long intervals. On Saturday morning we left, and floated down the river without the motor, Gerella hoping to see some deer to shoot in the early morning sun. We saw four barking deer (muntjac) about 200 yards away, and two strange dark duck with large white wing patches and silvery heads flying downstream. The trip back was as fascinating as before, and we reached the south bank just after midday.

When I reported to Telford and showed him sketch maps of the airstrip position, he wrote a letter to Constable, who was sending his car to collect me next day, asking him if we could try a landing on the strip, and let him know how it worked out. In the event I flew with Constable after midday, and after checking there was not much wind to worry about, we landed successfully, stopped the aircraft engine and walked back to check the depth of the tracks, deciding it would be quite safe to take off and land as long as there was no heavy rain to disturb the surface. We took off easily with at least thirty yards to spare, and found plenty of room to allow a slow climb away from the river. We landed back at Medeloabam where, as if he expected us, Telford was waiting at the strip. We told him how we had landed and taken off easily; and Constable told him to get in and I would take him to land at his fishing camp, then return for a cup of tea. Telford was intensely preoccupied, and let Constable strap him in. When we arrived I left the engine running as we walked up the strip and back; and then we got back in and I took the Cub off and flew back to Medeloabam. Telford climbed out and thanked us both for our help, his eyes burning with an intense private zeal. It was days before he referred to what had happened.

We seemed to concentrate on Monday on estate work, and Telford kept saying he wanted to cover as much as possible with me before Foyle came as acting manager, as Foyle would only be here for six months, and I would remain as the permanent and only assistant for a considerable time.

Chapter VI

In the weeks following the first landing on the fishing camp strip the news
broke of Mountbatten arriving to replace Wavell as Viceroy of India. When
Telford broke the news to me he was clearly shaken, and straight away
declared this was a slap in the face for all those who knew India, who had
lived so long here and become dedicated to the country, who knew how bad
it would be for the people of India to be deprived of the pax Britannica. He
was sure Wavell had said he could not agree to the granting of independence
because he knew it would lead to terrible slaughter, and they had put
Mountbatten in to make absolutely sure it would be accomplished, come
what may. Feeling this to be unfair criticism of Wavell I told him if Wavell
had been given the tanks, guns and aeroplanes which Montgomery had
been able to muster before Alamein, he would have hit the Germans and
Italians just as well, with Hitler having abandoned the support of Rommel
as he did. To this Telford made an astonishing comment, implying Hitler
was a national socialist, not a soft-romantic socialist like those in the Labour
party who were preparing to commit themselves to the vainglorious bloody
renunciation of power over India. He said Hitler would have improved
India faster than the British had done; he would have been far tougher than
the British, and made India into a powerful armed state with much more
industrial development and prosperity. He said Hitler would have cured the
sputtering Hindu-Muslim problem long ago; and what is more he would
have built up a massively menacing frontier facing Russia, from India to
Iran. He would have erased Russia, and its Bolshevism, and in time with
Japan would have erased China, and brought Britain to surrender before
conquering America. This took me aback, and had me wondering whether
his obvious passion was in support of Hitler and the Nazis, or at showing

how lucky we were things had gone the other way.

Before I could gather my thoughts he changed the subject, still with passion, and confessed he now had great doubts about going home to learn to fly: he might not be able to afford it if his career in India was going to come to an end. It had really shaken him to find how easy Constable and I had made it seem, to fly in twenty minutes to his own private little paradise in the wilderness. He asked me to ensure with Constable there would be no divulging of the location of the fishing camp, and no flying there ourselves or with others. It had taken him so long to explore and find it; there were plenty of other places people could find if they exerted themselves.

He asked me how long it would be before he was competent enough to land on such a short strip as the fishing camp. I said it was a matter of intensive practice, meaning it would be necessary to have a good landing strip somewhere conveniently near, which could be marked with short and narrow limits where one could do many hours of practice, perhaps about thirty to forty hours. It was also necessary to experience various wind and temperature effects, sufficient for reactions to be automatic. All the time we spoke I can only describe him as being so obsessed I felt as if I had to him become a book, or a voice, without any kind of personal relationship. Almost belligerently he said he was going to have to pay personally for learning to fly; he wouldn't have it all free as I did, at the expense of the British nation. I said I would be willing to help him if he were able to organise an aircraft, and I saw he was deeply in thought on how he was going to manage that. He said he was dam' well going to carry on as if nothing was going to change, and tomorrow he wanted me to go with him to look for an all-season airstrip site, as the one in the rice fields would be unusable for many months during the rainy season and the harvest. When we drove in to polo there was little said, but at polo and afterwards for about an hour at the club there was a great deal of talk, and it seemed to me people were mostly depressing each other, with very few being optimistic. George came up behind me and asked what I was thinking about, and I said I was sure there should be more patience and perhaps faith, although I was least qualified to pass an opinion; but I had a feeling there must be some kind of news forthcoming from the British government. He smiled his indomitable smile, put his chin up and surveyed the noisy congregation.

'There is nothing official yet, MacStorm, but we do know there are people in Delhi who are going to let us know as soon as there is anything worth knowing. Mountbatten holds a very difficult brief, we think, but although none of us agrees with the British government's policy, most of us think he will make a good job of it. You are right, you know: those of us who have been in the wars understand how optimism wins battles.' He laughed loudly, attracting curious glances, and said, 'After all, MacStorm, we're not going to be shot at dawn, are we?'

Telford was moody next day. Nothing was said of anything but the work in hand. He told me there was a special job for me that day: the tea companies had taken advantage of the government's offer to sell cheaply the large stocks of army medicines lying in Assam, and had bought huge quantities of anti-malarial tablets for workers and staff. The scourge of malaria was still bad, and led not only to serious loss of labour strength during the harvest season, but to deaths of anything from two per month up to four or five per month in places on the North Bank. All senior staff took paludrine regularly already; now the Indian staff and labour were to be given mepacrine. He told me the labour would be very glad to have wounds treated by our hospital, but they tended to regard the taking of medicines of any kind from our hospital with great suspicion. They preferred to use their own remedies, and there were innumerable peddlers of what they called *jangli dawai*, who were sometimes effective but sometimes dangerous. I was to supervise the issue of mepacrine tablets to the women and girls. When I asked about the men Telford said he would explain later. Thus it was that I followed instructions and positioned myself at the entrance to the northern area of the estate at seven in the morning, where all women and girls turning out to work were to form three queues and take their turn in opening mouths wide so that the malaria *babu* and two *chowkidars* of high caste could throw the round yellow tablets as far down the gullet as possible. After swallowing the tablet each person would receive a mark with an indelible pencil on the right wrist above the universal bangles, without which they would not be allowed to take up their work in the field when they arrived there. There was much merriment, and I was frustrated not to be able to understand much of the banter taking place. We were on the last few stragglers just before eight o'clock when Telford arrived to ask how things had gone. I told him everything seemed to have gone well with much good humour. With his panther stare he asked if I was sure they had swallowed properly, and I said as far as I could tell they had, with one or two cases of choking which led to much giggling and taunting from the others. He told me to follow him, and we walked after the stragglers. After about a hundred and fifty yards he stopped, looking down, pointing vaguely all over the track, telling me to see what had happened, moving slowly further. I was highly embarrassed to see mepacrine tablets lying in the dust, many little yellow discs which would protect them from the dread disease, wasted. Eventually Telford stopped and stood staring at me, holding his elbows.

'You see the problem?' he said. 'It looked simple, didn't it? It's a good experience for you. What I didn't tell you was that Banerji (the Head Clerk) told me some of the hotheads working for the Congress Party have spread it around the tea districts that these mepacrine tablets are intended by the British to make India's women barren. Let's talk about it this afternoon, and see if you can work out a better system.' In the afternoon one of the field *chowkidars* reported he had seen two youths picking up the tablets, and waited at a distance to see what they would do. They sat under the mango tree not far from the village store shop, and seemed to be cleaning the tablets with a cloth. They then took them into the shop and came out smiling, hands in pockets. Careful investigation by the *chowkidar* revealed he could buy anti-malaria tablets at one anna each, yellow ones. The Assamese villagers were keen to buy them for one anna per tablet, knowing how good they were for preventing malaria. After much discussion we decided to give the tablets into the hand of the person, who would be given water by the higher caste *paniwalla* (water carrier) and with it swallow the tablet, showing the mouth empty. It was interesting to note some women refusing to take the tablets on the next issue, and I had to learn to say in Hindustani if they got malaria we would know from the book they had refused to take the tablets.

Foyle arrived at Medeloabam with his wife that week, and I was invited to tea on the *barra* (big) bungalow lawn to meet them. Foyle gave me a broad grin of welcome, and introduced his wife Dierdre, saying, 'Be careful with him, my dear, he's ex-RAF, you know,' at which she blushed profusely and prettily, shaking hands with a smile after darting a sideways look at her husband, who winked with his upper lip drawn down. He had chosen well: she was beautifully built, with dark blue eyes, and the features of a Greek sculpture. Her shyness seemed to be infectious, and I sat quietly listening to Mrs Telford first quizzing, then encouraging Dierdre Foyle on how it simply took a little time to become used to life 'out here'. Telford spoke mainly to Foyle in his almost lazy drawl, which I was beginning to recognise as an affectation intended to soften the impact of what he had to say, to present orders and wishes less as peremptory orders than as gentle injunctions. When I heard Foyle say he thought he would like to start writing things down I knew he was already aware of Telford's style, knowing he must ensure nothing was lost in the quiet conversations. I was learning myself that the vaguest comments could be orders in disguise. After tea Telford invited us all to go with him to see the stables. Foyle had a large horse to stable, and Telford said he would show him where he could install it. There were eight stables, and only four were occupied, two polo ponies of Telford's, one mare of Mrs Telford's, and my AVLH horse 'Conker'. The stables were built in the English country style, with a Dutch gable in the centre of the row bearing a large clock. At one end was a storehouse containing food for the horses. Telford told us the maize was grown near Medeloabam, but the oats, bran and other foods we would have to buy fresh every fortnight from the millers in Dibrugarh, about fifteen miles away. Each horse had a large chunk of pinkish rock salt hanging on a front pillar, something they needed because of the high amount of sweating in the hot weather, when the horses drank a lot of water. Telford looked at me with his head down and said it was something I should remember: to drink plenty of water and have plenty of salt. He asked us to help his *daffadar* (riding boy) to exercise his horses whilst he and his wife were away on home leave, saying it was one way of ensuring they actually got the exercise. He also asked us to supervise the feeding, as it was a temptation to the syces to fiddle with the maize and oats to the detriment of the horses.

As the time for Telford's departure drew near he piled task and commitment one after the other upon me, and my rather battered small notebook which, because my shorts would not take kindly to stowing it in the pocket, had to be pushed into the breast pocket of my short-sleeved shirt. It was now so warm I dispensed with wearing an undervest, and changed my sweaty shirts two or three times a day. Whilst out riding with Telford and Foyle early one morning, to familiarise the latter with the general layout, Telford reined in beside a part of the estate workers' village-style living area, where there were many trees, bamboos, and vegetable gardens.

He pointed out several clumps of what he called '*ganja*', another name for marihuana, later to achieve notoriety as *cannabis indica*. He told me I should ride round frequently and note where these plants were growing, and arrange teams to uproot and burn all visible plants. He told Foyle he had almost obliterated *ganja* over the years, and now had no cases of broken families, ruined personalities or stupid behaviour. This was all interesting for me, and I felt as if I was indeed born into a completely new world; but for how long?

The following weekend was the last before the Telfords were due to depart for Calcutta, Bombay and England. Constable sent me a message saying he would not be able to fly on Sunday as he had two unexpected guests arriving for the weekend, but he would send his car for me as usual on Sunday and I should have breakfast with him. He would lend me the aeroplane to fly to the North Bank, perhaps to visit another ex-pilot he had heard about. Before Sunday arrived, whilst Telford and I were riding out to look for possible places to clear and level a permanent landing strip, there was an interesting incident. As we stood discussing a place which lay to the west of the tea area, our horses became suddenly restless, and swung their heads, with ears pricked ahead, to a clump of trees and huts about half a mile away to the north. We could hear faintly the noise of frenzied shouting, and saw cattle stampeding in various directions. Telford's mount became very restless, and mine became tense but still. Telford put his heels to his horse's sides and began to canter towards the clump, beckoning me to follow. We cantered across the dry rice fields through several islands of trees and scrub to the small village which stood in a grove near a promontory of woodland which connected with a wedge of forest stretching west towards the huge forest reserve. It was mainly an Assamese village, and the men were gathered around the bodies of three cattle, two dead and one badly injured, kicking in what looked like its death throes. We tethered our horses to a couple of small trees nearby and walked over. Telford spoke with them, and followed as they showed the tracks of two large and two small tigers, which had attacked the cattle as the herd was being rounded up by the cowherds prior to taking them out to graze for the day. There were two more calves killed, one carried into some scrub before the men raised enough noise to send the tigers off into the woodland, from where they were on their way back to the large forest by now. It was about six in the morning, and the men were angry and miserable at the loss of so many valuable beasts. Telford explained how tigers had become vermin ever since the last few years of the War. There had been ready access to ammunition, and the many army camps soon found it easy to pay local *shikaris* to take people to shoot wild pig, deer, and anything else edible or displayable, so depleting the local sources of the tigers' normal food, with the result that the tigers began killing cattle, far more than ever used to be killed before the War. Each of these small farmers possessed only three or four cattle, and the loss of one was a serious disaster. He told the people he would inform Gerella Shikari, but warned them there was no chance that the tigers would come at night into the village. They would have to give Gerella a large goat or a buffalo calf over which he would sit some way away on the edge of the larger forest. He told me it looked as if the tigers were encouraging their large cubs to kill, and were less concerned about finding food.

Two nights later I went out with Gerella to sit, not in a tree, but under one on a reedy ridge in the shadow cast by the moon, hoping a tiger would cross the clear land between the forest and the small ridge to take the buffalo calf, tethered some way down-moon from us. We each had 12-bore guns with SSG cartridges, which Gerella warned were not to be fired unless the tiger was no further than fifteen yards away, just beyond where the calf was tethered. He made me take off my dark blue silk scarf and tie it over my sun-bleached hair, which even in the shadow would have warned the tiger of an unusual presence. He was insistent that we should sit still for several hours, and if moving our heads to scan widely, we must do so very, very slowly. Darkness fell, and the moonlight gradually illuminated the landscape as if one could expect to see the tiniest creature move. The night noises were ghostly and intriguing. Once a huge owl came gliding noiselessly into the tree where we sat, and when after about an hour it suddenly launched itself into the air to fly back to the forest, Gerella squeezed my arm gently. I saw his head turned over his left shoulder, towards a large pale area of rice field, and slowly rotated my head to the same angle. I could see nothing, because I was looking for something recognisable. Two squeezes from Gerella seemed to indicate urgency or excitement, and I stared, moving my focus left and right, near and far. Then, after about ten minutes I saw, about sixty yards away, the vaguest shadow, drifting slowly across my vision, and I squeezed Gerella's arm twice. The blur stopped, moved for ten yards, stopped, and eventually seemed to dwindle to a quarter of its size. It had to be the tiger, and it now lay on its belly, obviously staring at the buffalo calf. The buffalo calf gazed as fixedly at the blur, remaining as a statue. I not only felt my heart thudding, but hoped the noise would not be heard beyond my ribcage. The moon was behind us, and some 200 yards away a nightjar began its ghostly jugging at long intervals. It began to seem that my eyes were no longer able to focus on the vague blur. I wondered if the tiger could possibly charge the buffalo calf, which would bring him straight in our direction, the calf being only twelve yards from us and four feet lower. It seemed like more than an hour without any movement from the tiger, or from the calf. I could imagine the tiger staring, scenting, imagining all the possible dangers surrounding this improbable find of an unprotected calf in the open, and understood patience was the most powerful asset for the hunter, be it tiger or man. After the longest spell the beast rose, and moved swiftly to the right, where it lay again. I could still not identify the blur as a tiger, and could only presume the fixed staring of Gerella and the buffalo calf as worthy only of such a threatening menace. This time the blur showed less patience; it was as if seeing the target area from a different angle he slowly convinced himself there was something not to be trusted about this apparently proffered gift, for he rose, wheeled away from us, and disappeared towards the further shadows of the large forest. Gerella made no movement except to rotate his head very slowly, as if to see if there was another intrusion of which the tiger had not approved. After another half hour Gerella rose, laughing quietly as I groaned with the stiffness of my limbs. He went to pull out the peg holding the tethered calf, and we walked the half mile back to the village. As we walked he told me I should find orange-brown garments to wear for night hunting, explaining the red colour of tigers and leopards was neutralised in moonlight, and scattered by their stripes and rosettes. Their white bellies cancelled out dark shadows in the way they did with fish. This was learning of a different kind, and it was to prove important.

As we drove into polo on Saturday I told Telford I had been thinking about the virtues of our large group of estates providing itself with something like an Auster as an official ambulance and transport for special purposes. From what I had been hearing about poor communications and lack of good medical contact, I said it looked as if it would save lives and time. He asked if this was my idea of keeping myself in the business of flying. I laughed and said I would not volunteer to be a taxi pilot, but since I was attracted to such remote places as the North Bank I would like to be picked up if I had a ripening appendix or such. He remained quiet, but on the way back he suggested I write down how I thought such a scheme would work. I said I would have to learn much more about the geography of Assam, and our estates in particular, before I could offer anything sensible enough, but given time and opportunity I would certainly do my best. I actually played my first chukka of polo that day, without committing any false moves or scoring any goals; but I enjoyed it hugely, and wanted more. Telford, when he heard me say how keen I was to live on the North Bank, commented dryly there was no polo over there.

That Sunday was another memorable day. I had breakfast with Bobby Constable, whose guests were recovering from a late club night. He gave me a map showing the Subansiri, with Bogahilonia marked, another Assam Lothian estate in our group of companies, where I would meet one Steve MacDonald, said to be ex-air force. Constable explained there was no easy quick contact with the North Bank: it would take more than a week for a letter to arrive there, and another for a reply to come, therefore it was worth buzzing what looked like an assistant's bungalow to see if anyone was at home. There was said to be a grass airstrip beside the river from wartime days, but I would have to have a good look at it before landing. He took me down to his airstrip and helped me push out the Piper Cub from the timber and bamboo hangar, do the inspection, and start the engine. He said the sooner I arrived the more chance I would find MacDonald at home, and I was soon climbing into the cloudless sky, aiming almost due west for the 70-mile flight. There was a light haze which disappeared as I crossed the Brahmaputra and drew nearer to the blue mountains, which rose like heaving waves, ridge after ridge. Far to the north, from 3,000 feet I could see the delicate tracery of the snow ranges. I could see one earth road on the North Bank, and saw one dusty plume from what looked like a military lorry making slow progress in the same direction as I flew; otherwise little sign of movement. There were vast areas of dense forest on the level ground, and except for a few rocky scars on the steep hills, they were covered even on the steepest slopes with huge trees. The rivers which came out of the mountains made their way to the Brahmaputra meandering in many curves for twenty or more miles.

The Subansiri was unmistakable, and I flew northwards along it at 800 feet, looking for Bogahilonia, a tiny speck on the small-scale map I carried. It was a breathtaking sight: the river was blue-green, leaving the mountains through a steep rock gorge. After about half a mile through the tall forest on either side, the force of the current was shown by the white plumes and dark rocks of various rapids, which were beginning to catch the sun. It then divided into several courses, running through four beautiful, slim, forested islands, with beaches of white sand, and boulders at the water's edge. The water was crystal clear, amber in the shallows, and showing all shades of jade in the swift-flowing depths. At that height the mountain ranges were huge, the trees tall, and the sweep of the landscape magnificent. There were no people to be seen until nearly two miles downstream. On the east bank I saw some small villages with houses built on timber piles, with several dugout boats pulled up on the sandy river shore. On the west bank, some hundreds of yards into the thick forest, I could identify what looked like a tea estate in paradise. It nestled in thick forest not far from the river, and I could see the factory's silver roof, and three bungalows, all standing in the pale green expanses of newly emerging tea leaf. The one nearest the river seemed the best to investigate, and I flew round it at about a hundred feet, delighted to see a man wave with both hands high. He pointed down the river, and I flew off to find the airstrip. It was an irregularly shaped patch of grass with many cattle grazing, and the river running very close to it, twenty feet below. Eventually I made out old markers, which showed part of the strip had been eroded by the river, probably during the monsoon, when this river would be transformed, no longer bringing this snow water from Tibet, but delivering the furious flow of the more than 200 inches of monsoon rain which fell from mid-June to mid-October. Wary of frightening pregnant cattle, I flew low at some distance from the strip, and waved, pointing downwards. There was some understanding, and some of the cowherds began clearing their beasts away. Before long I saw the hefty figure of MacDonald speeding along the strip on a bicycle, obviously making it clear to everyone what was going to happen. There was comfortable room to land, and although the surface was bumpy it was safe. I shook hands with the tall, bronzed, tough-looking MacDonald, whose first words were, 'Who the hell are you?' Once he had organised some men to guard the Cub, he gave his cycle to a man, and pointed saying, 'Bungalow!' He took me to his bungalow and gave me a cup of excellent tea, then took me to the river, further up where there were no people, showing me many tracks of tiger, leopard, elephant, wild pig, otter, and monitor lizard. The air was marvellous, coming gently from the north, over the snow ranges. We talked without pause, finding out about each other.

He had been in the Fleet Air Arm, and had been shot down when attacking shipping on the Italian coast by moonlight. He managed to reach the shore, but was soon taken prisoner, and spent years languishing in prison camps in Germany. Not long after Hitler ordered the execution of more than thirty air force officers who had made a mass escape, MacDonald and another pilot, knowing full well they would be shot if they were discovered, took the chance offered, managed to escape, and went through unbelievable danger posing as Dutch sailors. They reached a seaport on the German coast and eventually attempted to board a Swedish ship, but the Swedes ordered them back on shore. They tried the same thing about a week later, and managed to board and find a hiding place under the ship's boilers, where it was freezing cold for many hours until the ship began to prepare to sail, when it became unbearably hot. They knew they had to wait until they had sailed into neutral waters before giving themselves up, and Mac described how they at last came out, made it to the bridge, saluted and exposed themselves as British officers. He fainted from sheer exhaustion and exposure, and awoke in clean pyjamas in a snug bed, being brought back to a fit state before they docked in Sweden. It was not long before they were flown back to Britain in a Mosquito designed to carry them. The interrogations and suspicions they underwent were, he said, the most unpleasant part of the whole escapade, and he was glad when it was all over, and he returned to duty, to fly again. I could see what the years in prison camp had done to him, having learned from what Jag had told me, and how Jag had sometimes behaved under stress. Mac had been in Assam for six months, and had some interesting things to relate. I told him how marvellous I found the North Bank, and was glad at long last to see how splendid it actually was. He confirmed it was marvellous in the cold weather, but when the rains came it sounded pretty awful. All the bridges on the only outlet road for 170 miles to Tezpur were washed away, and the rivers could only be crossed by ferry. Even the bridges to the club in North Lakhimpur, fourteen miles away, were some of the first to come down, but he cynically said that didn't matter much anyway. His manager, that day visiting friends beyond the town in his Ford Prefect, was a rumbustious Irishman of eccentric habits who had promised he would take him to meet people at the club; but he had a bit of an argument with him, and he went off on Saturday afternoon to the club without picking him up. The next weekend his manager said the water was clearing and he was going to fish up the river, and so Mac decided he could cycle the fourteen miles to the club, and cycle back again by moonlight. The road was in his words 'bloody awful', and he had a puncture half way. A forestry lorry found him stranded, and the Assamese crew set abut fixing the puncture with their own gear, so that he could continue on his way. When he arrived at the club there were about eight people there. He described them as typical ancient elders of the kirk, with their quiet, suspicious wives, all of them looking down their noses at him and not offering to speak, let alone welcome. He said who he was, and where he had come from, and was told by one of the men he couldn't have a drink as he was not a member of the club, and should arrange with his manager to fill in an application form, have it countersigned by two sponsors, and sent to the club secretary. One of the ladies offered him a cup of tea, but as the men seemed to ignore him he thanked her and went out to mount his bicycle to ride back. He had to wait nearly an hour in the moonlight for several elephants to move off the road in the forest, and got home very late to find a note from his manager telling him he had caught a big fish, and to come and celebrate. He went, and had a good welcome; but he said this giant Irishman could drink Scotch all night long and never show any sign of fatigue or impediment. He asked him for some food as he was ravenous, and ate many pounds of grilled fresh river fish, drinking beer until well after midnight.

'The North Bank is fine in the cold weather; it's fine if you don't care for much social life; the fishing and the shooting are wonderful, which is just as well, as there aren't any shops around with the sort of food you long for, and wild pork, venison, duck, snipe and jungle fowl, all in season, are royal fare; but here I am, engaged to be married, and I just wouldn't dream of bringing my girl out here to live. Women who want to have babies here take their lives in their hands, or they go and stay with someone on the South Bank until it's all over, and then come back to live in this bloody wilderness.' He pointed to a small island on one of the smaller rivers running

110

through the estate towards the Subansiri, and told me what had happened not long before the War to an assistant manager who was a keen and accomplished *shikari*. A leopard had been causing trouble by killing goats, muscovy ducks, and dogs in the various labour lines. One of the Indian staff had tried, with a rather ancient single barrel hammer gun, to shoot the leopard over a tethered goat. The leopard was badly wounded, and lost a lot of blood. The Koyas and Mundas, both tribes being expert hunters and knowing the dangers of a wounded leopard near human habitation, went with their bows and arrows and beat the leopard eventually into the small island, hoping to move it from there to the scrub by the main river: but it wouldn't move, either because of exhaustion, or a dislike of moving away from the forest. Andy, the assistant, was asked by the Mundas to come with his rifle to see if the leopard could be moved. The animal was in cover so thick it could not be accurately located. Two other experienced estate *shikaris* told Andy they could hear from the noise of the leopard's throat it was still very much alive, and as it was now after sunset it was better to leave it where it was, either to die or to disappear overnight. Andy, being keen and intrepid, managed to have some of the Mundas cut a wide strip through the tangle of the island, isolating the leopard in a patch about twenty yards by eight, where it was agreed it was lying. He then stood watching down the path with his rifle ready, and had the other *shikaris* stand ready on the island shore whilst the Koyas and Mundas hurled boulders into the thicket, shouting and thrashing the tangle with bamboo rods. The leopard rushed out from one end of the thicket and launched itself at Govind *shikari*, who had no time to shoot, and dropped to the ground as if lifeless, with the leopard on top of him. Andy came round fast, and not wanting to shoot the animal for fear of harming Govind, he kicked it hard where it crouched, rolling the beast away from the prostrate Govind, but before he was able to fire the leopard hurled itself into the air with all limbs whirling, and gashed Andy's knee deeply. Andy shot and killed the beast, but had to be carried to the primitive hospital, which took the best part of an hour. The wound was cleaned and dressed, with iodine the only antiseptic available in those days. Next day the compounder confirmed that the wound was rapidly becoming inflamed, and that the sahib's high fever meant the onset of septicaemia. The nearest hospital which might be able to deal with such a case was about 170 miles away, in Tezpur. All the cold-weather bridges had been

111

washed away, and the delays with ferries taking the manager's car with the suffering patient made it impossible for Andy to survive. The following year another assistant manager went into his dining room on another estate not far from Bogahilonia, and had his kneecap slashed off by a leopard which was under the dinner table; the result was more or less the same: no penicillin, end of assistant. Mac said one of his manager's pre-war predecessors used to boast of how he had left the Assam Lothian North Bank doctor to deal with his wife who was about to give birth to a child, and on the way to the factory jumped out of his car and with a revolver killed two leopards not two hundred yards from the bungalow.

Such tales as these led me to offer to change places with him. I wasn't aiming to be engaged until I had established a career, certainly not of the damfool kind, in a working life I could enjoy. Then, with money saved, I would seek the kind of girl who would be happy to share a life far from the madding crowd. There was so much uncertainty about the future making it fairly sure it would take time, perhaps several years, maybe leading to some other part of the world. I dared not question Mac's obviously passionate desire to bring his chosen love out here, where so much hung in the balance. I hardly knew the man, but I did think his aim was magnificent When we arrived back at his bungalow for a good chicken curry tiffin, he showed me photographs of his fiancée, a very attractive girl who was obviously keen on sport. Most of the photographs showed her with several handsome young men of the Fleet Air Arm, she being the only girl in the pictures. We agreed he should write through his manager to the company saying I was willing to take his place when he wanted to be married. This also led me to discuss with him the idea of a company air service, which would at a stroke make life over here for married folk much more tolerable. It was something he immediately accepted as an excellent idea, and we talked long about Telford's request to frame a scheme. In the afternoon we cycled up the river, found a beautiful pool, and swam naked for about three minutes in the icy water, emerging mauve-pink to lie in the warm sun. He was surprisingly well informed of the senior staff establishment in the Assam Lothian group, having learned from his manager the numbers and length of service of the managers currently serving. There were six superintendents, each presiding over clusters of five estates; one cluster had only four. There were three estates on the North Bank which had no superintendents, beyond

North Lakhimpur, and four estates lying to the east, under a superintendent who ran one of the estates himself, and visited the others regularly. They were all First World War veterans, and they would begin to retire within five or six years, as would many of the managers. He reckoned there would be rapid promotion for people like us, in contrast with some of the managers now serving who had waited fourteen, fifteen years for a management. He quoted Paddy, his manager, as saying one never made much money until one became a senior manager or superintendent. I felt guilty when I realised I had not formed any such ambitions, but merely lived in hope of being able to work in a truly wild place, as the world used to be before the late appearance of the human race.

The talk ranged far and wide, discussing the prospects of Indian independence; the poor selection of girls at Bogahilonia of whom Mac said it was because they were married far too young; the possible effects of isolation if one stayed over here too long. He said malaria was awful over here, and was interested to hear of the mepacrine distribution, which had not yet reached these parts. After tea at the bungalow we went to the airstrip, where more than a hundred people sat patiently gazing at the aeroplane. Mac said many of them had seen aircraft landing in the later stages of the War, when a lodge once used by the Viceroy up the river had been converted into a convalescent camp for wounded soldiers and airmen of the Allied armies in Burma. It was still there, but quite abandoned. One lean, greying man with an interesting face and keen eyes, came up to us and made a low salaam to each of us. Mac told me this was one of the *shikaris* present when Andy was slashed by the leopard. He was a great friend of Govind who, although virtually without a scratch after the leopard had knocked him down and crouched on him, was taken into hospital with what would be called severe depression and delusions. He told everyone who went to see him how the sahib had given his life to save him, and therefore he was going to join the sahib when he was born again into his new form, which would be very great. They tried to make him eat, and had the compounder give him glucose and saline injections, but he died. Eventually we started the Cub engine, and took off together to have about twenty minutes reconnaissance of the river, where we saw huge mahseer fish in pools below the rapids all the way to the gorge. Mac made a good landing, and got out with the bright-eyed look of a satisfied aviator, giving a strong handshake and an invitation

113

to further visits, before the monsoon arrived. I flew back at a thousand feet, revelling in the appearance of the terrain with the golden sunshine lengthening the deep shadows, and darkening the green courses of the Brahmaputra through the luminous sandy islands. It was interesting to mark the existence of small villages where the clouds of dust raised by returning cattle herds formed flat sheets at about a hundred feet, like chimney smoke in Britain in autumn under clear skies. The mountain ranges, bright cobalt during the cloudless day, were now changing through shades of darker blue and purple, with the late sun gilding the higher ridges. The impact of having been at last in that beautiful place, for all its deprivations and dangers, gave me a great reassurance that such places did exist still in our crowded world, and that my yearning to live in such a place was more than romance.

I presented a sheet of foolscap to Telford on Monday on which I had written a draft of a possible company air service. I told him MacDonald and I had spent time in visualising what would be necessary, but neither of us knowing the actual lie of the land at each and every estate, it was not possible to suggest how many airstrips would be necessary. The North Bank estates being mostly spread out and cut off from each other for many months by swollen rivers, would need a strip on each estate, except for the two east of the Ranga river. An Auster aircraft, perhaps ex-service, with a Gipsy Major engine, would give good load-carrying and short strip performance. As for flying the aircraft, neither MacDonald nor myself would want to allow such duties to interfere with our experience and development as future managers of tea estates, and it would probably make sense to employ a full-time pilot who was also a qualified engineer. We thought there would be such people available in plenty who would not cost very much, with a commercial licence, and who could perhaps acquire other duties, or fly the aircraft on a charter basis for other companies who would pay for such a service, subject to the priorities of Assam Lothian. We would both offer our services for test-flying or emergency substitution if the company pilot was not available. He thanked me, and from the faraway look in his eyes I saw he was processing these ideas furiously in his brain. In the few days before he departed he never raised the matter again.

The factory overhauls were complete, and small amounts of tea were brought to the factory from the teams of women and girls who were carefully measuring and tipping the slender new tea shoots at a measure of eight inches above the pruning cut. I was encouraged to visit the factory to observe what was going on, and began to learn the names of the factory staff and the engineers, mechanics and carpenters, who worked busily and devotedly at the many tasks required to take the factory into a season which would reach its peak in August, and carry on running two shifts a day until October. One Birbal, a well-built engine attendant with curly hair showing a sprinkling of grey, struck me as being a happy soul, dedicated to his engines as he was to his family. One day when I did my afternoon visit to the engine room, he flashed his excellent teeth and said his children were at the factory gate, wanting to make salaams to the new *chota* sahib. I went to see them: three boys and three girls, from three to ten, well fed and smiling like their father. The girls put their hands together, and the boys saluted vaguely like soldiers. When I went back to congratulate Birbal on his fine children, he laughed and said there was another on the way. In the following week I was told he had stayed off work because he was not well. Only two days before Telford left, Birbal was carried into hospital in a bad state. Nunoo, one of my bungalow boys, had asked leave for half an hour to visit Birbal in hospital, which I granted. After dinner I went down to the hospital, and found Birbal groaning in agony, unable to recognise anyone. Dr Pal (pronounced Paul) appeared, looking upset and anxious. He told me Birbal was going to die of tetanus. Mr Telford had ordered him to give masses of penicillin from our precious supply, in a desperate attempt to avert tragedy. It had been a hot day, and all of Birbal's family and other friends and relations were sitting in the tiny ward, where a wood fire burned, giving off smoke. Dr Pal explained this was the way the people kept mosquitoes away, and grimaced as he pointed to the blackened roof and upper walls. The fire was used mainly for cooking the patient's food, and the single wards were the idea of Mr Telford which had helped to encourage people to use the hospital, as they could more easily be allowed to gather with the patient in such individual rooms than in a large ward. The people sitting patiently on the floor by the bed were sweating, and using fans on themselves and Birbal. They were all large-eyed with deep concern, and somehow knew death was lurking close. I saw Birbal's wife next to his bed, fanning the youngest child which slept with its head in her lap. She watched her husband with an expression of wondering disbelief, closing her eyes now and then as she moved her lips in what must have been prayer. Birbal's spasms were dreadful to watch, and there were soft moans and sighs from his family and friends. I had learned to be afraid of tetanus, but this was the first time I had seen what it did to a man, and I felt a chill of horror to see Birbal, who had exuded happiness only a few days before, sinking in agony to his death.

A stir behind me made me turn. Telford had arrived, and I went to him as he spoke to Dr Pal, who was confirming there was now no hope. He told Telford Birbal had months ago had a deep puncture in one of his feet, but had not reported it, which was why he had not had an anti-tetanus injection. He had kept the wound bound tightly in order to carry on with his work, which was the worst thing he could have done. Telford turned to me and said it was a damned shame a man like Birbal had to die like this because he still didn't have confidence in our system of medical treatment. He told me I should learn to recognise any signs of ailment amongst the estate population, so that immediate and early treatment could be given. I said I hoped I would be able to learn from Dr Pal the rudiments of what I should look for, and turned to the doctor babu, as he was called, and suggested he come to tea with me to start me off on the right lines. Telford said it was better to attend the hospital where the doctor babu would have his evening clinic, and would be able to show me things like anaemia, oedema, scabies, swollen spleens and so on. He said it was part of the scene out here. Hygiene was poor generally, and that led to problems of intestinal parasites.

As we spoke it hit me there was no electric light in the hospital compound, and I mentioned it was a shame, as I would have been happy to send one of the bungalow fans to keep these people cool. This seemed to embarrass Dr Pal, and irritate Telford, who said it was easy to think like that coming fresh from the UK, but these people live in their own way. They had their oil lamps, and were used to the heat, this being nothing to what you could expect in June, before the monsoon arrived. I said I had found in the Middle East that fans didn't suit me; I used to wake with pains in all my old injuries, and gave up the idea of using them. Telford then went to great lengths to describe how much he had been improving conditions for the estate population. He said the group had made great progress in the matter of medical facilities, some of the best in the industry. The villagers for hundreds of miles around would have to travel long distances to reach the Civil Hospital in Dibrugarh, but if they had no money there was little hope for them. There were one or two mission hospitals which were difficult for people to reach without transport, therefore most of them relied on their herbal remedies, not always with good results.

He showed me the new workers' labourers' houses he was building, with brick walls and corrugated-iron roofing, thirty of them in two lines, at opposite ends of which stood a large cowshed, with large compartments for keeping bullocks, milking cattle, and suckling calves separately. At each end of each shed he had built bays for cattle manure, collected from the byres and gathered from the nearby grazing grounds and roads through the housing areas; one bay was for the workers to use on their own vegetable patches beside their houses, and the other was to be used by the estate in the field. He explained there was opposition from older planters to this kind of housing, backed by many of the workers who were used to living in houses thickly thatched, with bamboo walls thickly plastered with a mixture of mud and cattle manure. These traditional houses were cooler in the hot weather, and warmer in the cold weather, and Telford agreed with this claim, pointing to his own bungalow which was thatched for coolness, and had lime plaster walls in timber frames. However, he said it was becoming difficult for estates to find enough thatch to keep workers' houses in good repair, because the War had attracted many building contractors who had made fortunes building for the masses of troops in Assam, and had stayed in Assam making a living from cutting thatch from river islands, and selling it to tea estates at high prices, from which the government took royalties. The people who lived in the outside villages always looked after their houses well, but it always happened if you gave them something 'on the company', they left everything to the company, and many neglected their houses, often reporting leaky roofs when it was too late for good repairs to be done in the heavy monsoon rain. He was very much bent on impressing me he was doing his best to improve things, and I had not seen enough of other places to know how far ahead he was in many respects. There was no doubt he had been upset at my attitude.

During that night Birbal died, and I experienced a funeral in this part of the world for the first time. The wailing and keening were quite depressing, and I could not forget the sight of Birbal's wife, watching her husband in agony, with her children. The oldest child being but ten years old meant she and her children were totally without support. I joined Telford and Foyle at the office the following afternoon when the widow came with all her children to the office. Birbal had been settled in the estate since he was a small boy, and had no contacts with any relatives in Bihar, whence he came. The widow's family had lived on another estate; both her parents were long since dead, and one of her brothers had died of malaria, leaving four children to the other surviving brother, who had three children of his own, and a wife with anaemia in pregnancy. Nobody knew of anyone who could support the widow. Telford said she could be given light work in the factory until her child due in August was born; until then the children would be given one good meal a day at the hospital, with the two older children looking after the younger ones. Meanwhile everyone who knew the family should try to find some of Birbal's relations, either in Bihar or in Assam, who could take care of the widow and her family. Telford said it was often a problem when people settled on the estates; those who kept contact with their tribal villages and went to visit them regularly, sometimes travelling nearly a thousand miles each way to do so, never had any trouble with cases like this. We would help them to repatriate a widow and her children to a community which would absorb them without any kind of reluctance, as a natural duty. 'We don't do them any good at all,' said Telford, 'if we disturb their ancient ways.'

Chapter VII

The Telfords departed with two vehicles at 04.30 in the morning to drive 250 miles to Gauhati, where they would take the train to Calcutta, the first stage on their journey to board the ship which would take them to England. It seems unfair to say of Telford's departure how a cloud suddenly lifted, because there had not been any noticeable awareness of a cloud; but within one day of their going the atmosphere changed. I began to find the staff and labour happily communicative and forthcoming, and felt the general tendency of people to converse as a marvellous stimulus to my learning of the language, or indeed languages. Louis Foyle made it clear he wanted to go round everything with me on the estate, until both of us were sure where everything was, and who everyone was. I hastened to tell him I had only been on Medeloabam a matter of weeks, and had found it difficult to keep up with Telford. I said I had told him I was still groping with the tremendous amount there was to learn, and was unsure of living up to his expectations during his absence. Foyle grinned and told me not to worry too much about Telford's style. He said it was well known how he operated: he had a good and very active brain, but with a very narrow focus, and lived very much in his own mind, not inclined to share his ideas and theories with anyone. He said he was a real old-fashioned baron-type, who looked after his staff and labour well; but the sad thing was they were all frightened stiff of him, because his word was law, and no-one got away with questioning it. They all knew they were very well off under him as long as they didn't upset him. I liked Foyle's style, and began to learn a great deal from him. He was neither dogmatic nor opinionated, but obviously knew not only a lot about tea in the field and in the factory, but he seemed to have a great gift of communication with all the people, old and young, male and female. In fact I found he had a Rabelasian humour which contrived to make people laugh, with no hint of disapproval, and for a Presbyterian with a straight-laced upbringing like myself it was fascinating to discover how there was nothing dirty about it. I found myself wanting to learn how he was able to adapt to the suitable style of conversation for each tribe, caste or rank, be it humorous or remonstrative, sympathetic or reproving. When I said he obviously spoke the language well he protested he was not a good linguist. He had picked up the vague type of Hindustani in the years before the War, and having been in the Army where Urdu was taught and spoken, he was now amusing the people by the way he mixed strange words with his sentences. When I told him I was very keen to learn various languages and would like his advice, he said I should concentrate first on learning to communicate in the language the people would use. He explained how very few of the immigrant labourers spoke their own language in Assam, except to people of their own tribe. There was a lingua franca used by the tribal people to speak to those of different tribes. Many planters called it '*coolie bat*' (coolie talk), and despised it, but it was in fact a proper language with a surprisingly sophisticated grammar. He had not learned this language except insofar as the estate language was thickly mixed with it. An Italian missionary had given him a book on this lingua franca, which was called Sadani, but he had not made much progress in learning it. He said he must have the book somewhere and would hand it over to me. He warned me in his arch, poker-faced way, that those who learned several languages were generally presumed to have used a succession of 'sleeping dictionaries', meaning mistresses, chosen from all the different founts of language. He said it must be an interesting way to learn more than just the language.

Foyle was keen to help me with polo, and I could tell by the way he sat his horse it would be worth listening to him. On the next polo day he took me with his wife in his large American Ford car. It was very hot, and they had brought plenty of cool water to drink. After I played in the first chukka, and before tea was ready, I mentioned to him I needed urgently to empty my bladder, and asked if the only way was to walk the quarter of a mile to the clubhouse. He told me to deal with the emergency by spending my penny against one of the huge 'rains' trees which stood in a row between the lists, where the horses stood in the shade, and the raised road which ran past the ground. There were as usual many Indians of all kinds sitting on the near edge of the road, keen to watch the sahibs charging around on horses and roaring swear words at each other. Foyle said not to worry about them; they wouldn't see me if I stood close to the huge trunk. Behind us the horses stood, and about fifteen yards away the ladies fluttered about, placing plates of sandwiches and biscuits on the table at which they were settling to watch the polo. 'Go on,' he said to me. 'The locals do this kind of thing all the time, but they squat down to do it. They won't notice anything unusual.' Being desperate I began 'slashing' (an air force term, which always struck me as slightly less urban than the spending of a penny) with glorious relief. Foyle had left me to it, I presumed in order to reduce my embarrassment. His voice came loud and clear from the tea table: 'Isn't that disgraceful now! Look at this! What kind of young men are they sending out nowadays?' There were shrieks of counterfeit outrage, and bubbles of soprano laughter, echoed by a gleeful tenor chorus of muttering from the spectators on the road. 'You wouldn't believe the way these air force officers behave, would you?' I felt myself blush from crown to heel, and had a few moments of uncertainty on how I was to come out of this with some dignity. Fortunately a chestnut mare, tail towards the tea table, decided to emulate my misbehaviour, and created such a diversion that I was able to involve myself in tightening Conker's girth strap, before merging with the other men, all grinning happily near the tea table. Foyle laughed apologetically as we drank tea together, saying one had to give the ladies a thrill, or a laugh, every now and then.

I played again, this time in the same side as Foyle, and he kept giving me quiet hints of how to anticipate where the ball was likely to go. There was still a lot to learn, not the least being the lack of speed of my otherwise experienced mount. It was a great thrill when in a scrimmage, virtually trotting on the spot about thirty yards from the Reds goal, the ball came out under Conker's belly, and I swung at it gently, to see it bounce through the posts. Drinking tea again after that chukka I was given faint praise by Dark Glasses Stapleford. 'Not bad for the only beginner we've got,' he said, smirking at the others. 'But you have made a big mistake, haven't you? No future in learning polo now, is there? Unless someone leaves you an awful lot of money when this all packs up next year, you won't be able to play polo ever again, will you?' Someone told him to stop being so pessimistic, for heaven's sake. I said to Stapleford I was prepared to go through life

121

trying whatever attracted me, however soon it might fold up, believing it would be possible eventually to find something worth doing which wasn't going to blow up, or sink. There were various points of view expressed on the future of tea in India, some very optimistic, others simply hopeful, and some downright pessimistic. Stapleford, casting a glance over his shoulder at the nearest ladies, leaned towards me, saying I should make no mistake about it; I should make sure to bed as many of these nubile tribal girls as possible, telling me as long as I was a bachelor there were great delights to be enjoyed. 'Once you're married that's the end of it all. You'll never enjoy it so much ever again. Get on to it now! They love it, especially if you give them three or four chips a time. Marvellous!' The way he said all this was so repulsive, and the fact that his wife, who sat only a few yards away, was surely one of the most attractive ladies present, and mother of two children, made more than me feel there was something wrong with this man's mind. Foyle edged close to Stapleford, winking at me, and murmured he was very sorry to hear what he had said, and told him he should go up to Shillong and see Dr Harry Gonzalez. 'He'll put you right again, dead cert, only fair on you know who.' He tilted his head and flickered a glance at Mrs Stapleford, who was bubbling with mirth amongst the other ladies. Stapleford swung sullenly away from our little group to seek other company, and Foyle murmured to us it was easy to see there was nothing wrong at all with that bonny lass.

The Foyles tended to stay longer at the club after polo, mainly because he said his new wife had to get to know the other ladies in the district, as Medeloabam was out on its own, and not easy for other ladies to call on their way to and from shopping in town. Although I had begun to drink the odd jug of beer in the Air Force after the War, I had decided not to begin drinking in Assam. This was partly because when my father heard I was aiming to become a tea planter he said, with some concern; 'Planters are a hard-drinking bunch, you know. Try and keep off it if you can,' and it was probably my Scottish tendency, reinforced by MacFortune, to wait and see how the money came and went on essential things before splashing it on booze. The trouble was, as I had discovered before, when even the nicest chaps drank more, and more, their conversation became louder and more boring to the sober listener as the evening progressed. I soon learned it was idiotic to stand with a group where, tennis having created a great thirst, one of the successive rounds of eight beers a time eventually landed on me. I decided to seek out quieter pairs or individuals, not so much through parsimony, but from a real need for more discursive and informative conversation. In this way I found a man drinking on his own who turned out to be very interesting. His name was Gurney, and he spoke in the way one expected to hear from an Oxford don, not only in diction but in the content of his almost reluctant conversation. I asked him what he thought of the coming of independence to India next year, and he said he regarded it as quite frightening. He was in his early forties, and I thought he was a 'tween war man, inclined to be timid, perhaps. He said there would be terrible blood-letting, but thought it wouldn't involve us very much; but what worried him was the thought of having to leave India. Assam was for him a refuge from civilisation, as he put it: with enough of civilisation's benefits to make it more comfortable. He liked the people very much: the immigrant tribal labour, the Assamese, the bird life, the wildlife generally, and would find it hard to leave it all. He was not married, but was very happy with an arrangement of what he called 'discreet immorality', causing no offence or suffering to anyone, nor any suffocating bonds. He did have a strong hope of remaining out here, perhaps if the tea industry were able to continue by agreement with the new government, which would make him very happy, or if it were possible to build a small bungalow in a remote place with good fishing and a small covey of servants. One thing he was sure of was he would not be able to settle in Britain, and we agreed it was an overcrowded country. He warmed a little as we spoke, almost as if he found I was not going to bore him or corner him. When I refused his kind offer of a drink he smiled and nodded, saying the longer I stayed off it the better. When I spoke to Foyle about him in the car going back, he told me Gurney had won a Military Cross in the first war. He was rather reclusive, and seldom came to the club. People said something happened to him at Ypres which gave him a strange complex. He had a terrible temper, sometimes for no reason that others could see, but all it did was to send him into several months of sulking. He lived a long way from other contacts, and seemed to be highly thought of by his company, which gave him a free hand and didn't regret it. It was rumoured he was a Buddhist or some such thing. He read lots of books. Which brings me to the subject of reading.

Now living on my own I found myself able to read a great deal. The store

123

of books I had brought with me turned out to be a treasure. Like so many of my age I had come under the spell of T.E. Lawrence, and finding a fascinating bibliography at the end of the book *The Letters of T.E. Lawrence* I agreed with two friends who left the Air Force to study at Oxford, who were similarly impressed with that unusual character, that this bibliography was a first-class list of books worth reading, more for me in the wilderness than for them tied to the wheel of intensive study, and I had brought many of those books as well as several others which suddenly became very significant. I had earlier began to read Mahatma Gandhi's autobiographical *Story of My Experiments with Truth*, bought in Calcutta and not on the Lawrence list, and found myself alternating between it and Russell's *History of Western Philosophy*, the latter a scintillating work of impressive and confident scholarship, which I found as gripping as any novel I had read. The former was a book of natural wisdom, steeped with a religious spirit which transcended organised religion, and embraced Christ's teachings in a way that warmed me rather than the reverse. The former feeds me with rich platters of knowledge whilst cutting me down to size with the realisation that at twenty-three I had already run out of time to read and learn enough of what human thought had been able to distil; but the latter gave me a strange hope there might be time enough to reinforce a faith in something good behind the mystery of life and death. Even at twenty-three I had somehow come to believe there was no final and conclusive answer or explanation in terms of human understanding to the mystery of life. Indeed to me the very mystery was created by the limitations of human understanding: the impossible concepts of beginnings and ends; the marvellous theories of morality, eternity, creation, re-birth and afterlife, which had been transformed into indefensible fabrications, misused and corrupted by ancient generations of power-poaching priesthoods. I was brought up in my tracks by the all-pervading religiosity of all the Indians I had been able to meet so far. It is true that whenever there are times of stress people tend to turn to religion, and because of the Hindu-Muslim carnage which had already frightened the people of India, there were, according to Foyle, widespread signs of stress, and although he confirmed India as normally pervaded by religious influences of many diverse kinds, he was sure there was widespread concern everywhere.

I had been able to converse in English with the head clerk, a gentle and conscientious man who gave very good advice. I asked how I should proceed with the learning of Assamese, and he named one of his clerks, suggesting I learned from him the Assamese script and its pronunciation. The young clerk's English was not very good, but he was very willing, and I had great trouble trying to induce him to speak slowly. I was able to begin trial conversations with the field staff, and made sure to compile different vocabularies and notes on grammar. My teacher passed the local Assamese newspaper to me so that I could study the script, and have him correct my reading aloud. It was very difficult learning the script, but I was attracted by its beauty, finding it easier to admire than the Hindi script, for which there was no pressing need to learn. I began learning the workers' names. Foyle was strongly in favour of this, and said it was clearly better to address a conversation, whether in admonition, inquiry or humour, to a person by name, rather than the equivalent of something like: 'Hey! You there.' Each day after work I would write in a ruled foolscap book the official work plan for the following day, using notes and discussions with the field staff and the *sirdars*. I learned their names quickly, as I wrote them each day when allocating the work for their teams, or gangs, which we called '*challans*'. The book was then taken into the manager's office and discussed before he either altered or signed it. There was always an alternative programme for work in the event of rain. The spring rain was expected, and such things as spraying insecticides and fungicides, application of fertilisers, roof painting, and road repairs would need to be called off, and substitute work given.

It was not long before I was settled into a regular programme: rising at 05.15 to ride on horseback a different loop each day; then to the office for dealing with workers' applications; complaints about housing repairs; water pump repairs; days off to attend sick relatives; disciplinary matters like absenteeism, insubordination, drunkenness; family quarrels, elopements; and many other matters brought for settlement by the manager. Telford was before his time in appointing a welfare officer, known as the 'welfare babu', who kept housing registers and dealt with house repairs and water supply, as well as doing the preliminary hearings of family quarrels before they were heard by the manager. These sessions lasted until seven, and were quite fascinating. Telford had not drawn me much into these on account of my inability to understand the language. Foyle was a delight to watch and hear as he dealt with people's problems. He took time to explain the development of cases and inquiries to me, and had me write down the various terms used in describing different kinds of injury, different relationships within extended families, and the words for various types of immoral behaviour, most of which were either promiscuity, seduction feigned or real, and occasional marital infidelity. The prevalence of these misdemeanours varied widely depending on the tribe; but Foyle pointed out how any tribals who settled and lost touch with their homelands eventually suffered as the years went by from a loosening of their morals and personal discipline. It was remarkable how it became easy to distinguish different tribes, not merely by the different styles of dress – or undress – but by their physical appearance. Foyle said although some toffee-nosed Britishers didn't like to be told, the breeding of these tribes was far purer than that of Europeans. There were cases of children born to be 'village idiots' as in isolated rural communities in Britain in earlier days, but this tended to happen amongst families who settled in Assam, and had too few of their tribe to enable correct marriages to be made. Some of these tribes were what the West would call 'primitive'; but their knowledge of the laws of genetics was impressive, and they were maintained by the division of the tribe into '*gotras*' with special totems to identify them, so that every mature man and woman knew who may marry whom without the risk of bearing an abnormal child. I found it very difficult to cope with the names of family relationships, there being different names for maternal aunts and uncles and paternal aunts and uncles, in all the different languages.

In the warm springtime, round about the Holi or Fagua festival, which was vaguely similar in basis to Easter, but much more a frank and rumbustious fertility festival, there were always several cases of illicit sexual exploits brought for settlement at the estate office. It was a time for asking the gods for a season of bumper crops, as well as for healthy progeny. There was much drinking, much dancing and singing, with drums throbbing all night long. By day, during the few days holiday, there would be a great deal of spraying each other with red fluid, supposedly made from sandalwood seed. The Foyles invited me to a picnic lasting most of the critical spraying day, which we spent miles away on a quiet spot with plenty of shade on the Brahmaputra. The water was cool, and we swam frequently. When we returned to our homes after dark, we found even the most sober of our servants had glazed eyes, and silly smiles.

Foyle predicted there would be, during this festival, several cases of youths and maidens found spending the night together, mostly when the parents had fallen deeply asleep after a lot of rice beer. If they were of the same tribe, and there was no breaking of their relationship tabus, it was a matter for both families taking two days to discuss the bride price and a marriage date. Sometimes the boy's family would refuse to fix a date until the girl was found to be pregnant. More difficult were the cases where each of the pair was from a different tribe. There were a few tribes which had acquired Hindu caste, but most of the others were followers of their own ancient religions, generally described by anthropologists as animists. Premarital sexual relationships outside caste or tribe were regarded, sometimes genuinely but often feigned, as outrageous, with the girl's family not only refusing to allow a marriage, but claiming huge damages which had become necessary by their daughter becoming more difficult to marry to one of her own tribe without double the normal amount of dowry. It was clear every pair had been drawn together by strong mutual attraction. Their ages would differ generally according to their tribe. The Mundas seemed to instil strong principles in their young, whether Christian or animist, so there were fewer cases of elopements or independent 'love' unions at ages less than seventeen or eighteen. It seldom happened that a Munda girl was enticed by a youth from another tribe. Foyle, like MacFortune, told me of the grim case before the War where a young British assistant fell for a beautiful Munda girl. She went at dead of night to his bungalow. Next day they were found in his bed with spear wounds which had killed them instantly. The Mundas are a proud tribe. Some communities of Gonds (pronounced roughly as Gores) were inclined to marry girls of as little as fourteen to much older youths. They were Hindus, and for want of a better word, were bordering on the ribald in their humour, and tended to promiscuity in their behaviour; but after a rowdy pantomime of outrage they normally settled things happily without delay. The Oraons, generally a handsome lot, seemed similar to the Mundas in physical type; but their languages were totally different, except for the use of the glottal stop, and their characters were distinctly different. The Mundas were almost as dour as Highland Scots, and although they seldom told a lie, they would be very difficult about producing the truth; but the Oraons, especially the unmarried girls, had what seemed to be a similar attitude to sexual activity as some of the South Sea islanders. Until they became pregnant they were happily, if somewhat secretly, promiscuous. Oraons tended to take an artistic view of the truth, and often told huge lies which they thought would be far more pleasant than an unpalatable truth.

One case came up where the girl had gone to the youth's family home, and claimed he had forced himself on her. Foyle asked the boy how he had silenced the girl, and he replied he had no need to do so. The girl, asked why she had not shouted or screamed, said she was terrified and could not utter a sound. Foyle, who was standing before his office table, took a five-rupee note from his pocket. He was wearing a safari jacket, with short sleeves and bag pockets. He told the girl this was company money, not his, and she could have it if she was good and clever in helping to settle the affair. He then put the note in one of his pockets, and stood beside the girl, looking at the large crowd of relatives and onlookers. He told the girl to reach out and take the note from his pocket. She demurred, saying she was ashamed, at which he told the crowd she was a good modest girl; but they should tell her there was no need to be ashamed, everyone knew the sahib had asked her to take the money for a good reason, which he would soon explain. The girl, beginning to smile through her expression of injured innocence, lunged her arm towards the pocket, and just as the hand was about to enter it, Foyle swivelled his body so that she failed to reach the money. There was a ripple of stifled laughter, and Foyle once more asked the girl to take the money from his pocket, and once more prevented her from making contact by twisting away. By the third time everyone was laughing and chiding the girl. Foyle raised his hand for silence. He told the girl to try once more. 'I am a girl now, and you are a boy trying to take my money.' He looked around. 'My money.' He slowly moved the pocket towards her, and with one hand over her mouth to hide her mischievous grin, the girl waited, the other hand poised, then suddenly thrust it, only to miss again; but this time Foyle called out in a loud high voice: 'A thief! A thief is stealing my money! Look, look! Help!' The crowd gasped, and the girl reacted as if stung. She turned to the crowd and appealed with both hands palms upward, in a plaintive high-pitched voice: 'He told me to take the money. I'm not a thief. I wouldn't have put my hand in his pocket unless he told me I should. He said he would give me the money, didn't he?' Foyle had features which radiated friendliness and confidence, with the sort of wrinkles at the corners of his eyes I had always hoped I would one day acquire. He swept the crowd with a dignified smile, and held the five-rupee note out to the girl, who looked at him with bewildered, dilated eyes, still shaken by his unfair accusations. 'Take it,' he said, 'you have helped to settle the *bichar* [process of justice].'

With an uncertain look she took the note, and looked at her father with a faint smile. Foyle then explained in a quiet voice to the fascinated small crowd how he had put the girl into the position of the boy, and himself into that of the girl. She, as the boy, would only attempt to put his hand into the girl's pocket (at this point there were two or three delighted shouts from one side of the crowd) if the girl had indicated she would allow him. He, as the girl, showed it was perfectly easy to move her pocket away if she really wanted, and that if she shouted, any unwelcome action by the boy would have wakened everyone, and probably led to the boy running off into the night. There was a chorus of approval from what appeared to be the boy's side of the gathering; but the girl's group stared wide-eyed and doubtfully at Foyle, still wondering if there had been a trick. The girl's mother, a woman still handsome except for the tense and twisted scowl she now wore, came briskly forward to snatch the five-rupee note from the girl's hand, and turning to Foyle she handed the note to him, explaining in a voice choking with emotion how it was impossible for her daughter, now having conspired like an idiot to ridicule herself, to take money for having done so. At this the girl burst into tears and sought refuge amongst the onlookers, some of whom made comforting noises, and others castigated her mildly for being so wayward.

As Foyle later explained, it was always wise to support tribal and parental authority concerning marriage laws and customs, because these had been developed over countless generations, always trying to reduce suffering, to protect women and children, and to strengthen tribal and family bonds against disintegration. They were all naturally dedicated to the care of their families and relations, and they had very strong objections to the breaking up of marriages which left wives and children without support. They were willing to care for widows and their children, but their attitudes to parental irresponsibility were unitedly stern. They were also conscientious about the need to keep their numbers and territories in harmony, so that either the crops or the game, or both, would support them; but as soon as they drifted away from their home lands there was a gradual collapse of these traditional values.

He told the people at the *bichar* there seemed no doubt about this beautiful girl and handsome boy being good specimens who had become attracted to each other by the qualities they inherited from their parents. Now it had been shown there was no unfair attack on the girl, it was necessary for there to be a *panchayat*: a court of five normally elderly wise men, chosen and agreed upon by the families of the boy and the girl, to establish what was to happen next. If the girl had been made pregnant it could be said the boy should marry her, but only if her parents and their tribe could be persuaded thus. This would mean an agreement must be made as to the amount of bride price to be paid, including a fine for the breaking of the tribal laws. It was always better to make an agreement which would keep the young pair with one or other family, rather than suffer their loss by an elopement, which often happened and did no-one any good. This was followed by much ritual protesting from the girl's family. The boy's family had little to say, but the boy was left standing on his own. He was in fact at seventeen earning a man's pay, and had a clean record. As there seemed to be a shortage of girls in most of the tribes, his family was, according to Foyle, going to be quite willing to support a marriage, but would have to go through a couple of months of mutual upbraiding, each side accusing the other's protegée of seduction or enticement. He explained how they would now arrange for the first *panchayat*, which would probably sit several times under the large pipul tree near the weekly market (bazaar), and when they came to a final conclusion which both sides accepted, the five wise men would appear at the estate office to have the agreement, the amounts of dowry and other payment, and the dates by which payments would be due, all recorded in writing in the agreements book. Their entry would now be signed by the manager as correctly written and confirmed by the *panchayat*, and would then be signed, usually by the thumbprints of both fathers, the one side's son, and the other side's daughter. It was not normally allowed for any European or any member of the Indian staff to be present at a *panchayat*, unless called as a witness. When I commented on the practice of taking fingerprints, I was surprised to learn from Foyle that the British Indian Police were first in the world to use fingerprinting in dealing with crime detection. Very few of the workers could write. Many of the Christian Mundas, Oraons, Parjas and others sent their children to mission schools, where they learned Hindi, and could write in that script.

All of this was typical of the early morning sessions which were part of tea estate life, and it was rather sobering to find I was expected to learn how to deal with such things wisely, in such a way as to maintain stability and confidence in the estate community. It would take years of experience under one's manager, and much depended on the quality of that manager. Foyle was right in saying he and I would have learned quite a lot about promoting justice during our time in the services, but I had to tell him I was much impressed by his judicial skill, which he assured me was the result of working for a manager on the North Bank before the War who had great gifts in the handling of people – of all kinds. It amazed me to hear him describe how Inverarity a giant Scot, operated. The only time corporal punishment was used was in cases of physical assault on women, children, or old people, and the punishment was by strokes of his thick leather belt on the bare backside of the offender; but the number of strokes had to be decided by the *panchayat*. Foyle enjoyed mimicking Inverarity describing in his rolling accent that most of the guilty ones would plead on their knees to take the belt on their backs, so that they could come out of it with scars they could show, and a reputation for bearing the punishment like a man; but one stroke on their backsides was worth ten on their backs, and the old men of the *panchayat* knew this well. 'I tell ye, Foyle, I learned this at school in Tobermory: one on the bare arse in front of your class mates would cure ye of any crime on earth: the sheer indignity of it!' Foyle said he had learned in the time he had been in tea how dangerous it was to use corporal punishment except in extreme cases, there being nothing worse than making enemies by insulting them physically in front of their fellows. But we agreed how strict discipline and good order were well maintained in the armed services without corporal punishment, and it would always be best to follow that example. This system of settling disputes, which I had seen in action under Foyle's management, existed because of the great tradition in remote, rural India, of settling things at source. If anyone wanted to use litigation through the courts, it was an awesome and expensive business, normally beyond the purse of small farmers, estate workers, or widows. The stories Foyle told me, and he was a splendid raconteur, indicated how many people had been ruined, committed to never-ending debt by a network of some unprincipled local lawyers who had developed the dark art found in shady corners all over the world, of keeping the milk flowing from their captive litigious cattle.

There came the time when I crossed the language hump, and after much pestering of Foyle to help me compile a versatile set of questions, I surged forward with these implements of rapid progress. The labour force seemed to enjoy having someone like me: a '*notun chota sahib*' (new assistant manager, literally a new little sahib), who was frankly asking them to teach him how to converse. The women and children were the easiest, full of humour and curiosity, drawing me out on questions only to be expected from people, some of whom in their own home lands lived lives described by anthropologists as not much different from the bronze age. Let me be clear on one point concerning the use of language: I was generally not a very talkative person, probably because in my early youth I had acquired the role of the strong, silent lover of the wilderness. I was very much influenced by such books as Ernest Thompson Seton's *Rolf in the Woods*, Thoreau's *Walden*, Fleming's *Himalayan Adventure*, reports of T.E. Lawrence, under other names hidden ultimately in the Air Force, *Scouting for Boys*, and many others in the same strain. In the years that followed I found many others of my own age who were similarly affected. We affected a stony-faced taciturnity, which seemed an effective armour for adolescent shyness. When I was about eleven years old, I was plunged into painful shyness by a girl of whom I was very fond, who told me that I looked cruel, with sharp features and cold grey eyes, and was seldom seen to smile. I began to believe this was true, because I found it difficult to mix, and was later convinced it was one of the reasons I yearned for the wide open spaces. I used to enjoy flying alone at great altitudes, above the weather, under skies so deeply blue even at midday one could see Sirius. Once I discussed this with Jag, who said he knew what I meant, but he was sure the feeling of bliss was something to do with oxygen lack, which was akin to intoxication. I was not a misanthrope, because it often hurt me to fail in forming wider friendships. Here, at Medeloabam, I was carried by a great wave of discovery: I was not only communicating, enthusiastically if rather disjointedly, but I was being drawn out. It was the easiest thing to make people laugh happily at descriptions of life in the West. The children were not only not afraid, but would lie in wait to scream salaams in the early morning when I rode past; and there was a memorable and reassuring discovery when a proud mother held out her three-month child for me to take. I did so, and the wee thing kicked and chuckled, beaming happily at what until then I had supposed to be a cruel, cold-eyed face.

One day not long after this episode ended, Foyle began by complimenting me on my progress with the language, but said it was important to remember the aim of the language was to communicate clearly what was necessary for the efficient control of the estates business, on which everyone depended for a living. He saw how I enjoyed chatting and laughing with everyone, and commended it up to a point, advising me there was much to learn, not only of the language, but of the psychology of each tribe, as well as the curious united psychology of the people as a whole, especially with regard to the difficult times which frequently occurred in life on remote and secluded plantations. One had to win the confidence and respect of the people before anything else. They would tolerate some things which we would find ludicrous, but they could dig their heels in over something long before you were able to work out what it was. There were around 1,500 workers and their families to look after, to keep in good health and good spirits, which was not the easiest thing in the world, especially when the heat and humidity rose, bringing tempers often to the boil. Between October and May people of all kinds were reasonably happy. Working hours were short, nights were cool, and skies were mostly blue; but the high season months could sometimes become difficult, and if you could not carry the labour force and staff with you it would make your life and work very difficult. His advice was to avoid becoming too friendly, because slowly and carefully I must learn the art of being strict about standards of work without frightening people to the point where they would believe themselves in danger. The more responsibility I had to take, and the more orders I had to give, the more people would try to test my strength, and if I was not well prepared it would be more difficult than it need be. One valuable hint he gave me was one he had learned from Inverarity. Inverarity was a linguist of repute, and Foyle explained with a wrinkled brow and a twinkling eye he was probably one of the early protagonists of the 'sleeping dictionary' idea, as he had at one time three mistresses, all from different tribes, saying it kept them out of mischief. Able to speak six or more distinct languages, Inverarity emphasised no matter how well one spoke these languages, it was absolutely imperative when it became necessary to create a really serious atmosphere of high importance or emergency, to speak Hindustani with the accent of an English speaker, and the cadences of a minister of the kirk. He said it never failed. I was always glad to have learned this early.

Foyle was a rich fount of information, of knowledge, and of abounding interest in everything to do with the growing and manufacturing of tea, and the people involved in it. His style was relaxed and apparently leisurely but, as with a good runner, it was clear he wasted no time or energy, and certainly stimulated me into wanting to do my best. He never bored me as Telford sometimes unwittingly did, by persistently dwelling on a subject until it palled, which led me to be self-critical, and suspect my time in the Air Force had blunted my ability to absorb new learning. Foyle showed no sign of stealth in the way he trained me. His habit of changing subjects frequently seemed natural, following his own instincts in registering all that could be seen about him. Interspersed with the great diversity of his teachings, ranging from the application and response of fertilisers to the various sprays required to prevent the proliferation of fungus diseases and insect pests, Foyle taught me a great deal, not only of the distinguishing differences of castes, tribes and religions, but their peculiar sexual attitudes, practices and proclivities. It was not only deeply interesting for me, but most important for my personal education that he was able to impart a vast store of almost encyclopaedic knowledge on the subject of women. Medeloabam had very high standards of what in the Air Force we called 'talent', meaning excellence of feminine beauty, build, and natural grace, which presented a wide field of interest, bound to capture perhaps too large a share of a young man's attention. The whole new ambience made Foyle's lectures both fascinating and credible. In a very short time it undoubtedly changed the structure of my stored intelligence, filling one particularly shadowy cave of my brain with a wealth of exciting and illuminating knowledge, where previously there had been little light except from furtive sparks, like shooting stars seen from the corner of one's eye, or suspicious dim lights like creeping glow-worms.

Perhaps the immensely detailed knowledge he imparted on the astute management of people, the learning of languages, the botany, plant pathology, drainage, surveying and accounting, enabled me to treat the absorption of all he imparted on women as another one of many subjects in an essential education, without allowing it to monopolise my thoughts. He

134

told me he remembered clearly how when he first arrived in Assam he found it very difficult to adjust to the fact that the womenfolk basically wore only two garments, and the men one. The women and girls on the estates wore a cotton blouse, and a cotton skirt, which was twice as much as they wore in their tribal habitat. The skirt was black, and the blouse of coloured material without a collar, and with short sleeves. They would add a sari, or a cotton stole for paydays and visiting the bazaar. Each tribe had its own style and colours of ornaments, mainly beads, with bangles of coloured glass or alloys of silver and copper or brass. Some wore necklet bands of black fibre cord threaded through silver coins, tied at the back of the neck, with tufts of coloured wool on the black cord hanging down their backs. According to Foyle the covering of womens' breasts was something the Muslim Mughals had brought, mainly in the northern territories where the Mughals destroyed innumerable Hindu temples, all of which were richly adorned with graven images, much less tragically holy and much more voluptuous than those that roused Cromwell's fury. In the southern areas of India many magnificent temples remained, and indeed Foyle had seen during his travels with the Army in rural South India a great deal of what he called healthy, unspoiled beauty, where the women were bare to the waist and totally uninfected by the shame-loaded prudery of the Christian missions, or the fanatical Muslims. He said since his early days in Assam, attitudes had been changing, to the extent that orthodox Hindus were almost as bigoted nowadays as the puritans and the Muslims. The facts of life, which were so little discussed in the West, and were known to very few children and adolescents other than those raised on farms or studs, were known to small children throughout rural India in surprising detail. I grinned as I remembered the cold sweats in fear of discovery whilst trying to read in hiding the books of Havelock Ellis or Marie Stopes, borrowed from friends lucky enough to find them in family libraries.

On the next polo day Foyle told me as we loaded our gear into his car that the wireless was reporting serious violence in the Punjab and the North West Frontier. It seemed the Muslims and Hindus were fighting, the former for a separate state, and the latter for the preservation of India. In the North West Frontier the Moslem League had sent agitators to stir the Pathans and other Muslim communities into violent agitation for a separate Muslim state. Whilst waiting for his wife, who was packing the sandwiches and biscuits for the polo tea, Foyle said we should do something about finding a wireless set for me, as it was important to know what was happening all over India. If the violence began to mount it was anyone's guess as to what might happen to the British, who had always been accused of exploiting divisions between Hindus and Muslims. Rumours were fed on the violence of communal riots, and the atrocities of the Calcutta killings in 1946 had propagated the most dangerous of all natural feelings: fear. Whilst passing through Calcutta a few months before, Foyle had seen a collection of photographs taken in 1946, showing the terrible mutilations of women, children and men, in the streets of that city where I had walked scarcely a month before it had happened. He said things could deteriorate suddenly and the worst could happen if the criminal elements saw opportunities for looting, and the otherwise quiescent public followed their example, watching for people of the opposite side fleeing in terror from threatened bloodshed and rape, and moving in like hyenas for rich pickings in abandoned households. He was just saying how so far we were lucky no anti-British action had taken place, but if it began we would hear instructions on the wireless, when his wife came down from the bungalow with two servants carrying the baskets. He winked at me to signal a change of subject.

At polo I was lucky enough to be offered an old Ferguson wireless for fifty rupees, by a chap called Colly, who had just acquired a new set which his wife had brought out from England. The play was good, and I enjoyed it more as time went on, learning more about the game and the other players. One of the elder players with whom I had not yet spoken called me aside for a chat. He was a distinguished-looking man, very much the picture of the British sahib in India: ex-cavalry officer of the First World War, well built and bronzed, with broad shoulders, wearing a military moustache of silver, and a proper polo topi. He asked how I enjoyed the game, and I responded enthusiastically. He said it was essential to keep it all in perspective, never to take it too seriously. I had watched him play, and observed how he rode in a similar style to Foyle: from the waist up showing little movement except when hitting the ball, hardly showing any movement of the left arm on the reins, fused to the horse like a centaur, seeming totally integrated in body and mind. He said one must always be careful to distinguish between sport and business; if there was no happy relaxation in sport there was no point in it; enthusiasm is quite a different thing from the hard determination of business or war, where you have to win or go under. I assured him I was certainly not in danger of making any mistake about sport, and he seemed pleased. As we spoke it occurred to me he was probably preoccupied about Telford and the young Turks, testing me to see which side I was on. He gave me some good tips about how to handle Conker saying I shouldn't try to keep up with the faster horses. I should let others do the riding off, and follow in the hope of picking up a poor reverse shot when going at a good speed, whilst the spearhead of faster nags went about and found the ball going the other way again. He said he had played Conker a lot when he and the horse were a lot younger. He said it was a good idea to carry on for another month or two using Conker to learn more about the game, and then find myself a faster, stronger horse. It would know less abut the game, but could be bent to the will of any keen young player. Being unsure of the financial implications of buying a new polo pony as well as the uncertainty of the future, I said I felt rather wistful about the ongoing possibilities, not just for polo but for the planting life, which I was really beginning to enjoy, and asked if it was wise to bank too much on continuing for a worthwhile period. His hand came up with index finger extended, and he fixed me with a fierce stare.

'Young man,' he said in clipped tones, 'you surely know the words "carpe diem". Now it might seem to be cut and dried that India will be given independence, but no-one should take it for granted. My family has been Indian Army for three generations. I know this country and its people well, and I can tell you whatever happens will not be as bad as most people think. Even if they get their independence, and they've waited a long time for it, mainly because there are many among them who enjoy corruption as a kind of game and got the rest a bad name. I feel in my bones there could still be a future for people like you out here. Unfortunately nothing is certain in this life except death, and you never know when you are going to die. You should either give yourself to this life wholeheartedly or pack it in and go elsewhere. My brother was in the Indian Army, and transferred to the Indian Civil Service after the War. He wrote to me saying he could not possibly work on under an Indian government, and would only stay long enough to secure his British retirement terms. It's a damned shame because he loves his job, and the people he deals with; but he can't stand the idea of politicians suddenly diving into the running of India. The Indians in the ICS are first-class men, but they will either be corrupted or sacked by politicians. My advice to you is: get the most out of this unique life. There is a strange magic between the British and the Indians out here: they each bring out the best in each other in so many things. You will find yourself wanting to earn the respect and the admiration of the Indians you deal with, and it will make a better man of you if you are the right stuff. There are rogue Britishers and rogue Indians, but I tell you I have the greatest admiration for the Indian Army from top to bottom, and my brother almost weeps when he praises the Indian judiciary, who will yield to nothing but the letter of the law. Nothing is lost if you fill your current life with valuable experience, either in work or play; take my advice, young man, because however it goes you will never regret it.'

Chapter VIII

The planters all said Assam was never as hot and humid as Calcutta, and as the days went by I tried to remember how Calcutta had been a year earlier when I had passed through. All I could be sure of was that Bahrein had been insufferable and Calcutta had been much more tolerable. As May progressed the heat rose, and at night cotton shorts and a sheet were enough for comfort, with the sheet over the middle, to keep the stomach safe from chills. The cocks crew earlier, and I became used to the system of time which began the day with 'first cock crow', followed by 'second cock crow', and then by the hours of the day, which were struck by the watchmen in the tower on the highest building in the factory, clanging out the time from six onward up to eight, by which time everyone would be at work, and the hour would not be struck until next morning. Cock crow varied with the seasons, and generally suited everyone. When it was overcast the cocks crew later. There was a tradition in the tea areas of keeping clocks ahead of Indian standard time by one hour, something to be remembered when one wanted to catch a train, or attend some government office. We began to have more cloud in the rising humidity, and the sky was hazy. The showers made everything begin to grow, most of all weed, in my own vegetable garden and in the tea areas. The tea itself began to grow vigorously, and there began a race to cope with the increasing amount of weed and keep enough people plucking leaf so that it didn't grow too long and become woody. The best women and girls were those selected to pluck leaf, which required experience and a good eye, keeping the plucking table as level as possible so that it would not rise during the ensuing season, causing loss of crop and difficulty in plucking.

I spent many hours in the tea, checking the level, and making sure the sides were not plucked low, which would result in a domed bush instead of a flat one. The plucking table, once carefully established, resembled a lawn at waist height, and the beautiful pale green shoots gave an attractive reflected light which was easy on the eye except in the late afternoon when plucking into the sun. Foyle made it clear to me our plucking should improve, both in the standard of leaf, which tended to be too long, and in keeping the plucking 'table' level. This would improve efficiency in plucking and give better liquors from tender leaf. There was always a controversy among planters as to whether coarse plucking gave more crop than finer plucking, but Foyle said it was a matter of fine tuning: not plucking too fine, nor too coarse. With the right standards the pluckers would find they would actually earn more money from leaf which grew at a much more constant rate than coarse plucking, which led to high peaks of harvest interspersed with periods in which there was far less leaf available. It was necessary to use much circumspection when altering plucking control, because if pluckers were frightened into radically finer plucking they would suspect they would lose money, and start moaning, perhaps going slow to let the leaf grow bigger ahead of them. It sounded complicated to me, especially as Telford had clearly preached his policy of plucking longer leaf as very successful, saying his quality might not be as high as many of the other estates, but he gained in the extra crop he made.

Foyle taught me to recognise the various pests which could threaten our crop. Red spider mite was one which, in the early season was not always easily seen, but its presence could be detected by the sweet scent of the fermenting tea juice where the mites were busy puncturing the tender leaves and imbibing the sap. If it was not controlled by spraying it soon became embarrassingly visible as an unsightly rusty stain, and if not controlled would lead to a purple-brown hue which began to show leaf dying. Pluckers and weeders moving through the fresh green bushes would unwittingly carry the mites on their garments, spreading it widely. I learned how the spraying of lime sulphur was organised, and how often infected areas had to be sprayed, depending on the average day temperatures which speeded the hatching of the tiny red spider eggs as the season progressed. There were various caterpillars which ate the tea leaves, some of which, called nettle grubs, were amazing to behold with their iridescent colours of brilliant green, yellow, purple and red, and curious arrays of spiny antennae; but the sting on any flesh coming in contact with these antennae was an initial shock followed by intense irritation from the blistery rash. The bigger species could sting through the women's thin cotton skirt wraps, and we had to organise special teams of youngsters, protected by wraps of sacking, with tongs made from thin bamboos to pick the caterpillars from the underside of the mature leaves. The presence of these caterpillars was detected by *sirdars*, not only by the expostulations of people like me who traversed the area behind the pluckers uttering barks at each sting, but from their own sharp eyes noting the leaves being eaten by what the pluckers called 'leaf scorpions'. The fascinating thing about these insects was the name given them by planters and scientists: they were the caterpillars of the 'Tea Seed Moth', which pupated in a round, hard case resembling the seed of China Hybrid tea plants. The caterpillars would descend from the bushes, bury themselves in the leaf mould and earth, and make these round shells. The only way to deal with these was to send people to fork the earth round the base of the bushes, and collect all such round objects, seed or otherwise, a count of which would indicate whether we should persist with the operation. There were times when at the end of the day's plucking I stood watching individual baskets being weighed and entered in the leaf book, and the women and girls, observing the weals raised on my thighs by the leaf scorpions, would either show sympathy or scold me for wearing such short '*patlons*' (pantaloons = shorts) in the tea. One old lady told me in a stage whisper how these stings would make me very full of energy, at which there was much giggling and hiding of mouths by the girls.

Flying with Bobby Constable continued with much progress being made. The humidity led to plenty of turbulence, and we practised landing on the very hot concrete landing strip at Dinjan, where the turbulence was violent as one neared touchdown. After an hour of this in the heat, we did a long climb to 10,000 feet, cruising northwards in the direction of the snows, which were no longer clearly visible with the prevailing wind taking the haze of the plains towards them. It was delightfully cool at that height, and we made a habit of landing on some river island beside a deep pool, where we were able to enjoy good exercise in cold water before having a picnic lunch. Many of the places we found showed tracks only of wild creatures. We found areas of thatch grass where from a hundred feet we saw wild buffalo with great horns, and various deer. Constable told me there was a single buffalo horn in the Natural History Museum in London measuring seven and a half feet, which had been picked up on the cold weather shores of the Dihang river, over which we flew. We marvelled at the prospect of seeing a bull buffalo with a horn span of nearly fifteen feet. These creatures were far bigger than the domestic water buffalo, and had legs which were white from hoof to knee. The tracks showed hoof diameters of about the size of a soup plate.

One Sunday Constable organised a party at which I met about a dozen other ex-service officers of my own age group. One or two I had met before, and I was pleased to meet MacFortune, the oldest of the guests. He buttonholed me and asked how I was enjoying life at Medeloabam. I told him I was really enjoying life, and making good progress with the language. He said he had meant to come to the club early to see how I was making out at polo, and to have a chat with me. He reminded me how he had warned of the rumours which spread about people in this part of the world, and said he had heard stories about me from people who had never even seen me, let alone met me. 'You're supposed to be a socialist, you know. They say you had a row with Telford about the poor labour not having any electricity, and you wanted to take the fans out of your bungalow and put them into the hospital. You're supposed to have lots of books by Bertrand Russell and Bernard Shaw, and you're keen on E.M. Forster. All that sort of thing, you know?' My reaction was of intense irritation. I said I couldn't believe Telford would propagate such nonsense, or was I wrong? He laughed his husky laugh and told me it needn't have been Telford. Any of the Indian staff could have overheard some conversation and passed it on as 'three and fourpence instead of reinforcements', that kind of thing. He told me not to worry too much about it, but to remember how to tailor things so as to make it difficult to alter meanings. He told me he was going to sell his Mauser 10.75mm rifle, and his Zeiss Ikonta camera. He named the prices, which seemed rather cheap to me, but I jumped to an unwelcome conclusion, too fast. He laughed and said he was not contemplating resignation or emigration, not for a while. He said I could pay him fifty rupees a month for so many months, and he wouldn't charge me for thirty rounds of ammunition, ten new, twenty old. It seemed he had done enough of killing, and thought there must be plenty of younger people, like me, to kill tigers, leopards, and elephants which caused serious trouble for the labour and the villagers. He added if I went over to the North Bank it would help to provide food too. I said I would buy both rifle and camera, and he said he would arrange in the court to have the rifle licence transferred to my name. I was hoping he spoke the truth about not preparing to leave India.

One of the other guests at Constable's party was Joe, whom I had met in the club some weeks before. He greeted me as an old friend and began introducing me to various other people, some of whom I had seen but not met. On hearing my name they either said, 'Ah! The chap who flies,' or 'the chap who plays polo', and one actually said, 'The chap who is supposed to he a communist'. There was one tall, dark, strongly built fellow who said I looked like a tennis player, to whom I confessed I had played very little, regarding it as rather a clubby kind of a sport. This drew the comment from Constable that nothing could be more clubby than polo, and perhaps I meant something else. Ultimately, being baited for what might be snobbery, I confessed it seemed to make more sense to say I would keep tennis in reserve for when I got married. Someone then said, 'Ah! Like bridge, you mean?' To which I had to reply I intended to be happily married, with no place for dangerous sports like bridge. Joe introduced the tall chap as John Corders: 'A bloody fine tennis player. He can take his pick of any pretty wench in the fishing fleet. They love him and his excellent tennis.' Corders was like a tall, dark-haired version of T.E. Lawrence, with a strong lower jaw, and a face not given to much expression. He spoke a clear, clipped, military-county kind of English, tending to look down his nose. Constable eventually had us all sit in a loose ring on his verandah on cool, cane chairs. He had a red light burning in the verandah area, which drew ribald inquiries from several rather tipsy pongos (army types) who were then enlightened by Constable as to the virtues of red lights which provided illumination without attracting insects; but above the eaves were three bright lights to which the myriads of winged insects ware attracted, kept thus from worrying us by falling into our drinks. This was very important at this time of the season when the disreputable 'stink bugs' abounded. One of these in a glass of any drink rendered it totally undrinkable, the odour being vaguely like hot shellac. Two bearers kept a constant supply of snacks: pieces of tinned Frankfurter and sardines on toast, and small pieces of curried chicken, which we all ate hungrily.

Our host then announced we would all take it in turn, round the ring, to say in a few words why we had chosen to take up a career in Assam. This provoked loud protests from most of us, with Joe, whose habit seemed to be to represent the 'damfools', standing like an elder statesman to make a speech on our behalf to Bobby Constable. He said he felt it was unfair to expect a group of fugitives from justice – or injustice – to expose their reasons for seeking remote anonymity. He said for his part he would rather be thought an escaped poodle-faker than be proved one; rather be thought disinherited than born in poverty; rather be thought a gentleman driven mad by the War than a jumped-up bank clerk trying to be a gentleman. This last sentence led to raucous cheers and clapping as Joe bowed and resumed his seat. Only two of those present did not applaud: our host, and Corders; and Constable pointed at him. 'The only one who doesn't find our friend's oratory amusing. Let's start with you, and go round clockwise.' He was a man who exuded authority, and sensing the strange hush as Corders stared at him with drooping eyelids, he added in a quieter tone: 'No compulsion, of course!' He grinned. 'When you have all either confessed or funked, I shall tell you why I came out to Assam.' Corders held his empty beer mug up towards the bearer, and when he was replenished he began to speak. To begin with there was much banter and mockery, but it died out as he spoke on.

'I decided to come to Assam to escape making a proposal of marriage. I had met several fellow officers during the War who were planters, and I was struck by their attachment to a life they described frankly as tough, but worth all the worries and deprivations one had to accept along with the unusual quality and character of the life. My father was killed as a corporal in the Yorkshire Light Infantry on the Somme. I was lucky to have a mother who gave me, her only son, a good education, achieved by her persistent efforts to make me able to get a scholarship to grammar school. She died of TB when I was seventeen. I failed to get a scholarship to Durham University, and worked on her brother's small farm for five years, until war broke out. I joined my father's regiment, and ultimately landed up in the Middle East as a corporal with the Desert Rats. I won the Military Medal at Alamein, and my CO recommended me for a commission. He was a gentleman farmer from Yorkshire, and he told me to begin learning to speak with less of a broad Yorkshire accent before I went for my interviews, warning me it was a sad fact that too countrified an accent would be a definite disadvantage. I rebelled, but he was wise, and helpful, and I was a good mimic. I got my commission, but I eventually got into trouble for not wearing my MM, and when I told him I was fed up to the teeth with fellow officers often looking down their toffee noses at an ex-ranker he told me to be proud of wearing it, and to behave like a gentleman and put them to shame. In time I found it paid to speak like an officer and a gentleman, not so much in dealing with the toffee-nosed bastards, but in dealing with the troops. They are a bunch of bloody snobs, you know. The posher I spoke the more they seemed to like it. I transferred to the Punjabs, and really began to enjoy life. Eventually I was posted back to my own regiment just after the invasion. It was a different world: I was a captain, and trained people in the arts of infantry warfare. We were stationed in the West Country. I found I was good at tennis, and had some good coaching from a fellow captain who had played county tennis up north. We played a lot in '45 and '46. The CO was a regular officer, and I got along well with him, played tennis with his wife and daughter. The daughter was a beautiful girl and a damned good tennis player. I fell for her, but didn't show it, being sure there was no likelihood of happiness ever after; my instincts told me. Sadly, she fell for me, and the parents noticed it. Now if you are thinking faint heart never won fair lady, listen to this. I know some of you, like me, are great admirers of Lawrence of Arabia. We lapped up his marvellous *Seven Pillars of Wisdom*, and we were shattered yet deeply impressed when he made his mystery withdrawal from society, from an establishment which offered him choice scholarly rewards. This chap had all the intelligence, dedication, courage and willpower that go to make a uniquely valuable human being. We liked to think he opted out because of the way the British and French treated the Arabs after the War. Rubbish! He was clearly very attractive to women, and he loved them; but he knew he would not be able to marry a girl of his own class, of his own intellectual level, because he was a bastard: illegitimate!' There was a long pause. 'I didn't discover until after my mother's death that I was a bastard. When my colonel told me he was sure he could use his influence to secure me a permanent commission, so that Jane and I could marry into the security of the family's traditional profession of three generations, I knew there was no future in that direction. I thought of eloping rather than presenting my birth certificate to the selection board; but without a secure career it was going to be unfair to Jane, and I had

145

convinced myself she would never want to marry a bastard. I know this because I used to speak often about Lawrence, and one summer's evening I heard her say: "It is so sad, such an unusually accomplished man, but no girl could be expected to marry a man who is illegitimate, could she?" I wouldn't be surprised to find I had some fellow bastards sitting with us here and now, but whatever they might think, I am here in Assam because I shall find a beautiful and complaisant hill tribal girl to love and to treasure, who lives nearer to the way life was before civilisation mangled it. I knew I would be able to play tennis most of the year round, and have a wholesome job working out of doors, with plenty of good books to read. I finish by telling you: you might not be illegitimate, but you're the sort of bastards I would rather mix with, otherwise you wouldn't all be here.'

Joe began clapping, and others joined, but the clapping faded into a rather awkward pause. Constable broke the silence with what sounded like a callous judgement, saying he thought Corders had become over-obsessed with the curse of illegitimacy, and asked him if he hadn't even thought of waiting until he met a girl on home leave, or someone's daughter visiting Assam with the cold weather 'fishing fleet', to whom he could announce his illegitimacy before he let himself be too deeply involved. He said he knew several people who had done just that, not just in Assam, and had made very successful marriages. He told Corders he should be careful not to stumble into a liaison with a woman in Assam too soon. 'You stand out to me as the marrying type,' he said, like a headmaster dealing with a boy not concentrating on his studies, 'and I can't see you being happy with any other arrangement. For heaven's sake be careful!' This moved the sad cynical expression from Corders' face for a brief interval before he took a deep draught of beer, and turned to the man next to him, telling him it was his turn. There were no more such interesting explanations after Corders had thrust upon us the drama of his situation.

When it came to my turn I felt by impelled the sympathy he had aroused to tell of an incident which would make sense of his change of accent, almost in the way it made sense for British soldiers to change their traditional red coats for khaki to avoid being massacred by their enemies in the mountains and the veldt. I said there was a rugged Geordie on our pilots' training course in Rhodesia: he was a tough wing-forward on the rugby field, the best shot-putter on the course; he was a brilliant mathematician, and a great humorist. We had difficulty in understanding his broad and guttural Geordie accent, and pulled his leg about it, much to his amusement. He gained above-average flying assessments, and came top of the course in all written exams. We all expected him to be one of the officers created from our course when we were awarded our wings. No cadet had any idea or indication of whether he would be called forward for his wings as Sergeant X or Pilot Officer X. It was kept a tight secret until the names were called out in alphabetical order on the final 'wings' parade day. He was called out as Sergeant Cuthbert, and we were all shocked. The seven of us who had been called out as pilot officers all agreed Geordie was in every way superior to us, and felt guilty we had somehow been awarded a privilege we deserved less than him. He was killed in action in Burma within a year of leaving flying school. Corders gave me a poker-faced wink. Constable asked why I had said the Geordie had been killed within the year: did I mean it was because he had not been made an officer, and he had taken chances to prove himself distinguished in combat, or what? I was still trying to become used to his sharp questioning, sometimes very astute, sometimes annoying, but generally a refreshing stimulus to the avoidance of platitude or irrelevance. I said I had simply rounded the story off, the relevance of the story having survived the termination of the character. Constable looked at Corders with his piercing stare, and said we could all understand the problems of innocent offspring being stupidly punished for the sins of their fathers; but what was to be done about it? After all, it seemed illegitimacy was instituted to avoid murder, mayhem and worse in the matter of establishing who was the rightful heir to family estates and fortune. Some royal bastards didn't do too badly, probably because there was plenty of spare wealth to mollify them, but things had changed. What was to be done about it? Joe, laying aside his mock ceremonial manner, suggested India had the right idea: hardly any of them tell you the date of their birth, only their sign of the Zodiac. His office staff either didn't know their ages, or pretended they were younger than they actually were; they certainly didn't have any birth certificates. Constable said one could sometimes actually find the year and the month of people's birth by questioning. The other day he wanted to find the date of birth of the son of one of his engineers in order to help him join the Air Force, and his parents worked it out, remembering he was born a week before the Kali Puja in the year after the Constable

147

Sahib arrived on this estate. There was a gust of delighted laughter which Constable slapped away with a mixture of disgust and humour. Corders came up with the idea of abolishing birth certificates altogether, but this was proved impossible in Western countries where all kinds of legislation and entitlement depended on accurate registration of dates of birth. I asked if marriages were registered in India, and Constable clarified very few actually were, mostly by higher caste and income groups and where a lot of land was involved; but the millions of what in Europe would be called peasants, had no marriage registration. Most of them remained in their villages all their lives, where there would never be any question whether or not a pair had sworn complete dedication to each other.

The discussion continued until very late, ranging from Hatter's Castle to Polynesia and back, dealing with the way tribal people looked after their children and treated their marriages extremely importantly, less concerned with the so-called legality of births, and greatly interested in accepting as many children as possible, sometimes from any source, for the good of their tribe. This led to the problem of high death rates from disease, and the tendency of 'nature' to exert over all species its uncanny control of population balance. We all argued about whether it was in relation to territory or to competition with other species; but we were united in agreement that nature's methods, although sometimes without recognisable ill effect, generally used disease and starvation to control populations. Humanity in its private wisdom, presuming nature to be at odds with God, resolved to protect humanity from such cruelty. Constable was a splendid, laconic chairman, and I think the cold beer brought forth debating skills and wild speculation under his relentless demands for logic and reason. The required explanations of why the rest of us had chosen to come to Assam were forgotten, and the company broke up well past midnight. Constable thanked me for flying with him, and sent me home in his car. On the way I resolved I would seek out my Darwin's *Origin of Species*, the Everyman edition someone had promised would be easier to read than the full original. It seemed to be one of the many books everyone discussed, but few had read, and I continued to hope I would be able to cope with the supply of such well-known books I had brought with me: Carlyle's *French Revolution*, an abridged *Decline & Fall of the Roman Empire*, *The Story of San Michele*, and many more. The trouble was finding time to read before sleep intervened.

148

It was a couple of weeks later that Nicky MacFortune met me at polo and told me all had been arranged to transfer his firearms licence to me. There was a date to attend the District Commissioner's Office on the following Wednesday before polo to complete the paperwork, and Foyle said he would drop me off before he and his wife went to the store, and MacFortune would deliver me at the club when we were finished. He gave me the rifle and the camera, both in beautiful condition, wrapped in cloth in an old, washed fertiliser sack, padded with old newspapers. He explained it was best not to show the shape of a firearm in what could be described as times fraught with danger. The ammunition he said was safe enough hidden with the connivance of the servants, and was not as much sought after as shotgun cartridges. Within another couple of weeks, after having used three old rounds to check the aim at different ranges, there came an unexpected need to use the rifle in an unforeseen necessity. Foyle and I had walked from the office to the stable, discussing a report of villagers cutting what we called 'goat-proof' fencing at the south-east corner of the tea area, and had stopped at the stable to watch the syces brushing down Conker. Just as Foyle looked at his watch and said we should go and have breakfast, I saw his wife come from the bungalow, ducking under an arch of deep crimson bougainvillaea to enter the stable forecourt. She wore a cool, pale green summer dress, and to me was the picture of blooming womanhood; yet nearing us she gave no radiant smile of greeting as I had grown to expect, but looked at her husband with large, moist eyes. The wireless news said there was increasing communal violence with many deaths around Delhi; and Mountbatten had flown to London for discussions with the British government. They said British troops were being sent to areas where trouble was breaking out. Foyle took her hand and spoke reassuringly to her, saying there was nothing to worry about: just a lot of politicians stirring trouble about who was going to take over whose land. She turned her pale face with deep blue eyes which were wider open than I had seen before, and the glance set some tiny nerve in my own gut vibrating as I recognised fear. I smiled and suggested I went off to breakfast, but at that point a man came running from the office, wide-eyed and panting, and salaaming Foyle he spoke rapidly, breathlessly, gesturing at his shoulder and head, until Foyle raised his hand and told him to go back to the hospital. We were coming now. Still holding his wife's hand he told us some Assamese villagers had brought a badly injured man from their village, six miles away. A couple of hours ago a bear had killed a man in a grove of reeds, right in the middle of the village. We began to move back to the office, making way to the hospital. I saw Mrs Foyle show reluctance to go with us, but Foyle patted the hand he held, and said it was always good for his lady to come round the hospital with him when there had been an accident. He told her not to worry; the man had walked in with the others. It was his brother who had been killed.

When we reached the hospital Foyle waved the crowd of curious onlookers away as the doctor came to meet us. We went with him into his surgery, Foyle still holding his wife's hand. A man sat moaning softly on a bench; the doctor, the compounder, and two nurses busied about with bottles, needles and bandages. Blood was running through caked runnels of older blood from his face to his waist and loincloth. He raised his hands, palms together, to each of us in turn. His right ear hung dangling from the rear point of his jaw, and his collarbone on the same side was standing out from his skin in a green-stick fracture. As the doctor worked Foyle spoke with the villagers who had brought the man, and explained to us what had happened. About dawn someone had seen this man's brother enter the twelve-feet-tall reed grove. Later, when the man was not to be found, his brother and some others shouted, but had no reply, and taking their *daos* (bush knives) they went into the grove, following his tracks in the dew. They found his brother lying dead, his skull crushed in, and raised a shout, which brought the bear charging. This man slashed at it with his *dao*, but went down under the great beast's weight, and suffered this dreadful mauling before the others returned with long, sharp bamboos, and were able to turn the bear away. It must have come out of the nearby forest by moonlight, and decided to sleep in the very thick cover of the reeds. The men say there are two large honeycombs in the trees, which probably attracted him. It was a Himalayan bear: black claws like pruning knives, a white horseshoe on its breast; it sounded like a big one. They wanted someone to go and shoot it; Gerella was away visiting his relatives near Sibsagar. Foyle looked at me with wrinkled forehead, and said it sounded like a nasty kind of playground for a game like that. The men said the paths in the grove were very narrow, and arched over at about five feet. He said he didn't think Dierdre would like him to go, and he thought it a bit unfair if he went and got himself killed by a bear, leaving the poor girl on her own so soon.

Dierdre went pale and stared at him in horror. He grinned and winked at her. What did I think? I had been thinking of the handsome Mauser rifle, but as the description of the situation became clear it seemed to me not so much a case of using a powerful rifle as a case for experienced craft in close cover. I said it would probably be best to leave the bear in the grove until nightfall, when the bear would be likely to find its way out and return to the forest; but when Foyle put this to the villagers they were strongly opposed to this idea, saying their women and children were in danger until the bear was destroyed, and they were quite adamant in their belief of killing any animal which had killed a human. The *Jemadar Babu* (head field overseer) had arrived, and he spoke with the villagers in rapid Assamese, finding out as much as he could of the lie of the land. Ultimately he gave Foyle his view it was a dangerous situation, and said perhaps the villagers could use their buffalo herd to drive the bear out into the open, or one of the timber contractors' elephants could be used to carry me into the grove in order to find the bear and shoot it.

Within the hour we had organised ten Koyas and their diminutive terrier-like dog. I was scarcely able to speak their language, and my Hindustani was hardly up even to their not very fluent standard. They went off gleefully, loping on the route explained to them, each wearing a tiny, tight loincloth, red beads, and carrying four arrows. These arrows had points of steel five inches long with two barbs, sharpened on river stones until they could penetrate the thickest skin of boar or bear. The small terrier was their best hunting dog, and it seemed to converse with them in a strange falsetto tongue as they moved off.

Foyle and I rushed a quick breakfast, and he took me in his jeep with two of the villagers to show us the way to the village. We didn't see the Koyas, who were trotting across country, and we bumped over cattle tracks and ditches where no wheeled vehicle had ever been before, frightening cattle and buffalo along the way. I wore washed tennis shoes, and a dark khaki shirt and shorts. I had five rounds in the magazine, and one 'up the spout'. My practice shots had all been with the old ammunition, which had proved good, but MacFortune had warned the old stuff was unreliable, therefore I made sure the first round was bright and new. We arrived at the village well beyond my furthest wanderings, and found it was very close to the tall forest. The people were worried, and it took some time to quieten them down. The grove was about an acre in size, with five tallish albizzia trees standing in it. We asked if there was a usable elephant to be had, and we were shown one young female, but it was not trained for *shikar*, and would panic if a shot were fired from its back. The buffaloes were grazing not far from the village, and I suggested they, being reputedly afraid of nothing, could be driven into the *kagri* (reed), to force the bear out on the side nearest the forest. I could wait there and shoot the bear when it appeared. The Koyas would take some time yet to arrive, so we briefed the headman and his sons on what should be done. By the time the buffaloes went in and I took up a position where a stream came out of the forest, it was steaming hot, with bright white sunlight making one's hands greasy with sweat: not the best weather for taking a firm grip on a rifle. By the time the Koyas arrived the buffaloes seemed to be stuck, but the Koyas, bouncing with hunters' delight, said they would send their little dog in to nip the buffaloes' heels. When I resumed my position in the scrub on the bank of the small river, I found many people had congregated at both ends of the grove, watching to see if the bear would appear. I had to tell the villagers and the Koyas to move them away, because I could not shoot in either direction if the bear came out in a rush, for fear of hitting someone with the powerful rifle bullet. After more than an hour, when tension was beginning to flag, Foyle said he would have to return to Medeloabam. It was pay day, and the money would be arriving soon, demanding his presence at the counting. He went off saying he would send the jeep back for me in a couple of hours.

Hardly had the sound of his jeep died in the distance, when there was commotion on the other side of the grove, and a Koya appeared on a flank waving urgently for me to come to the other side. I ran round, feeling the tension rise, and waved for the men to clear the people away from the flanks. I went carefully along to where three Koyas were pointing into the *kagri* with strung bows. Inside the kagri I could hear some kind of commotion, and saw the reed tops waving about eight yards in. A buffalo was snorting, and suddenly I shouldered the rifle as a huge bull buffalo crashed out of the grove some twenty yards away. He pranced out about fifteen yards before swinging round to face the thicket, snorting, shaking his head, and pawing the ground. I waved my arm and shouted for the people beyond to move away from my line of sight along the edge of the grove, and as I was doing this the killer ambled out, shuffling like a jovial

152

circus bear right up to the buffalo, who lifted his head until his horns touched his back, and stared showing the whites of his eyes at the black, furry creature with the white horseshoe gleaming on its chest as it rose on its hind legs, close to the buffalo, a perfect target but for the thickening crowd of spectators less than sixty yards beyond and directly behind it. I dared not shoot, and saw the bear almost lazily swing a great forepaw, slashing the buffalo's nose easily before swaying back onto all fours. The crowd yelled and screamed, and the bear ambled past on the other side of the buffalo, back into the close cover of the *kagri*. The villagers went wild with disappointment. The bull buffalo, with blood gushing from its nose, head tilted to one side, trotted erratically into the village, where it stood for another ten minutes before collapsing. The village men were yelling at each other, at me, at the Koyas, and I felt hopelessly tongue-tied in a situation where only words could have helped. I felt as lonely as a marooned sailor. The Koyas were not at all embarrassed, nor need they have been, and they took me aside, trying to explain their proposals. Eventually I began to understand their gestures, which were powerfully explicit in some strange way.

After another half hour we managed to convince the villagers silence was essential. By cheer competence and intrepidity five Koyas managed to reach and climb into the upper branches of the five albizzia trees. Three Koyas were to patrol the edges of the grove, listening; and I, with two Koyas and their small dog, entered the grove by one of the narrow paths, meaning to creep carefully along, listening for movement and watching the Koyas in the trees whenever the *kagri* was thin enough to allow sight. The Koyas in the trees were to point with their arrows to show where they could see the bear or its movement in the *kagri*. We had not been moving for long, but just long enough for my thudding heart to slow down and leave my hearing unimpaired, when there was frantic shouting from the people outside: they had seen the Koyas in the trees point. The noise abated, calming my nerves, and we took time to find a good view of the trees. To our delight we saw the Koyas, as still as the branches of the trees, pointing silently, their extended arrows aiming at a spot not more than twenty feet from us, moving slowly in unison as the bear moved on a path which seemed to be converging with ours. We came to a widening where three paths converged, and I stopped. The Koya behind me squeezed my arm, and I saw his hand point down: the little dog which had kept station perfectly until now moved slowly forward, the hair on his back rising, his nose pointing into the right-hand path. His ears trembled as he leant with raised muzzle at a thin screen of *kagri* blades, twelve feet ahead of us. Without warning, it seemed, a tank, or a railway engine, had suddenly launched itself to crash at speed through the screen, straight at us. The little dog sprang nimbly aside. I had been holding the rifle at my hip, safety catch off, and as the bear broke cover I sensed the familiar feeling of something taking over my actions: there was no time to shoulder the rifle, and I rotated automatically to face the bear and fired, aiming from the hip. As the shot burst forth I was marvelling at the width of his head, which suddenly went down to the earth about five feet away as the charging bulk somersaulted, his hindquarters knocking me over backwards with domino effect on the two Koyas. I leapt to my feet reloading, and put the barrel in his ear, squeezing the trigger, just in case he was only stunned; but the old round did not fire, and so I reloaded with the next old round, which fired reassuringly. As well as the kick of the shot I felt a sharp pain between thumb and forefinger, and found the weight of the somersaulting bear had cracked the neck of the butt in his final inertia, and the crack had bitten into my skin. The first bullet had broken his chin and entered his body, slashing the heart. I was amazed at not having felt anything when the butt was cracked, but within an hour the pain at the base of my ribs on the right reminded me, and kept reminding me for a week or two, of what had caused that surrealistically coloured bruise. Pandey, the rearmost Koya, suffered the worst injury of the hunt, excepting the bear.

Later we spent a jovial half hour removing cruel thorns from his naked back, buttocks and legs. The villagers were mollified when the bear was carried out. He measured six feet six inches from nose to toes, beautifully muscled. It felt somehow like a terrible accident, in which the first killing was committed by a frightened animal to whose rightful territory humans had laid claim. The second killing was the passing of judgement on the innocent animal by frightened humans, whose side I had taken in executing it. I found myself taking refuge from this dilemma, counting myself fortunate in having put a new round first into the breech. If it had not been there, the bear would have been upon me, and remembering the death of the first man, and the sad mangling of the second, I wondered if the Koyas would have been able to kill it with their arrows before his furious strength killed me.

This episode created, whether I liked it or not, a sudden reputation for me as an intrepid *shikari*; but it did more for my appreciation of what was involved in what promised to be necessary security operations. I couldn't believe my folly in undertaking so dangerous a task in such a state of ignorance, and counted myself lucky beyond belief. Without the Koyas I would have finished up as a laughing stock. I was struck by the immediate behaviour of the Koyas, when they rushed in to find us and saw the bear lying dead. In their melodious language, vaguely reminiscent of Italian, they seemed to salute and comfort the bear, and whilst the thorns were being removed from Pandey's back I learned from Poyami Adma, the senior of them, they were apologising to the bear for its death, explaining they bore him no ill will, and had not intended him to die, having always respected his kind, and always would. That night before I slept I understood what they were doing. The display of grief was either authentic or expertly mimed; but I think I shared what surely was a mixture of guilt and regret, perhaps larded with the Koyas' animistic fear of the dead animal's spirit. We managed to load the bear into the jeep, and took five of the Koyas with us, the others trotting behind, all the six miles to Medeloabam.

It was late afternoon when we arrived, and we almost ruined the normal good order of pay day, which was about to begin. Foyle congratulated us on the successful outcome, and put two *chowkidars* to guard the bear in the shadow of a building conveniently distant from the pay tables. I was becoming experienced at payment, and although hungry and thirsty took pleasure in carrying out my duties in an aura of general adoration. I saw Dierdre Foyle come with two visitors, man and wife, examine the dead bear and take photographs. Payment took an hour and a half, after which Foyle went with me to look at the bear and measure its length. We were horrified to see what had happened to it. Its teeth were intact, but only three of its large black claws remained; tufts of its fur had been cut from all over the body, leaving it looking like a huge, mangy dog; even its scrotum had been stolen. All this, Foyle explained, was because everyone believed there were magical properties in any part of a bear, tiger, leopard, or wild elephant. He showed anger with the *chowkidars*, who said whilst they were keeping people away on one side, others were darting in, and there was nothing they could do. They were afraid to disturb pay day, which the *sahib-log* always treated as a special occasion, never to be interrupted. I was sad to see the majesty of the great dead animal so rudely destroyed, and tried to convince myself I was not disappointed at losing the magnificent skin, with the pure white crescent on its breast.

Charlie Mason, who was visiting the Foyles, said the bear was certainly a big one. Foyle said he was a *shikari* of many years experience. When I recounted what had happened the ladies were horrified and impressed, but Mason nodded with a tight grin and said so long as I understood how lucky I had been I would do it better next time. After some biscuits and a cup of tea I excused myself, refusing a drink, and went off to my bungalow for a much-needed bath, a square meal, and a quiet spell with a book and some quiet Chopin before bed. When I reached the bungalow I was rather irritated to find the bear's carcass had been placed under the bungalow, and was surrounded by about forty people. I managed to instruct my servants to take the head, and the remaining three claws, and said I wanted the carcass taken away. As soon as they understood what I had said, they excised the head and claws, and the body was raised by many hands, and carried off gleefully into the gathering dusk. They told me it would be eaten, and '*dawai*' (medicine) would be made from the bones and other parts. When I stripped for my bath I saw the great bruise on my side, and sat shivering in the heat, savouring the sweetness of survival.

The euphoria passed, accelerated by attempts of the disgruntled owner of the buffalo which had been killed by the bear, who demanded I should pay him damages for the loss of his much-admired bull. He began to spend money on a local lawyer, framing a claim which was to be made through the court in town. Foyle told me this was a frequent thing, and, as the claim was against me and the company, asked our company-retained lawyer in town to compose a good letter to all the villages around the estate saying if this kind of claim were pursued there could be no question of the estate helping either with the eradication of wild animals endangering life or property, or with emergency medical treatment after attacks by violent wild beasts or rabid dogs. This had the effect of changing the mind of the would-be litigant. Meanwhile the family of the villager who was eventually discharged with his arm in a sling, and his head wounds healing well, brought gifts of eggs, four chickens, an embroidered headcloth, and a *chadur* (stole) spun from a mixture of tree cotton and silk and woven into a cream-coloured heavy cloth in their own home. They took these to Foyle, who sent them to me. I wanted to say I should not accept such beautiful gifts from people who had suffered such loss and injury, but my Assamese was still not good enough. Their gratitude was clear, in spite of their loss; they were thanking me for the retribution I had so narrowly made on their behalf.

When Gerella returned from Sibsagar he came to see me, listened to my account, laughed at the difference between what I said and what the villagers had said, and told me never to go into close cover after a dangerous animal with anything but new ammunition. He said the villagers had described how I had wrestled with the bear, which had struck me on the side with its huge paw, throwing it down before killing it with the rifle. I asked what he would have done if he had been asked to deal with the situation, and he said he would have told everyone to go to bed early and leave the bear to find its way out quietly during the night. This left me with mixed feelings: I was happy to learn my first inclinations had been sensible, but I felt sad to have been carried into the violent alternative. Gerella had a delightful habit of pronouncing on moral issues with much laughter. He said the villagers would always call for death if such things happened, but as a *shikari* he knew it was best to forgive animals which had made a mistake, particularly animals one could not eat.

The heat continued to mount, and every day there seemed to be plenty of cloud development. The rate of leaf growth on the vast areas of tea was to me quite astonishing. In seven days shoots would grow four or five inches, and had to be plucked within this time in order to make good tea from it. Foyle took me along to the factory after dinner to check how the leaf was spread in the tall leaf houses, where there were four main floors, and horizontal racks spaced above each other at just over three feet. The racks were of strong wire mesh, covered with hessian cloth, on which the plucked leaf was spread thinly or thickly, depending on the weather and the humidity, so that by five in the morning it would have lost about a third of its moisture, becoming like very soft chamois leather, still juicy, but able to be bent without breaking. The scent was very attractive, something between apple juice and orange blossom. The youths who spread the leaf would move in the racks in a squatting position, and be careful not to squash or break the leaf whilst spreading it evenly, according to the guidance given by the factory staff. Foyle told me how the amount of leaf would increase from now on until all space would be full, and whenever there was rain it would become difficult not only to wither the leaf which came in soaking wet, but to make a good wiry tea when the rain continued for days at a time, preventing a good wither.

Listening to the wireless news I sensed the general feeling of unrest. The reports of violent conflict were rather terse but not detailed. The office and field staff had acquired reports, perhaps from Assamese and Bengali transmissions, or from people arriving by train in Dibrugarh from Bengal or the Central Provinces, which were highly coloured and explicit as far as apportioning blame went. They spoke of rape, of women having their breasts cut off, of children dashed to death against walls. Foyle said such things had certainly happened in the Great Calcutta Killings: he had seen photographs, and one of the Calcutta executives who had been called up as a reservist had told him the dreadful details. There was plenty of cause for fear. Remembering the man on our ship who had walked out of Burma to escape the Japanese, I began to walk barefoot more, and bought the various things he had recommended. I found an Assamese villager who gave me lessons in throwing a net in the shallows of the Brahmaputra, and decided to buy such a net, just in case.

One day a letter arrived from Jag, with a photograph of five of the squadron's pilots leaning in various nonchalant positions around a Spitfire. He gave me many details of what had happened since I had left. I had a photograph of myself leaning nonchalantly against the cowling of Constable's Piper Cub, and began writing about my new life. I had not yet completed six months, but it seemed as if years had passed since I had last flown in those sleek, powerful aeroplanes. Jag announced his engagement to a delightful WAAF intelligence officer called Helena, a development I found exactly right for that splendid pair. I was able to wish them great happiness. To his question of when I was likely to have a leave in Britain, I could but say it would probably be after another three and a half years: a long, long time at the age of twenty-three, yet strangely enough I felt only a slight twinge of nostalgia, but did not say so.

Chapter IX

By the time we entered June it was decidedly hot: up to 96° Fahrenheit by day, and 72° by night. These temperatures did not look very hot compared with Allahabad, and Karachi, but the high humidity made the heat feel more than it actually was, although I felt nowhere nearly as uncomfortable as I was in the steam-oven summer of the previous year in Bahrein, on my way to India and beyond.

I found it odd that there were hardly any showers in planters' bathrooms, especially as one needed cold baths at least three times a day, to wash away the mixture of dust and sweat. People said this would change when the monsoon arrived to lay the dust and cool things down. The monsoon was said by everyone to arrive on the fifteenth of June, and I wondered if this could be invariably true. It was tiresome having to wait a long time for the bath to fill with cold water. When I asked Foyle if I could have a shower fitted he said it was notoriously difficult to find shower hoses of satisfactory quality. There were few to be found in Assam, and those from Calcutta were small with tiny perforations. We managed to fit an old rubber hose to my bath tap, enough for me to hose myself down thrice a day. Not having a refrigerator now became very inconvenient. Mrs Foyle was very helpful keeping my milk in an old gin bottle with a screw top in her refrigerator, whence my servants drew a small jug twice a day for tea. Her refrigerator was too small for anything else to be kept for me, and my tinned butter, tinned bacon, and drinking water were kept in screwtop jars, lowered into my deep well in an old leaky bucket. I once tried to keep milk that way, but after about six hours it came up like yoghurt.

My diet was spartan, mainly controlled by the impossibility of keeping food for more than a day. I had plenty of eggs: small tasty eggs from village bazaars, with rich orange-red yolks. The only trouble during the hot season was the frequency of finding bad eggs. I had chicken: roasted, boiled, curried, made into rissoles; they were mostly small and rather thin village chickens, but properly cooked were very tasty. I had lentil soup and lentil 'rissoles', mixed with onion and spices. The bread from town was made from white flour, and was unsubstantial, unsatisfying, and when toasted broke into pieces, therefore I very much enjoyed plenty of chupattis, made from rough-milled unsifted wheat flour, and on Saturdays had four or five for breakfast, into which I would roll a lot of my tinned bacon, nothing like the bacon we dreamed of, but very welcome. I was several times offered beef, and I refused this on Foyle's advice. The butchering of cattle was clearly not in keeping with life in a massively preponderant Hindu area, therefore beef would only become available from cattle which had died 'by accident', so to speak. The best and safest would be the result of a lorry or train killing a cow on road or track, usually at night; but the worst could be a cow which had died from some undiagnosed affliction, too often anthrax. Many of the tribes which were not Hindus suffered sometimes very badly from eating such diseased beef. There would often be goat meat available in local bazaars, where goats would be killed after inspection by my cook. This meat was acceptable when curried, but was too often tough, and needed plenty of spice to make it tasty. Being close to the Brahmaputra meant fish was available at a price; but I was told when the monsoon arrived and filled all the smaller rivers which flowed into the Brahmaputra, there would be abundant tasty fish except when violent floods disrupted the fishermen's efforts. With the onset of the hot weather my supply of things like cabbage, carrots, Brussels sprouts and beans, most of which we grew in my vegetable garden, eventually ran out; but instead there was a good supply of spinach, tender shoots of an edible fern, pods of a long bean, and things like 'ladies fingers', onions, and various aquatic vegetables, safe to eat once the rains made the rivers and streams flow vigorously.

For several weeks, following occasional showers of rain, there would be huge hatches of insects after dark, round about the time I finished my bath and sat down to dinner. There was the night of the yellow wasps, hatching from nests made from mud which they built mainly in houses; they could sting viciously. There was the night of the green beetles, handsome insects just under an inch in length, bronze below, and a metallic dull green above.

Their noise was intrusive, and they would congregate around any light at night except, of course, red bulbs such as Constable used, which were impossible to obtain. There would be several nights of cockchafer beetles, the heavy bombers of the Assam night, which made a loud, deep buzzing; blinded by the lights they would crash into shades, walls or mosquito netting with dramatic noise, falling on the timber floor where, mostly unable to recover from landing on their backs, they would spin and 'rev their engines' in a snarling noise reminiscent of someone in a lorry bogged down in mud. There would be several nights of white ants, mostly an inch and a quarter long, with heavy sausage bodies and long diaphanous wings. Although they seemed the stupidest of all insects, they seemed able to penetrate to the interior of any room, and could be infuriating bed companions at dead of night when all lights had been extinguished, and a torchlight patrol of the bedroom had shown no more intruders. It was always a sight which gladdened my heart, to find anywhere on the estate a hatch of ants or termites just before sunset, when a huge ascending spiral rose into the western sky, attracting multitudes of birds of all shapes and sizes, many of which I could not identify.

The least welcome insects of all on these hot, humid nights were the cockroaches. They were never as big as the ones I had seen in Calcutta, but they were all sizes, and seemed able to pass through the closest door, the smallest crack, and were so fast once they had landed it was extremely difficult to kill them. The local name for them was '*telpia*', meaning oil drinker, and there were stories of how they would actually feed on naked feet, in some cases eating away the horny flesh of the toes and sole to the raw flesh, more likely to happen to those who went to bed after a heavy drinking session. With the heat, and the insects, the evenings could not be spent in reading, much as I wanted to explore the many books I had brought with me. It was generally too hot to sit inside to read, and although it was cooler on the open verandah, a light for reading would attract insects of all kinds. I began to follow a routine which, after my evening shower and change, led to a light supper – which made me sweat more – and then to the extinguishing of all lights except one beneath the verandah, where the insects swarmed and several large toads gorged themselves on the many insects which spun blinded to crash on the concrete floor. I would put records to play on my handle-wound gramophone and sat, with long sleeves down to protect from mosquitoes, in the relative cool of the dark verandah. Sometimes the competition of the frogs and bullfrogs, in small bogs at the outlets from drains, or puddles near the vegetable garden handpump, prompted me to stop playing Mozart, Chopin, or Debussy, and listen to the amazing sound of hundreds of them in chorus, vaguely like something by Delius. In the heat, waiting desperately for the rains, the night sky would be bright with myriads of stars, and the high-pitched sound of smaller frogs, augmented by tree-frogs around my bungalow, somehow seemed to be coming from outer space, as if the stars were singing in mysterious harmony. Whether I was able to sit inside and read, or do what I have just described, I would find myself fighting to remain awake until nine o'clock, and would retire to instant sleep under the mosquito net, with all doors and windows wide open until the first cock crow warned of the coming of dawn.

I listened one night to the radio news saying Mountbatten had returned from London, and would hold a press conference next day, and wondered if there would be a postponement of independence until the increasing communal violence between Hindus and Muslims had been controlled by the Police and the Army.

The following day was busy. Foyle took me with him round the factory, which was now running longer hours as more and more leaf was harvested. It was fascinating to be taught by a man who was expert at this kind of thing, and although the idea of having eventually to work for a year or two in a factory was something I regarded with horror, something I had only become vaguely aware of whilst travelling out on the ship in January, I began to be deeply interested in all that was entailed. Foyle said I should make sure to have a look round the factory once a day, for about half an hour, to familiarise myself generally with the people, the machinery, and the processes. There were several things which dispelled my fear of the factory: the first was my ignorance of what it would be like in the high season, when huge daily harvests would frequently mean the factory would not cease running for a week or more; the second was the delightful aroma, beginning with the plucked leaf, some arriving in lorries from the estate during the day, and some arriving in the afternoon, carried in baskets on the heads of the women and girls; and the scents during manufacture coming from the rolling machines which expressed the juice from the withered leaf; and from the leaf which was spread on polished cement floors to ferment

– a mixture of apple juice with something like grape juice – and finally the rich malty scent of the tea being dried in machines like continuous transit ovens. There was a familiar pride amongst the men who looked after the diesel engines which drove the factory machinery, reminding me of the teams which maintained our aircraft in the Air Force. They tended the all-important water pumps for the whole estate, and the generators which provided lighting for the factory and the bungalows. The men working in the tea processing were, as Foyle pointed out, bound to the wheels of the manufacture, and only when the black tea was loaded into the sorting room would they be able to relax and rest before the next day's crop was ready. In the sorting room there were about eight well-trained ladies who worked every year at their jobs of feeding the sorting machines, and about another twenty assorted 'light workers', several in advanced pregnancy, and others with injuries or infirmities who were unable to work outside on the estate all day long; these would sit and pick stalk from the sorted tea. Foyle moaned there was too much stalk because the plucking was so coarse: one of the effects of the British government's price support for the tea industry, which tended to encourage those who believed coarse plucking would increase the crop. He showed me where the stalk was being picked by the pregnant and out-patient women and girls, who sat on the timber floor with a small mound of black tea on one side from which they took a few pounds at a time in a kind of winnowing tray, and stirred the particles lightly with their fingertips, picking out the reddish-brown stalky particles which they each placed in a small basket of woven reeds. Foyle stopped beside a girl of about seventeen, too pale to be a tribal from central or south India, well built, with hair worn in a large chignon on the back of the neck in the Assamese style. When he spoke to her she did not look up, and I noticed her long eyelashes as she shot a glance sideways at an older woman sitting near her. The old woman glanced up at Foyle and me, and spoke waving one hand at the girl's right foot which we noted was bandaged. Foyle explained she had suffered for weeks from a thorn in her foot which had gone sceptic and had to be cut out by Dr Pal.

We left the factory, and Foyle said I should take a ride the length of the estate on the earthen road, to look for red spider in the tea, more easily seen from the elevation of a horse's back than from a jeep or bicycle, and I went off to my bungalow to change into breeches and boots. As I cycled back to the stables I passed the factory workers making their way home, and saw, among them the girl with the bandaged foot, limping slightly. The men and the older women smiled and raised a hand calling *'Salaam, sahib'* to which I replied *'Salaam'*, raising my hand to the others.

When I dismounted from my bicycle at the stable a servant came running breathlessly from the Manager's bungalow, telling me *'Bara sahib bulata hai!'* The manager was calling me. I walked quickly into the beautiful garden compound, over the smooth lawn between the clumps of foaming bougainvillaea and hibiscus. Hearing the wireless speak on the verandah where Foyle stood beckoning, I ran up the stairs, sweating in breeches and boots, to find Foyle staring at me, and his wife sitting wide-eyed watching the wireless set as if hypnotised. 'You know Mountbatten has just come back from London; well they've just announced today he was revising the date of granting Independence. It's not to be June 1948.' He paused, shaking his head slightly, and I thought to myself: it's off, it's off! My heart leapt. Foyle continued, speaking slowly and emphatically as if issuing a warning: 'India is going to be given its independence on the fifteenth of August this year: in ten weeks' time. He must have gone mad!' I was literally speechless with surprise, or shock, and my thoughts began spinning, shooting in all directions at once. The voice on the wireless went on, talking about the reactions of Congress, the Muslim League, the imminent possibility of turbulent disorder over the decision to partition British India into Pakistan and India.

Eventually Foyle switched off, and sat down with a grin which belied his pale face and tightened lips. He took his wife's hand and spoke to me as I folded my arms and leant with my backside on the verandah rail, suddenly remembering the feel of what we used to call 'the icy hand of panic stroking the lower bowel'. 'When you look at it,' he said, 'they must be thinking of handing over the keys and making a dash for it before the whole thing becomes uncontrollable. Nicky MacFortune had a visit from one of his friends who was a colonel in the regular army and was saying neither officers nor men wanted to be told to try and stop the fighting and looting that'll surely break out between the Indians and the Pakistanis, especially now they've confirmed there will certainly be partition. It'd be a dead certainty that both parties will turn on the British for taking sides, and that would make things . . .' he paused, mindful of his wife's presence, '. . . a little

164

difficult; but there are plenty of British troops and aeroplanes still in India to deal with anything like that.' I said I hoped the tea estates would be able to have contact with Calcutta through some of the army signals units, so that someone could tell us what was going to happen now. Foyle laughed, and said he didn't think the signals units had anything good enough for that, except maybe from Shillong to Calcutta. Dierdre Foyle took her damp handkerchief away from her face, where she had been dabbing up the sweat gently, and said in a low voice that everything had turned very quiet: no-one seemed to be cheering. Shouldn't that be expected? Foyle said it was most likely everyone was as shaken as we were. 'After all, the educated people, our staff, had all become accustomed since they were boys at school to dates being given, commissions being organised, plans being made for independence, which in the end came to nothing for all kinds of reasons. They must have thought, especially with young chaps like Hamish here coming out to make a career in tea, that it was just another promise, and would get lost like the others. Lots of folk didn't care much about independence anyway, only politicians and Bengalis seemed to be worried about it, mainly because the British always dragged their feet about stupid things like club membership and salt taxes. It's a helluva big country, you know, and it was always frightening to let it off the leash, remembering how India used to be many different nations who were always fighting each other. It is quiet though,' said Foyle. 'I think we just have to do what we did through the War many a time: carry on as normal. Let's walk down to the hospital, and then have a look at the leaf spreading.' Turning to me he said, 'You won't want to go riding now. The sun will be down in about twenty minutes.' He winked over his wife's head, and asked her to join us, 'just to show how really relaxed we are.'

We crossed the lawn where the gardeners had come late to begin watering the flower beds in the lengthening shadows. As we went past the stables my syce came out of Conker's box with a currycomb in his hand, salaaming us each in turn. I told him I would not be riding out after all. He spoke to Foyle in a rapid low voice, looking worried. Foyle turned to me and asked if I knew he was a Muslim. His name was Ramjan, and I said to Foyle I had always thought that indicated he was a Hindu. Foyle said Ramjan was very frightened. He said someone had told him there had been some 'town people' in the Saturday bazaar who had been asking about Akbar, Telford's chief riding boy, an ex-cavalryman, wanting to know where his house was. Telford had sent Akbar away on furlough for six months. Ramjan was worried about himself, with a wife and two small children. He had been born on the estate and didn't want to leave it, but he was very afraid. Foyle told him not to worry: there would be no trouble in Assam, and he would tell the watchmen to report any trouble-seeking strangers immediately to the office. I was deeply impressed when Foyle explained he would tell Dr Pal to give Ramjan a certificate dated five years ago saying he had had his foreskin removed because of phimosis and infection. He explained to me there had been incidents in Calcutta and the Punjab where foreskins saved lives.

When we came to the office there was a gathering of the Indian staff, obviously deep in discussion which stopped as we were seen to approach. There were about twenty others: *sirdars*, *chowkidars*, and some villagers, all standing in the cool shade of the large pipul tree. The Head Clerk came forward, wishing us good evening. He said everyone was in a state of amazement. All were in one way very happy and very grateful for the idea of having independence; but in another way everyone with some education was very worried at how soon it was going to happen, especially with the decision to divide India into one Hindu state and one Muslim state. This was not what Mahatma Gandhi, not what the Indian Congress wanted. The Muslims should not have been afraid of one India for all. The British united India out of many nations, and although there had been some very bad disorders, these had been caused by unscrupulous Muslim politicians, frightening everyone. Bengalis were worried about their families and relations in Calcutta and East Bengal. There was bound to be terrible bloodshed, in spite of what Mahatma Gandhi had been doing. He said although they were worried, they did not know what to do. The Head Clerk's English was excellent, and he spoke with dignity. The *jemadar babu*, senior overseer of the estate, put up his hand in a reassuring gesture, saying in Assamese there would be no trouble in Assam. There was quite a large Muslim community which had been built from the Mughal army officers and architects, invited by the Ahoms to work for Assam; they were Assamese; they would be safe. This did not solve the problem of Bengali Hindus in their own habitat, where there were areas densely populated by Muslims. Banerjee, the Head Clerk, said the big problem with partition was going to be the coveting of land where the majorities who were safe would do everything to get rid of people who were of opposing faiths, even their neighbours who had been friends for all their lives, so that they could take over the land adjoining their own. He said, 'People were afraid if the British Army was going to leave so soon: who will keep order? Who will restore peace? If you all leave us who will be our employers? We are fearful that the wonderful idea of independence will be a terrible loss for all of us for at least a generation.'

Foyle put up his hand, and explained the news had been most unexpected for us, and we waited now to hear how things were going to be organised. He said it was very worrying for everyone, but we should not imagine the worst was going to happen. We should be calm, and carry on as usual, producing tea, which would bring wealth for India. At this point an old man, with a neatly tied white turban and a large Victorian silver moustache, came out of the crowd, salaaming each of us in turn. His bulging eyes showed a redness, and his diction although clearly understandable suggested he had taken rice beer before the sun had set. He spoke to Foyle in good Hindustani, and turned to point at some of the clerks to emphasise what he said, which was that we should not leave the estate to such people as these, who in spite of the way we ran the company, were up to such mischief as writing in daily pay for people who didn't come to work as shown in the account, but went to work for some of the pay clerks, and others. Loud murmurs of protest began, and the old man hit himself on the chest, saying that he, Bhimlal *sirdar*, who had worked for forty years for the Damfool (Dalrymple) sahib, the *Makai* (= maize = Mackay) sahib, and the Telford sahib, and although he had retired ten years ago, before the War, he still kept the manager informed of all the *badmashi* (roguery) going on at Medeloabam. His voice strengthened and his eyes gleamed as he told Foyle he could tell him at any time just who was up to mischief. The Head Clerk was a good man; the *jemadar babu* was a good man, now he was properly and respectably married. At this there were laughs and grins as the *jemadar* shouted at the old man to be careful what he was saying. The *sirdar* pulled his moustache, with a crafty gleam in his eye, gave a desultory salute to the *jemadar babu*, and muttered that he himself had also been young once, like our new flying *chota sahib*. He leaned towards me with joined hands to his forehead, and when he turned stiff-necked back to Foyle his eyes remained on me with what I took to be a knowing smile, making me wonder if he had the gift of telling fortunes, or perhaps simply knew the inevitability of my age and circumstance. At this point Foyle raised his hand, showing his palm to the *sirdar*, and said he should not forget how times changed, how those whom we criticise today might become our *burra sahibs* tomorrow. He said we did not want to leave. His new *memsahib* did not want to leave; she liked Assam, so did the pilot *sahib*. We didn't know what would happen yet, but we hoped we might stay. At this there were many voices raised, telling us we should not go. Foyle smiled and raised his hand, saying we must get on with going round the hospital, then see the leaf spreading in the factory.

The Head Clerk said, 'Thank you, sir, for speaking so sensibly to us. Thank you. If you will go away who will speak to us like this?' He and his staff put hands together in the '*namaste*' or '*namaskar*' sign of greeting, and the various others raised single arms in salute. Their expressions were serious. We three moved on with Foyle and myself wearing the smooth brows and vestigial smiles of British officers trying to put up a good example to the troops; Dierdre Foyle managed a very pleasant expression of sympathy.

Next day George Fraser sent a letter, saying he had heard nothing yet, but expected there would be some kind of communication very soon. Meanwhile everyone should carry on as usual, letting him know immediately if any difficulties arose from any quarter. There would be a Circle meeting at the club on Saturday after polo.

'That's the spirit!' said Foyle. 'We're all right with George as our Brigadier: right up his street. Plenty of stiff upper lip, backs to the wall, to the last man sort of thing. How do you feel about going on with polo?' I said I thought it was a good idea, but I would bow to his advice. It seemed to me, I told him, as if the Indians were taken aback with the sudden change of plan, as if they were a crowd of students who had been belly-aching at their housemaster for not letting them out into the fresh air, and he suddenly opened all doors and windows and pushed them out in their pyjamas without time to put on their clothes; it did seem a bit unfair. Foyle was sure, having lain awake most of the night thinking about it all, it was bound to be Mountbatten having told the British government the same as Wavell must have done, that having told India we would grant independence, and if we waited too long before giving it, the communal conflict, the civil wars, would become too difficult and too dangerous for the British and Indian armies, and the Police, to control. This idea of partition made it all even more difficult; but if one thought it out, if the British didn't allow partition, we would be blamed for the terrible massacres bound to result, from handing over the Muslims to the Hindus. Having granted partition to this bloke Jinnah there were still bound to be massacres, and Britain would still get the blame, but for having granted partition. The main thing was basically to get the British out before the blood-bath became their responsibility. It didn't leave us much time to make a painless evacuation.

'Still, we have to wait and see. They were saying on the wireless early this morning the fifteenth of August is astrologically a very bad date for granting independence, but it is doubtful if it'll be changed. One of the Delhi newspapers is blaming Gandhi for agreeing to partition; apparently he was prepared earlier to fast to death, rather than agree. They say he got Congress to offer Jinnah the first Presidentship of India if he renounced partition, but Jinnah refused, maybe because he would get the blame for any communal violence.' Foyle said he was sorry for the whole lot of them. We were talking at the stables, a good place not to be overheard, and he said we'd be even sorrier for them if we were safely evacuated, leaving them to sort themselves out. He told me old Huntingdon-Smith, the senior British lawyer practising in town who had been in the Indian Civil Service for many years, reported very bad morale amongst the ICS people. They were with few exceptions determined to leave India by the 1948 independence date, despite offers having been made for them to stay on, helping to make a smooth transition. He said too many of the Congress politicians had been put into jail for causing disturbances, and they would surely be itching to get their own back on those who had done this to them, which meant most ICS people would now want to leave their posts by August 1947.

We got on with our work for the next few days. I had a feeling of sadness about my growing fluency with various languages: to what end now? Various members of the staff and the labour force confided they were frightened: people who had been punished for thefts or other misdemeanours were saying, 'You gave evidence against us, wait until the sahibs leave, and then we will fix you.' Some of the tribal workers who had one or two years to wait before they would return home, either for holidays or to settle, were worried what would be happening in their own homelands. Foyle was able to tell them their tribal lands were not likely to be given to Pakistan, but they were worried about unscrupulous moneylenders taking over their lands, with no-one left who was able to resist accepting bribes from them.

When we visited the hospital to inquire why there had been a few cases of malaria in people who were supposed to have taken mepacrine, we had an interesting chat with Dr Pal. He said there were many of the Indian staff who had always tried to make trouble for him, and if we were to leave, who would protect him? 'Mr Telford was a very strict' – he pronounced the word like a whiplash – 'person. He keeps us in order by making us afraid to do wrong, and this is correct; but there are so many jealous enemies. If I do not give them the special medicines they want, they offer me bribes. If I refuse they tell Mr Telford I have demanded payment for special treatment. They tell Mr Telford I am treating villagers with company time and company medicines, and charging them money which I keep. They once tried to spread rumours that I give estate workers injections of boiled water, and keep the drugs they should have had, to sell for my benefit.' Dr Pal placed his hand on his heart and shook his head, saying he had suffered from high blood pressure only because of these people who made his life miserable. 'Every time Mr Telford tells me what they say, and he warns me if he ever finds I am misbehaving he will not only kick me out but put me in jail. I have wasted money on litigation against these false accusers. I have a large family to educate.' – I noted: not 'to feed', but 'to educate' – 'and I must not waste money; but what am I to do? If Mr Telford and your goodselves leave Assam, what hope have I?' He put both hands forward, palms upwards and said, 'Surely now that Britain is presenting India with its independence, India should be grateful, and there should be no need for you all to go away. Surely you do not want to go, even if the government changes.' After this outpouring I noted his pale face and bluish lips, and pitied him. Foyle simply resumed his inquiry into why there were these cases of malaria, and said it was time we tightened up on this. He asked Dr Pal to think about it and let him know within a week what we could do to make the system work better.

When Saturday came the horses went off early in the morning to cover the twelve miles or so to the club, four horses and three syces, including Ramjan, for whose safety the other syces said they took responsibility. Several of the regular players had not turned up for polo; some had come leaving their wives behind, but we had enough riders and horses for the usual number of chukkas. There seemed to be many more spectators, despite the heat, sitting on the roadside in the shade. I was very pleased to see Nicky MacFortune there, and told him so. He said he was very sorry he didn't play polo, because in times like these it was just the thing: 'Like Drake playing bowls, you know.' Before the polo began three players cantered over the field, each with a ball, practising shots. MacFortune pointed to one of them who wore dark glasses, and asked me if I knew him. I said I did: his name was Stapleford, and that was his pretty wife with the other memsahibs, preparing the tea table. Nicky told me he was an odd chap: furious temper, always upsetting staff, labour, and the Calcutta office. He said Stapleford was being posted to take over Baorijan, and he was himself posted to Panitola. He said he didn't think the Baorijan labour would take to Stapleford, and I had to say there didn't seem to be many people who took to him at all, and I felt sorry for his wife. Nicky gave me a sideways look, and seeing my expression patted me on the shoulder, saying he would sit with the ladies and watch the polo, enjoying excellent tea, sandwiches and cakes, and the charming company. He chuckled wheezily as I went off to mount.

After playing in the first chukka I joined Nicky at the table, glad of the refreshments. Stapleford was in the second chukka, and his wife was attentive to our needs, sitting beside us to talk. She said her husband was very upset about the date of independence being brought forward, extremely upset, and was talking about getting out quickly before things became too difficult. She showed signs herself of being very tense, and Mrs Foyle said the people at Medeloabam seemed to take it all seriously enough, but were hoping we would stay at our work. Mrs Berry, a tall, lean lady, wrinkled prematurely by the sun, said that sort of thing was just sycophancy; they were always saying things to please us, in case something could be gained from it. The chukka was warming up, with much shouting and more than usual expletives. As we watched the ball was cleared from a group of five horses in the near corner down to the right at the club end. Straight away the field spread out, and Colly on the far wing, intercepting the ball but losing his speed in doing so, smote the ball to the opposite wing, where Stapleford stretched his gallop to receive the pass, but missed the ball, which went under his mount's belly, bouncing into touch on our left towards the clear ground near the spectators. Several youths darted forward to field

171

the ball and return it to the field in their accustomed way. Stapleford, furious at failing to hit the ball, swung round on to the field in a tight circle, then rode off the field after the ball, riding fast at the three or four youths, screaming as if in a cavalry charge, with his stick aimed forward at the ball. The youths fled the thundering hooves, up onto the road, scattering the onlookers. Stapleford shouted in fury. As far as I understood him it was something like: 'What do you people think you are doing? Leave the ball alone, idiots! Who are you to touch the ball? Do you think you can do what you like nowadays?' The 'older statesman' with whom I had spoken not long ago was referee, and he cantered off the field to where Stapleford, with a tight rein on his unsettled horse, stuttered in his incoherent efforts to find more to shout, his voice cracking and his whole body quivering with blenching anger. The referee quietly pointed to the ball and asked him to bring it back to the field, where everyone was waiting. Stapleford kicked his horse to a trot, and made for the field, leaving the ball forgotten on the turf. The referee walked his horse to the ball and called softly to the crowd for someone to pick it up and hand it to him. Someone shouted they were afraid, to which the referee said, 'Yes, but I won't bite. Surely someone who is not afraid will bring me the ball.' A portly greyhaired spectator began striding purposefully towards the ball. Suddenly encouraged and recovered from their shock half a dozen youths sprinted for it, competing for the kudos. One, faster than the others, snatched the ball and handed it up. The referee held it up and uttered a loud '*Shabash!*' (Well done!) at which the onlookers cheered as he cantered gracefully away to put the ball into play.

MacFortune, Foyle and some others expressed their distaste for Stapleford's exhibition. I noticed his pretty wife had become as pale as her husband, putting a trembling hand under her chin. I wondered what was wrong with the man, but decided it was not the time to ask those who knew him to explain. When the chukka finished Stapleford handed his horse over to his syce, shouting at him because the girth strap was loose. He came across for some tea, still quivering, and picked on me, the others being suddenly engaged in conversations with someone else. He spoke with teeth clenched, eyes hidden behind his dark glasses, and began lecturing me on how to prevent these bloody people from thinking just because our idiotic Labour government has decided to give then independence they can write us off as nobodies. I said I couldn't understand what had happened, and had many a time seen the youths retrieve the ball and return it; was there something else that I missed? 'You don't know these people yet, do you? It's a damned good thing we are leaving them all to get on with it themselves. It's no place for people like us. Have you ever read the account of the Mutiny? By God, they should have made you read it before you came out to work here! They are deceitful, lazy, dirty, and corrupt. When I think of the years I have wasted in this bloody awful country it makes me ashamed of myself, that I didn't get out sooner.' He paused as he gulped his tea, and I asked him where he had got to in the War. He stared at me with what I took to be infinite scorn, then suddenly removed his dark glasses, revealing one good grey eye, and one useless, disfigured eye which showed mostly bloodshot white, with the pupil almost hidden, permanently turned outwards and upwards. 'I volunteered for service as a riding instructor at the remount depot near Faizabad,' he said, replacing the dark glasses which had taken on a new meaning for me, 'but it didn't work. I carried on working through the War up here. My wife stayed the whole in time in England with her parents, with two small children I didn't see until early forty-six. I got my own back on whoever cursed me with the fish-hook that fixed my eye when I was twelve. Hundreds of our younger labourers were recruited on good pay to work on the Ledo Road. Before they departed the young men asked me to look after their wives and kids; I did. I was one of the few planters not suitable by age or – ha! – visual acuity, who was not sent to supervise the road work.' He was now leering. 'I damn nearly needed a stick to keep those young grass widows from climbing into bed with me. No-one was annoyed to find a few "cafe au lait" kids waiting for them after a year or so away. The happiest days of my life; but I did miss the polo. I'll miss it more when we leave here; that'll be the end of it.' I said I thought he managed remarkably well to hit a polo ball, with only one good eye. Wanting somehow to mollify his anger at missing Colly's long pass, I said his one serviceable eye had certainly been good enough to find a lovely wife. He smiled at me with nostrils dilating and said: 'Don't rush into marriage too soon, young man. Take my advice and go for the wenches for as long as you can.' He strolled off towards the ladies at the table, and I heard him say to his wife she hadn't saved him any sandwiches before the hungry bachelors took their fill. I went on to play another chukka, which was as much as my ageing Conker could cope with in the heat.

I remember not being able to sleep for thinking about that man, and his sweet wife. It went to show how even with a ghastly disfigurement love can conquer huge obstacles.

The tennis people, although not as many as usual, made it impossible for the almost as sweaty polo people, smelling strongly of horses, to have a bath or shower. Many people had come to attend George's meeting, and drink flowed. It was hot, thirsty weather, and beer seemed to be the emollient best suited both for the slaking of thirst, and to smooth away the worries and uncertainties of imminent independence. As chairman of the local circle of the Indian Tea Association George Fraser obviously felt it important to hold the tea people together with a pep talk, despite the total lack of any information concerning their impending fate. He did it splendidly, managed somehow to breathe upon the few glowing embers of hope that all was not as bad as it might sound. He said his bit about carrying on with our best efforts in producing tea, because it could well happen we might be expected to carry on longer than some people thought. He said no-one must dwell on the possibility of disaster. 'There are many Britishers, and Indians, in Delhi, all talking together to work out the best way to bring independence in with the least possible pain and suffering. If one thinks about it, which is something most of us cannot help but do, even at the expense of sleep, one can see whatever the virtues of ideal aims on both sides, there are many problems for both Britain and India, which they surely want to settle to mutual advantage. It would be foolish to place too much hope in the fact that apart from the great disappointment with partition, it seems the very voluntary nature of the granting of independence has totally extinguished the tiresome "quit India" agitation. Here in our remote and peaceful province of Assam, which was so close to the desperate battles with the Japanese, we cannot gauge the situation in the rest of India; but the newspapers, and the wireless, although depressing us with news and comment of the terrible conflicts between Muslim and Hindu, give an impression that Mountbatten has captured the confidence of everyone, and can be trusted to do his best for India; and this redounds to our credit in ways unexpected, and could be seen as something to ease our worries about the immediate future.' He said there were many present who had fought under Mountbatten, and knew he was not the sort of person to throw them the keys and disappear leaving people like us abandoned. 'No!' he said, 'we do not yet know what is going to happen to us, but we are sure we will not be let down. What is more it is sure from our experiences through two crippling wars, that we shall never regret carrying on with our jobs, giving confidence to all those who work for us, and never forgetting: all political aspirations are nothing without a reliable flow of money. Thank you, ladies and gentlemen.' There was good applause, and many voices raised in appreciation; he certainly knew how to capture an audience, and had the gift of finishing his speeches with what I can only describe as an inspiring grimace, pretending it to be a smile. I heard MacDonuill, having made one of his very seldom visits to the club, say in his deep melodious tones, there was nothing very special in his words when they were written down – George had asked him to read his speech the day before – but it was the sheer excellence of his magical ability to use all the notes of his vocal chords, all the clever pauses, to cast a spell on his listeners. Months afterwards people remembered his prophetic and encouraging speech, and some were sure he must have known something of what was being discussed in Delhi; but I always thought he was a master orator, who had the art of having people think he was promising milk and honey, although he only sketched the vaguest possibilities, enough to make people hope things were not as bad as they had thought. I have not remembered at all accurately what he actually said so many years ago, and my attempts to emulate his style should not lead you to conclude he was hardly as good a master orator as I have tried to portray.

Although George's speech had raised my morale, the behaviour of Stapleford still dragged it down. As Foyle said next day, there were people who worked out there who spent their time criticising everything: the people, the weather, the food, the company, and seemed to live from home leave to home leave. There were little cliques of them who seemed to get together to enjoy being miserable. He mentioned having heard this bloke Delapere moaning his head off about coming independence. '"After all I've done for India," he was saying. Him! One of the most incompetent, ignorant, and lazy planters you could hope to meet; and a helluva boozer into the bargain. It makes you want to puke. They keep posting him around as often as they can, because he is hopeless with labour and staff. Always moaning, criticising, and lets people get away with terrible slackness. They say his uncle has a lot of shares in Assam Lothian; he went to the same school as our group chairman. He wears his school blazer and tie whenever there's a cricket match or rugby match: you should just see him. The tie is like a greasy bootlace, and the blazer is covered with so much spilled curry and ice cream it looks like Yankee camouflage. He showed me a first edition of some book of kid's poetry, presented by some aunt of his, signed by the author. It was falling to pieces, eaten through and through by white ants, and he said, "You see! This country ruins everything. It's ruining us, you know. Every time we go on home leave we find just how much it's ruining us. Don' t you find that?" I told him I had only had one home leave, having joined the Army after three years in tea. He's one of those 'tween war types, always telling you how lucky you were to be able to get in and fight.'

Bobby Constable came the following week into the town on business with the Planters Stores. He sent his car on to catch us before we left Medeloabam for polo, with a note inviting me to go back with him after polo, rather than early next morning. Foyle was having guests at Medeloabam, and gave me leave to accept the invitation. I gave Constable's driver a note, and packed a change of clothing: slacks for the evening, and shorts for flying on Sunday. The weather was very hot, and even the mornings were hardly cool enough to give Conker the vigorous regular exercise a polo pony needed. One or two showers fell, but I was told the monsoon would arrive punctually on the fifteenth of June. There was no doubt about the longing of everyone for the big rains. On that day after the showers we played polo in an ambient temperature of 96^0 Fahrenheit: not very hot as hot countries went, but the wet bulb temperature was just over 80^0 Fahrenheit, and this kind of thing affected everything one did. The happy, carefree days of the cold weather had given way to persistent marginal irritation with the many effects of heat and sweat. Everyone had a greasy look, with slightly sunken eyes. The Europeans lost their bronzed appearance: the sun no longer bronzed, but reddened, especially noses, producing anything but a handsome appearance. Polo was rather tedious for horses and riders, and I think we were all pleased when it was decided to give the horses a break and send them off home sooner.

Bobby Constable watched the last two chukkas before taking me off in his car, with all windows open, and the small triangular windows at the front of cars in those days were adjusted to act as scoops to bring in air as we drove along. It was after sunset as we approached Dikom station, but still quite light. The Dibrugarh train had passed us some miles back, and there was a crowd of passengers now on the roadside with piles of baggage and children of all ages, seeking transport for onward travel. There were many cycle rickshaws, and one dilapidated lorry, with people milling around, for fares. Constable suddenly braked, and stopped on the side of the road, opposite the melee. He called out of the window in a loud voice, and I saw a tall turbanned Sikh come swiftly across, waving his arms in greeting. As he salaamed each of us I noted the handsome, bearded man of about forty-five, with deepset eyes and hollow cheeks, who began in rapid Hindustani to speak to Constable, too fast for me to catch more than a few words and expressions. He was near to tears, and as he spoke others congregated: two teenage youths, a woman probably his wife, and three smaller children, all carrying bags and bundles. The woman was weeping softly like someone bereaved, and the children were wide-eyed and sad. I heard Constable say, 'Good God!' and 'Dear God, no!' and eventually, giving the man a couple of notes told him to wait at the adjacent tea stall for an estate lorry to collect him. The man saluted with tears in his eyes, screwing his face into an attempted smile, and turned, spreading his arms to gather and guide his family to the tea stall. As Constable drove away he explained this Sikh, Tej Singh, was a carpenter on his estate who had decided in May he would have to visit his family home near Lahore, from where he had heard there was increasingly serious trouble. There had been a massacre in March in which thousands of Sikhs had been killed, and although after that there had been signs of things quietening down, his father had written for him to come home to help him do something about the dangerous situation now developing. Tej Singh had gone, taking his family with him, only to find his parents and brothers had been killed, and his sister abducted by Muslims; the homestead was burnt to the ground, and most of their Sikh neighbours were either dead or in flight. It was all done by stealth. There were police patrols, touring with vehicles, but they were ineffective. He managed to move nearer to Amritsar, where other Sikhs wanted him to join in night forays against the Muslims, but he was afraid to leave his family unattended. He had been in the Army, but he was not married then; and now with the responsibility of his family he did not choose to take the chance of being killed and leaving them without anyone to look after them in what he described as a mad jehad. Constable said he was a first-class carpenter as

177

well as a builder and gunsmith, and he was glad to have him back. He had been a *naik* (corporal) in the army for seven years, and was good with discipline and organisation in the factory. It would be easy to blame this kind of thing on the British government, on Mountbatten carrying out orders; but it had already gone too far and couldn't be turned back now. He said it should be clear even to the Yanks now that the Hindu-Muslim trouble was not a British device to divide and rule. It went back a long way, started by the Mughals, and would have gone on and on in an undivided India before eventually fizzling out. But the agony of what was happening to these people was one of the oldest things on earth, even when there had been less than a tenth of the present population. Tej Singh said he was lucky to have been able to get back to Assam. Delhi was having trouble, he said, and Amritsar. This chap Tara Singh was plotting to raise a Sikh army in the Punjab, to wreak vengeance for the March massacres in which he and many others lost their families, and to drive Muslims out of what would remain as the Indian Punjab. Tej Singh blamed Jinnah for what was going to be the bloodiest massacre in India's history.

Constable remained silent for quite a distance. When he spoke again, he said Britain had managed to unite an incredible number of different tribes, nations and races in India under a government less violent than the Mughals or the Romans, but did so by a rule of law, and the use of prompt police or military attention. India would have trouble if it thought it could rule itself without such methods, and would be at a disadvantage without the neutrality of the strange Britishers. God help them! He said Tej Singh was a really tough character, but it was heart-breaking to see what this tragedy had done to him: his family was nearly starving, he had lost his heritage, and his morale was almost destroyed. That evening he suggested we had a drink and listen to some records. We listened to his favourite Beethoven sonatas, which for the first time since the War struck me again with their profound and portentous gravity.

Chapter X

In mid-June the rising of the heat and humidity brought with it remarkable changes, not only weatherwise in the atmosphere of my new damfool ambience, but in the behaviour of everyone with whom I was more or less in contact, and of myself. The high humidity filtered the sunlight so that it was no longer golden but a harsh, grey-white glare. Instead of cool blue shadows there were grey smudges, and the whole aspect of landscape and people seemed to lose its usual rich colour. The distant ranges of the Himalayas were spoiled by haze, and were shades of dull grey instead of cobalt. Everyone's mood seemed to change, and I wondered how much was caused by the weather, and how much by the relentless progress of what had suddenly become known in English as 'partition', and in the other languages as 'Pakistan'. From newspapers and wireless it was learned that the actual details of how the boundaries between India and Pakistan were to be drawn would not be made known until after the celebration of Independence. Because such news was spread by word of mouth or letters from distant provinces, there was a mixture of truth, lies, misunderstanding, and fearful hysteria, all of which was leading to perplexing uncertainty and insecurity. Foyle said he had heard some of the tribals say they were thinking of returning to their own districts, most of which were between one and two thousand miles away, and others were asking if they could call their brothers and their families to what might be the relative safety of Assam.

In the hot, steamy weather the growth of leaf on the tea bushes seemed to accelerate. More and more of the labour force was now being used to harvest the rising surge of crop, and the fresh green of its vigorous growth seemed the only bright colour to be found. There were 2,722 tea bushes in every acre, planted four feet by four feet, and in the thousand acres of the estate

179

under tea there had to be 2,722,000 bushes. By now the bushes had filled their available space, and the whole area was like a lawn two and a half feet above ground level, through which one moved as if wading against a stiff river current, thrusting through the branches gently enough to damage neither the bushes nor one's own clothes and thighs. This, on Foyle's advice, was my main occupation now, roving through the level stretches of green behind the advancing line of pluckers, trying to ensure the bushes were plucked to the prescribed height, eight inches above the November prune, ensuring the level did not rise so high that plucking would become difficult, and crop would be lost. I had also to watch that no-one plucked too low, especially at the edges of the bushes, which would both spoil the level plucking table and prevent weaker bushes from managing to join with their neighbours and cover the ground, an important way of preventing weed competition. It was now that the virtues of the shade trees became fully understood and appreciated. Just as people sought the shade of trees as protection from the harsh sun, the tea plants needed such provision of trees in this highly humid climate, where their normal ability to cool their leaves by transpiration was no longer enough to avoid sunscorch and maintain growth. These trees were all leguminous, bearing seed in pods, and having foliage which was feathery with never too dense a shade to cut the sun out excessively. They also had the characteristics of the time-honoured green crops, and in similar ways to clovers, lucerne and such, they formed on their roots nodules of bacteria which absorbed nitrogen, the prime plant nutrient, from the air in the soil, and not from the soil itself. The leaf of the shade trees gave welcome shade in the growing season, and in the cold weather the leaf would fall, adding fertility taken from the air as a welcome mulch.

It was on the fifteenth of June that I stood, admiring the alternate rows of shade trees whilst the pluckers moved from the field or section which had been plucked, to empty their leaf into their cane baskets on the road before moving to the next section. The trunks of the koroi trees (*albizzia procera*) were like old ivory, and their foliage was a delightful pastel green, with new shoots tinged with the palest pink and covered with a velvet pile of silver. They looked well against a sky of grey cloud. I asked Anulall *sirdar* if he thought it was likely to rain. His wrinkled face was like carved ebony, shining with sweat and adorned with silver brows and stubble. He touched his shoulders with his carved stick and said for two days now his shoulders had told him the big monsoon was very near. Within half an hour a strangely cool breeze began to waft towards what was now a darkening, almost purple wall of cloud, and the few little dogs which accompanied their owners stood staring at the dark cloud with cocked ears. Women and men had begun talking, calling to each other, with occasional laughs and shrill responses. Then came the distant sound, which seemed a long way away, like the sound of the surf in an onshore wind. The pluckers began moving back to the road to take from their leaf baskets their round '*jhapis*' woven from palm leaves, cane and bamboo. They were about two and a half feet diameter, with drooping rim and a rising cone in the middle where the head would fit. Balia *sirdar*, a younger man who always wore a neat military upturned moustache, and a spotlessly clean, well-tied turban (*pagri*), came offering me his umbrella, which all *sirdars* carried, saying that heavy rain was coming. I laughingly thanked him and said I was not worried about rain and would be all right; but I noticed his expression as he looked over his shoulder at the advancing dark wall, nodding gently, either in acceptance of my eccentricity, or thinking he could do no more than warn me. I remembered landing at Alipore in the heavy rain of last year's monsoon, my ears covered by the earphones in my helmet, the noise of the engine eliminating external sound, and the almost shameful joy of having broken cloud over that airfield with an almost empty petrol tank.

The noise increased, and I confess to being a little anxious that it was so loud now, without the slightest drop of rain to be seen. I saw the rain, and the spume of the rain at the foot of the dark curtain several minutes before the first large drop hit my head, and within a minute of that happening the full force of the monsoon descended in a powerful torrent, drenching, splashing, cooling deliciously, but drumming its large drops on my head and shoulders almost like a hosepipe.

There were yells from the men on the next section, and screams from the women, which led me to wonder if they were in distress; but I soon realised their tones were in fact joyful and full of fun. Foyle arrived in his jeep, and I thrust out of the tea to greet him. He laughed when he saw me, and handed me his umbrella, telling me to put it up so that he could talk to me. The *sirdars* came out and gathered round the vehicle, saluting Foyle. He told me it looked as if the rain was set to last all day, and before long the pluckers would feel the chill. It was well past midday, and it was best to tell them all to carry their leaf to the factory, weigh it in, and make their way home. It took about three or four days until they were used to the rain again, and the sun would keep warming them up. The *sirdars* called the pluckers out, and over the sound of the rain the sounds of jollity rose as they found their leaf baskets, placed the *jhapis* atop them, and helped each other to raise their baskets, the men to their shoulders, and the women to their heads, cushioned with rolls of cloth. I began helping to lift the women's baskets, made dizzy by the fact that their thin cotton blouses, soaked and running with rain, were virtually transparent, exposing breasts of more differing types than I realised existed, some intensely attractive, some sadly deteriorated, some neat and small even in fully mature women, some large and heavy even in girls hardly out of puberty. The cool rain was indeed welcome for someone caught in the lifestyle of the West, who had not yet learned to appreciate the wonder of how the babe in arms, born with the love and desire which draws it to the mother's breast, becomes the man whose first newborn desire is what gives him the marvellous urge to find his life-mate.

Rain in the West is revered for its power to produce food crops, reviled for its fickle appearances, and cursed for its failures. In Assam the heavy monsoon rain arrives well before the southern plains of Bengal, over which the moisture-laden air mass moves without giving up its moisture until it meets the hills of Sylhet and Assam, which raises it to the critical height where rain forms. The effect on the heated earth, irrigated by the copious rain, brings forth not only the growth of vegetation, but the hatching of myriads of all kinds of insects, some earlier described, in huge quantities. It also brings the blessing of wide distribution of fish, whose life cycle is harmonised with the seasons, and sends them frantically moving from stagnating marshes into streams, and from great rivers into streams which come to life in the hills, and fill the great rice-growing plains of Assam. Fishes, frogs of all kinds, and insects seem to take over the world, and ignore humans in their appropriations of living space and feeding grounds.

All this was new and fascinating, but the exhilaration of discovery became almost like the imagined enjoyment of some forbidden pleasure: intermittent and furtive, spoiled by feeling guilty and stupid: a damfool allowing himself to fall in love with something that wasn't going to last. There must have been some inextinguishable hope, for I could not believe it sensible or reasonable to continue learning languages, absorbing more and more facts

182

about tea, the local geography, and staring at the distant mountains whilst yearning to visit the North Bank again. The time passed rapidly. Polo was cancelled once or twice because of too much rain; we only played on Saturdays now, as the increasing amounts of leaf coming in meant Wednesdays were full working days. Flying was similar. We did longer cross-country flights, landing on polo grounds at more distant clubs if the weather permitted, and climbing a few thousand feet into the cooler air when there was a clear enough sky.

June and July passed incredibly fast. The news from Delhi and Lahore was grim, and Bengal seemed to hang in the balance, with Gandhi joining Surawardhi in Calcutta in attempts to prevent Hindus from launching a massacre of Muslims in retribution for the killings of June 1946. Hindus stoned the house occupied by Gandhi and Surawardhi, the Muslim leader, in the centre of Hindu activism. People all over India were blaming the Mahatma for yielding to the Muslims, for asking the British to allow them to have their separate Pakistan. When I heard this from our Bengali clerks, most of whom seemed to have turned against that saintly man, I hardly slept that night for thinking how Jesus Christ suffered terrible rejection and loneliness when trying to save the people with love and non-violence. It became depressingly real when one thought of Gandhi maintaining his faith in the jaws of massacre.

It must have been about two weeks before the fifteenth of August when a stipendiary of the Indian Tea Association flew up to Assam and gave talks in various planters' clubs supposed to be reassuring and instructive as to what was likely to happen. It is a long time ago, but as far as we who are alive today remember, the message was hard to grasp: the British were discussing arrangements with the future Congress ministers of India, and as these talks continued it was difficult to be positive about anything; but there was an implicit resemblance of agreement that the tea industry should carry on as before, and continue to produce tea. Although there were communal problems in certain areas of India, Assam was regarded as one of the places where there was little risk of civil disturbance, and the British establishment in India was ready and willing to establish air transport should such an emergency so demand. British companies in Calcutta were to continue working so that their many employees remained in employment, and ships would continue to arrive and sail for export and import needs. At the meeting we attended someone asked if the British price support for the production of Indian tea would be likely to continue, and the speaker, an ex-Indian Civil Servant, said he felt sure this was one of the important subjects currently being discussed. George Fraser was magnificent in his speech of thanks to the speaker, and from feeling on the verge of being abandoned in Assam, everyone felt after George's short speech that this was actually what we wanted, to stay in the place we loved and keep the thousands of tea workers, including ourselves, working for a living; but for how long? After the talk the bar was opened, and as the beer flowed various stories came out from those who were in touch with Delhi and Lahore, and they were depressing. The Police and the Indian Army, which had operated many mixed units of Hindus, Muslims and other, could no longer trust their men to act impartially. Many Sikhs had deserted with their arms to join bands to protect their own people, or to wreak vengeance on Muslims who were being encouraged by their leaders to eradicate Sikhs from what were guessed to be areas of the future Pakistan. I heard one corpulent, red-faced planter say it was time that crafty old bastard Gandhi got his come-uppance from his own kind after all the trouble he had created. Someone else said if it hadn't been for Gandhi we'd be staying in India and stopping them from killing each other. The tall ex-cavalry officer who had spoken to me at polo about treating the game as a sport to enjoy, held up his hand, pointing at the roof, and said 'Just a moment, gentlemen. One must respect the man. He has won Independence from the British without firing a shot, putting himself at considerable risk many times, including now. That's more than any other nation has ever been able to do to the British by force of arms since the Norman conquest.' I had the impression that the loud chorus of those of us who said 'hear hear' were ex-service.

A week before the fifteenth George called a meeting for his managers, and when Foyle returned from it he really enjoyed telling me we were to arrange sports, wrestlers, sweet meats for children, dancers, and to help in arranging a flag ceremony, lowering the British Union Jack, and raising the Indian tricolour of orange, white and green. The whole day was to be a holiday, after which work would carry on as usual. Local politicians had indicated there should be a definite appreciation of British action in handing over to an Indian government, coupled with a celebration of the achievement of freedom. Foyle called a meeting of the seniormost Indian members of the staff: the head clerk, the doctor, the head factory supervisor, the three field supervisors, the welfare officer, the factory engineer, the stores clerk, the head driver, and four senior *sirdars*. The meeting lasted a long time, and dealt with the sudden problem of acquiring a Union Jack and an Indian national flag, the ways and means of contacting dance groups, wrestlers, musicians, the sports programme, and the provision of sweetmeats for children. It was the head clerk who wisely suggested using family ration cards for the issue of sweets. These cards were used for the drawing on payment of paddy, dal, salt, mustard oil, and kerosene oil every fortnight from the estate stores, which was a system introduced to make available such commodities on the remote estates where there were few shops within reach, and in an economy where frequent failure of supplies caused serious disruption of employment, either through contrived shortages, or floods, droughts, and violent fluctuations in prices. The ration cards were durable small panels of plywood, with the details printed on thick paper, pasted to the wood, and then thickly varnished.

I was asked by Foyle to organise the flag ceremony, and promised to do it so that the rolled Indian flag would be hoisted in a small, rolled package, and unfurled at the masthead, which I had learned as a Boy Scout. There was no easy agreement as to who should raise the Indian flag, and the manager and the *jemadar babu* (senior field supervisor) were appointed to select some appropriate person. Foyle and I drove into town to investigate the entertainments possibilities, and managed to organise a team of wrestlers who also had three dancing girls. Foyle demanded to see the dancers before agreeing to accept them, and was told they would have to come from Bihar with their own musicians. As the estate was going to pay the bill for this Foyle said he would pay half the cost, and then ask the people who watched the show if they deserved the other half, but the team leader said he could not agree to such an arrangement, and showed us a letter offering to pay a hundred rupees less than he had asked from us, which he said was a safer arrangement than we suggested. Foyle then said he would accept the whole group, but could not guarantee what might happen if the people were disappointed by jaded old dancers who couldn't do better than our own tribal girls. We had to agree to send a lorry to the railway station to collect the team on the fourteenth. The estate produced its own music and singing troupe, led by one of the carpenters.

185

The sports programme was given to me to organise, and as the rains were in danger of rendering most fields unusable without warning we finished up with long and high jumps, an archery competition at stakes, and a race of about three quarters of a mile down the main road of the estate. That was about all there would be time for, and prizes were arranged. All this, and the increasing tempo of leaf harvesting and manufacture, passed in a whirl. The staff members were all in a mood of enthusiasm, and the workers seemed to become more relaxed, although still bemused as much as I was as Independence Day came closer. The men and the women kept asking if we were going to stay and look after them, to which one could only reply we ourselves were still not sure what would happen, but if the Indian government wanted us to stay we would certainly like to. There was one lady, a Gond (pronounced roughly as a nasal 'go(n)r') from Bilaspur, who spoke a well-enunciated kind of Hindi-cum-Sadani-cum-Bilaspuri which fascinated me. Her name was Sukhwaria, and she was probably beautiful in her early days, but having had seven children by her semi-alcoholic husband had lost her bloom except for her heavily lidded eyes, which when she was sober were large and luminous; but she had become as heavy a drinker as him, which led to her role as the mouthpiece of the female community, mostly amusing all concerned with her oratory, but sometimes invoking reactions from some of the Indian staff who, after pay day each fortnight, were her favourite targets. She publicly and blatantly denounced the idea that there would be a '*babu ke Raj*' (government by clerks), and said they were so corrupt they would ruin the estates, the farms, and the fishing, and no-one would listen to them. She named various clerks who were always bribing their favourites and making false accounts, and when Foyle told her she should be careful in what she said, she boldly told him the Telford sahib had decided to leave because he knew what was coming. He knew how corrupt the *babus* were, and kept them from stealing and corrupting the others. Foyle told her to come to the office next morning when she was sober, as he wanted to speak with her. When she arrived, much subdued, Foyle called the head clerk, the *jemadar babu* and the welfare officer. He told everyone he had decided this lady, who had been living on the estate for nearly twenty years, should enjoy the honour of raising the new Indian flag on Independence Day: the mother of seven, a plucker of high ability, and as someone proud of her family and her place of work she would perform the act as one of the people who wanted to see India go from strength to strength in a way only possible with the support of the workers. It shook the staff, but the *jemadar babu*, a tough Assamese with a good sense of humour, nodded his head vigorously, approving the idea. He said in English it was very necessary to make sure these people understood they were going to have to make freedom work, for everyone's sake. The others relaxed a little, and the head clerk said, 'Look, Sukhwaria, make just one promise: that you will not take drink before coming to the flag ceremony at eight o'clock on the day. Afterwards you can drink and be happy, and the people will be proud of you. Right?'

Whilst we were in town the Foyles and I met several polo-playing planters on similar quests, and the subject arose of how polo would be affected. Foyle said that 'carrying on as usual' surely meant just that in every way. There was only one polo day left before Independence Day, but the very day following was regarded by some as perhaps better cancelled. After pointing out that the new Indian Deputy Commissioner was invited to the Planters' Club on the sixteenth, which was the first time any such thing would have happened, there seemed to be a feeling in favour of carrying on with polo as usual, weather permitting. This was reinforced at the next club night after polo, when it showed very clearly that the general attitude of the British community, planters, merchants, lawyers and solicitors etc., had changed significantly. Although the future was by no means clear, the realisation that Indians in general, at least in Assam, were taking what someone described as 'a damned good sporting view' of the handover of power, it shook even the hardened sceptics and pessimists, who seemed to be modifying their reactions and expectations of life after Independence, for some time anyway. Poppy Fraser, keen to assess what I, one who had adopted the soubriquet of 'damfool', now thought of the whole thing, told me she was touched deeply by the Indian attitude. 'It doesn't matter what happens now,' she said with stars in her eyes, 'even if we are told after two or three months that we have to clear out, what they have said now will stay with us. For people like George and his contemporaries, who have set their roots down here, it would have been disastrous to have been ordered out as if they mattered not at all. We would all have slunk away to a dim and sinking life with the feeling it was all pointless and worthless. What do you think?' After I had spent about ten minutes trying to explain how I had stupidly fallen in love with this new life she laughed, and warned me to think it all out quite clearly, to identify exactly what I really loved, and how long it could last; and how I would last without finding that suppressed sex was an awful lot to blame for such far-flung affection. George was in excellent form, delighted at his contacts with the new DC, and spent his time encouraging shrewd optimism, and the demonstration of determination to carry on doing our best in the jobs we knew so well. He moved from group to group with his chin up, a broad smile on his lips, and bushy black eyebrows producing a scowl under which his eyes twinkled brightly with confidence and zeal.

'I have some news for you,' George said. 'Telford is learning to fly. What do you think of that?'

I said I thought it was a very sensible idea, and asked if he would be able to buy an aeroplane for himself. George said the way things stood at present didn't make it likely any planter would splash out on an aeroplane, not even a second-hand one.

'You know, it is quite extraordinary, MacStorm. John York, who gave us this talk, left the ICS some months ago about the same time as B.P. Kentwell when it became known the British government was bent on giving India its independence. These chaps were all dedicated to India. The cream of Britain's best universities, who had this marvellous idea of honourable service, and spent their whole career working for a miserable salary, and a pension at the end of it, getting out of it a splendid sense of achievement. We call them the 'heaven-born', because of their absolute impeccability, their spartan way of life. You know, all the best books on plants, and birds, and many notable works of history were written by these chaps as their hobby. B.P. was a brilliant linguist; many of them were; but the sad thing is that they are most of them already moving out. They simply can't face carrying on under an Indian government. York says he has heard that Nehru wanted as many of them to stay and carry on serving until there were enough Indians experienced enough to replace them, and Nehru is very upset that they won't stay; but one can see their point of view. The Indian civil servants who had been rising into posts as judges, magistrates, and local administrators, are all very unsure about their future. You see, MacStorm, the British civil servants were very tough on the Congress political agitators, and wouldn't let them get in the way of the country's administration. Now that these agitators are likely to become powerful politicians, they are likely to be corrupted by their new powers, and they could make life for the lackeys of British Imperialism very difficult. We, the planters, are already showing willingness to carry on, you see: we whom the agitators criticised and vilified!' He laughed heartily. 'You know MacStorm, York said the tea companies were all founded on British capital. India could, if it were bloody-minded enough, simply expropriate them, but they are clever enough to see that what the government wants is to collect fat taxes from the tea grown in India, and must keep the tax coming out of the well-established companies without taking any risks.' He gazed around, raising a hand to hold my attention. 'York said Kentwell is really deep into discussions with the Congress pundits on the subject of the value of British industry, especially tea, to the new state of India. Eventually Kentwell will be coming to see us, to explain the shape of things to come, but it might take months to settle things properly.'

I felt honoured to receive such a meaty helping of information and forecast, which George was able to deliver expertly. I thanked him, expressing my appreciation for some aspects which were not actually brought out in York's talk, and casting his eyes around as if to see who might have overheard him despite the high level of noise, he then stared straight at me, his spectacles magnifying the wide, dark pupils of his eyes in the dim rosy light of the crowded bar. 'All I have told you is strictly confidential, MacStorm. It is for your own digestion, and I have told you because I have a funny feeling you might suddenly decide there's no sure future for you here, and as much as you like it you might convince yourself you should get out while the going is good. I think there is a damn' good chance for us all; but you'll have to make up your own mind, and don't forget: time is on your side.'

On the way back from the club Foyle said he thought York spoke well, but didn't really say anything positive because even at the top no-one is sure of anything. He said George was very good at encouraging people to believe everything was going to be all right, but there were quite a few saying afterwards they thought it was time to go, because there was going to be a terrible civil war once the new boundaries were made known. He named several people who said they would certainly not turn up for polo on the day after Independence Day, because that was when the trouble would begin, even in Assam. They were saying there were rumours that the southern borders of Assam were likely to be changed, with the Muslim areas of Sylhet wanting to go into Pakistan along with much of East Bengal. Foyle said he very much admired Mountbatten, but he thought his idea of dividing India into two was either plumb crazy or, more likely, a deliberate and clever move calculated to produce a result none of us who lived out there could fathom. When we spoke next morning, I asked how his wife was taking it all now, as I noticed she was very quiet in the car all the way back. He said surely she was worried, but all the time he had been in tea he had noticed the memsahibs were always worried about something after a club night. 'You get those unfortunate women who have never been happy since they first set foot here, and they're always complaining about the heat, the servants, the insects, the other companies paying similar men more than theirs, and their husbands not being promoted because they complained about their bungalows to Calcutta. Anyway,' he said 'Dierdre's just a bit worried – and don't mention it to anyone – because we found some weeks ago she's expecting our first child. All she says now is that she hopes we menfolk know what we're doing, and just remember when our child is due to be born, God knows where!' This made me very conscious of the difference between the married men and bachelors when it came to the approach of life's frequent storms, and I almost asked him why he didn't at least ask for his wife to be evacuated, but thought such a question would not be helpful.

The weather on August the fifteenth was bright and hot. Although it had rained heavily during the night the sky was actually blue, with fairweather clouds drifting in a welcome breeze. The Foyles and I arrived at the office, where the flagpole base had been decorated with various flowers, and the Union Jack stirred lazily at the top. There were many people there, but not all of the people on the estate. The staff, the *sirdars*, drivers, carpenters and builders, and many of the field and factory workers, and a surprising number of villagers and others, some Assamese whom we did not know, mostly dressed in their best clothes, all stood quietly outside the office compound. As we arrived three women came in through the compound gate, clad in saris of purple, green and red, silver earrings showing under the part of the sari draped over the head, arms heavy with bangles of silver, ankles heavy with bent oval-shaped silver bands from which many silver drops dangled in a fringe, making a soft jingling as they walked gracefully forward. Foyle's first impression was the same as mine, that these were the three dancing girls, and he muttered something like 'a bit long in the tooth for girls', as they came towards us with broad smiles and hands together in greeting. Then 'By God, its Sukhwaria.' She had come with her two friends, all three dressed in their best Gond style and ornaments, looking remarkably dignified and elegant in a way that suggested pomp without pomposity. They came to us and with palms still together touched the feet of Foyle, his wife, and myself, smiling almost mischievously, but without the slightest trace of drink carrying on the breeze. The head clerk asked Foyle kindly to speak, and he spoke only a few words in Hindustani. He pointed to the Union Jack and said we were now going to lower it for the last time, after nearly two hundred years. 'We have not long ago finished fighting another great war to bring peace to the world. Where there is peace, there can be freedom, and this is the day India's freedom begins, with the raising of the Indian flag. If we stay here doing our work, with you, or if we leave you for any reason, we want India to live in peace: peace amongst the people of India, and peace with India's neighbours.' He then smiled and nodded to me, and I went forward, beckoning to Sukhwaria, who stood beside me with palms still together. I murmured she should wait a little. Although I did not wear a hat (and never did since leaving the Air Force) I saluted the flag, and lowered it slowly. In English a few voices said, 'Thank you, sir!' and I undid the toggles, folded the Union Jack and placed it on the table behind us, then tied the new flag carefully to the toggles, wound the lower part of the line round the folded flag, looped the next few inches under the tightly wound line, and put the upper run of the line into Sukhwaria's hands, murmuring she should now pull slowly downwards, watching upwards. There were a few excited murmurs, but otherwise there was a tense silence. I heard an Assamese villager say he could see no flag, only a bundle, and someone told him to wait. When the bundle reached the top I held the upper line and told Sukhwaria to pull the other downwards, moving my wrist to show how to tug with the hand only, hoping she would not pull too hard and bring the line and pulley down. She had to pull a second time before the green, white and orange flag opened into the gentle breeze. At this point one of the estate's better voices began singing the Indian national anthem, which lasted for about three verses, only the staff and some of the

Hindi speakers knowing the words. Following this the head clerk led the shouting of *Jai Hind* three times, followed by cheers, after which three beautiful girls, schoolgirl daughters of the Indian staff members, came forward in their beautiful pale blue silk frocks with three large garlands of various flowers and blossoms, including jasmine, and placed them round the necks of Foyle, Mrs Foyle, and myself. This had not been shown in our programme, and we each placed palms together and said '*dhanyabad*', to which the sweet girls responded by the same gesture, saying 'thank you, sir' before fluttering shyly to refuge amongst the staff wives and mothers. The head clerk came, moist eyed, and shook hands with us, followed by the other members of the staff, and suddenly the office compound was full of all kinds of people shaking hands with us. There were some Christian Mundas and Oraons, who shook hands saying not *Jai Hind*, but *Jai Jesu*. It seemed to me like a strange dream. The Assamese *jemadar babu*, whose voice was loud and clear, announced the issue of sweetmeats for children at the gates of the factory compound, where appropriate pay clerks were to supervise correct issues according to ration cards. We could see large crowds of mothers and children already gathered in queues along the factory fence. The entertainments were to begin at ten-thirty, and the Foyles invited me to have a cup of tea with them before we returned to see the fun.

'I don't know how you felt,' said Foyle, 'but I found it quite moving, that flag hoisting. I was thinking here in Assam we were always in contact with the local people, mostly our labour, but with the villagers, the shopkeepers in town, all going about the business of growing food and tea. I wonder how everything is going in Calcutta, Delhi and further west. The civil service chaps loved being posted to the wild areas, the hills, where they spent their time talking to people who wanted them to settle their disputes, and then went off for their shooting or fishing, similar to here. The people serving in the crowded towns and districts were the ones who didn't enjoy their work at all: the continuous thieving, which one seldom had in the rural areas, the political agitators who were not only agin the government but agin their rivals, and the awful processions where the Hindus and Muslims seemed to taunt each other regularly, with the Police being called out to restore order. Those are the chaps, who spent their years trying to do their best, they're the ones who are right now on their way out, and you can't blame them. But you know, they're not going to believe what's happening here today.'

His wife leaned forward and knocked softly with her knuckles on the heavy timber tea table on the verandah, made from a slice of a huge tree trunk, and said it was very kind of them to put these garlands round our necks, and shake hands with us all. 'But you've kept telling me you can never really tell what these people are thinking about, and I wonder what they really think about it all. Can they make a better job of ruling India than the British? Poppy Fraser said her uncle had written a long letter to her from Australia, where he settled after retiring from the ICS, saying the big problem for India is that ninety-five per cent of Indians don't have enough money to pay income tax, and one of the reasons Britain is handing over is that it is making a big loss in running the country, and hasn't got the money to develop any kind of improvement.'

I said I thought that was one reason Gandhi preached a return to the simple village economy, with everyone producing his own needs. This led to a discussion of the rising Indian population, in most places except for Assam, and this kept us going until we decided we should investigate the sports, the wrestlers, and the dancing girls. We went down to the area chosen for the entertainments which was the site for the weekly bazaar, where once a week villagers, barbers, fishermen, farmers, sellers of cures, herbs, aphrodisiacs and cloth would set up their stalls. Now there were other booths, for wrestlers, dancers, singers and musicians. There must have been a booth or two selling rice beer and perhaps illicit rum, because several of the tribal workers, treating the day as just another festival, were slightly pink-eyed and merry, mixing happily with the crowd. When we arrived at the wrestlers' pit the leader, a hefty broad-shouldered man, made a deep salaam and spoke with Foyle, who said he was a Bihari Nunia, of the kind the tea estates would hire in the early part of the year for digging drains, throwing up embankments, digging water reservoirs and such other work demanding muscle and stamina. The wrestlers' heads were all shaven, except for the long thin tail of hair which was the sacred Hindu lock by which their souls would be rescued from death, and would not be touched even in a wrestling contest. They wore the briefest of trusses and nothing else as they went through their exhibition of exercises as a preparation for the wrestling to follow. In pairs, one would put his hands on the ground and throw his legs up for the other to catch, whilst he bent and stretched his arms. As we watched this, one of my gardeners came swaggering up with two friends, and as far as I could gather they were loftily telling the wrestlers that was nothing compared with what their *chota sahib* could do, which they began to describe to the cheers of the many people surrounding the booth. My servants had seen me walk on my hands on the lawn, do handsprings, backflips, and running front somersaults in the air, something carried over from schooldays which I thought was good for keeping me agile. Foyle addressed the crowd, asking them if they wanted the *chota sahib* to show the wrestlers how to do it, and evoked loud and jovial demand for me to perform. I felt this was hardly what was required for the dignity even of a *chota sahib* on a day like this, and said so to Foyle with some embarrassment.

'You never told us about this before,' he said, and turning to his wife said, 'You'd like to see him perform, wouldn't you, dear? I certainly would. Come on then, otherwise you'll let the British down, you know!' He was laughing the way I envied: a really happy, crinkly smile. 'But for goodness sake be careful, we're short of assistants, you know.' Taking a deep breath I asked him to explain I would do a very quick routine in the ring, but no wrestling. Thus it was that I took off my shoes and stockings, and in a space of reasonably clean ground I walked on my hands, did flying springs, back flips, hand springs, and a running front somersault in the air, the last with so much vigour that I bounced after landing and ended in the brawny arms of the wrestlers, colliding amid cheers from the watchers. Dierdre Foyle said I was fantastic, and Foyle said it would be all round Upper Assam inside a week; but I said I could imagine all kinds of garbled versions of how I performed like a street acrobat in front of the crowd, letting the side down. I went off on the third clerk's bicycle with my shoes and stockings in my hands to wash hands and feet, and have a shower before returning to the show.

The dancing girls turned out to be tall, handsome but not beautiful women, who were brought to show themselves to us before they danced. They had several young girls, daughters and pupils, who were like large-eyed captured fawns, shy and anxious about the crowd of strangers. The dancing was fairly good, with musicians playing reed pipes and drums, and it lasted a long time, so that the crowd changed often enough for everyone to have a good view. The archery was fascinating, but tribal pride in the competition threatened at one point to fracture the general goodwill of the day. At about twelve-thirty we were invited into the pay clerks' office where a table had been set for tea and snacks. The overhead fans were working full blast, the current coming from the diesel generator in the factory. Mrs Foyle was introduced to the wives of the senior people, who were all very shy, and as they spoke either Assamese or Bengali, and Dierdre Foyle spoke some Hindustani which she learned from her husband and developed with her servants, there was not much opportunity for conversation. Being unmarried I was not introduced to any of the ladies until later when the *jemadar babu* and the third clerk who had been teaching me Assamese, introduced me to their wives, who were delighted at my embarrassed efforts to speak with them. It was the first time I observed how the Assamese ladies had none of the shy inhibitions of the other Hindu communities, and had a very happy style of communication, with many questions about myself, especially on the subject of my failure so far at my age to have married. The wives of the head clerk and the factory supervisors, both past the age of forty, spoke with me in slow but good English in a very dignified and quite charming way. They asked if I would learn Bengali, and I said I was willing, but must first learn the language of the province I lived in. They smiled and nodded, but I sensed by their flickering sideways glances at their husbands there was a need for them not to pursue any discussion too far. We retired for our tiffin at about two in the afternoon, and I found my servants ready to serve cold roast chicken with potatoes and spinach, followed by papaya.

I switched the wireless on later, to hear a rich, deep, and rather sad voice speaking; it was a replay of Mountbatten's speech on the actual handing over of power. I have forgotten his words in detail, but remember that voice, speaking to the Indian people, full of feeling and expressing hope for the future well-being of India as an independent nation in a way that was sincere and free of affected patronising. Later the commentator said Lord Mountbatten had accepted the invitation of the Congress Party, in the person of Mahatma Gandhi, to become the first Governor-General of the new state of India, and this gave me a warmth of the heart that seldom comes in life, for the discovery of something very special, not just in Gandhi, but in the huge country of India.

I went across to the stables and told Ramjan I would not take Conker out for exercise that evening because there would be polo at the club tomorrow. He looked pale, and said he wanted leave tomorrow as he felt unwell. I asked if he had been to the hospital, a mere hundred yards or so away, and he said it was not that bad. I felt his pulse which was strong and regular, and told him he was not ill, whereupon with an agonised expression he told me he didn't like leaving his wife and children on their own, not yet. I said to him if he showed he was worried it would attract attention; someone would take notice who otherwise would never take interest. I told him the stores clerk was a Muslim, and he was quite happy there would be no trouble. In the morning he should talk with the Foyle sahib, and we would see how things looked. I told him Gandhi had managed to ensure peace in Bengal, which meant Assam would remain as peaceful as it had ever been, and hoped it made him feel better.

Ramjan took Conker along with the other two syces and horses next morning. After a good day's work trying to catch up on the plucking area lost on the fifteenth, we drove in to the club. In town there were many people, generally in a relaxed and celebratory mood. About twenty girls with their thick black hair in a single braid down their backs, dressed in pale blue and pink blouses and golden silk *mekelas* (similar to a sarong), walked clapping their hands rhythmically and singing along the main street. Foyle said they were Assamese college students, and I agreed they were a beautiful sight. They waved honey-coloured arms and trilled their voices as we passed slowly, with Mrs Foyle waving gently to them. The sheer effervescence of the Assamese girls was a delight to see, and had the effect on me of two or three turns of a spin in an aeroplane. It was sunny and quite hot, and there had been isolated rainstorms.

At the polo field our numbers were fewer, but there seemed to be many more local spectators sitting in the shade of the large trees on the road along the north side of the large field. We felt our decision to play polo as usual on that day was right. I heard the ladies who were busy laying out the tea things and plates of sandwiches exchange stories of how the ceremony had gone the previous day, and later heard from the other men that the picture was so far very similar everywhere in the district. One of the planters who was an enthusiastic amateur wireless operator told us of the terrible things which were happening in the Punjab, but so far Bengal was not too bad. They were changing a lot of the Calcutta street names down there already, but apparently it was otherwise business as usual. I went on to the field with Foyle to practise some hitting, and he said we would have to watch the ground, because it was still quite wet after the early shower. Play soon started, and it seemed the crowd was cheering more than I had heard before. In the third chukka I think the cheering, and the feeling of relief that Independence had arrived without any of the feared disappointments or worries of the past two months, put me in a mood of bumptious over-confidence. I had been playing better than ever, gaining praise from team-mates, and as Conker was performing well I rode harder than I ought, hit a ball backwards, and reined Conker about in too steep a turn on the wet grass. He went down on his knees in the turn, nearly tipping me off, but then somehow managed after a few seconds to regain his forefeet, but it was clear he was not moving happily. Colly, who was refereeing, cantered over and told me I should walk him off and give him a rest, saying he'd probably pulled his belly muscles. 'You're not flying a bloody Spitfire, you know!' he said with a scowl, making me feel like a dim-witted fool. After the chukka, the last of the day, the others had a look at him. He walked well enough, but the trot was clearly not to Conker's liking. In the end, when Foyle told Ramjan he should walk the horse slowly back, and not keep up with the others, Ramjan came to tears, and I said I would walk him, mounted, slowly back to Medeloabam, and Ramjan could go back with the other syces and horses. Someone said I shouldn't go through the town, but take the road round the outskirts. Foyle said that would add another half an hour to the three-hour walk back. I said I would start straight away, and hope to be back by about ten p.m.

I set off in the saddle in my polo kit as the others went into the club, and in a fit of mixed curiosity and over-confidence decided to take the shortest route through the town; perhaps I hoped to see again some of the merry student girls. Many of the spectators who had left the polo field were on the road, and waved happily as I overtook them. I took heart from Conker's quick stride, with no sign of a limp; he seemed to want to reach home as soon as possible. Along the road where the government offices lay I passed the main police station, and heard a shout. Out of the main building came about eight policemen, wearing red *pagris*, and the oldest of them, with a large grey, bristling moustache, threw up a smart salute which I returned. Riding along the main shopping street I saw a party of about twenty men coming towards me, out of the sunset, singing and chanting slogans. As they neared me they ran across to my side of the road, and I saw they were in a festive mood, with garlands of flowers. They stopped me, and all talked

197

and shouted happily, eventually indicating they wanted to place garlands about the horse's neck. I told them to do it slowly so as not to worry the horse, and they went ahead, placing four garlands as if Conker had been used to it all his life. I placed my palms together and thanked them, and they shouted happily as Conker and I moved on. The light was going fast, but as long as we passed people who were able to see the garlanded horse ridden by a young sahib they waved happily. Soon we were on what was called the trunk road, where it was dark except for the oil lamps of people walking to their villages. Eventually I managed to identify the turn-off for the last three miles or so to Medeloabam. About fifteen minutes before I reached my bungalow it began to rain, and at my gate was Ramjan, with his umbrella, and one for me. He was delighted Conker was going so well. I had a shower, a light late supper, and went to bed dazed with wonder at how Independence had actually arrived.

Chapter XI

Although the way Independence actually happened led to a great reduction in tension, not only in general but particularly amongst the planting community at large; there were still worries about the news of terrible slaughter in the Punjab, for fear it might spread like wildfire throughout India. It was well known how fanatics intoxicated with hate and blood lust, finding themselves in powerful majorities, began their campaign of carnage by blatant murders in the open, thus sending into hiding or siege large numbers of terrified families which could not identify their attackers as either Hindus or Muslims. Others, being Parsees, Buddhists or Christians, were unsure if they would be spared by whichever attackers came upon them. In the trail of the slaughterers came those intent on plunder, knowing there were rich pickings not only from the corpses, but from the terrified families, regardless of their religion, locked in their upper rooms, hoping to save the lives of themselves and their families by leaving their material fortunes below to divert the armed looters until they disappeared with their loads of booty and peace returned.

It was confirmed as feared that Sylhet and East Bengal became part of East Pakistan, and some British companies were split between Sylhet and Assam. Much came over the wireless news on the subject of the princely states, which led to sad headshaking by some of the older planters; but it was something I was poorly informed on, and there was little hope of understanding what was happening. Some said there would certainly be trouble over Kashmir, where a majority of Muslims had always been ruled by a Hindu maharaja, yet it appeared Kashmir was to remain part of India. I tried to pick up as much as possible from the wireless, which was less lurid than what was coming in the staff's letters from Bengal, Bihar and the

Punjab. It was pleasant to find everything progressing normally on Medeloabam, and the news seemed to be the same from other estates and districts.

I was becoming more able and involved in managing my servants, who took a pride in polishing the good timber floors on my bungalow, keeping everything smart and clean, and feeding me well. I seemed to be managing happily on my salary, able to save something each month with a view to buying a mattress, bedclothes, towels etc., so that I would be able, as Foyle said one should within a year, to accommodate overnight guests. These would be company visitors of insufficient rank to stay at the manager's bungalow: accountants, engineers and such, and occasionally a catholic priest or a missionary, come to meet the Christian estate workers about once a quarter. My ambitious savings plan had gone well for the last few months, but my heart fell when Foyle said Conker was really not fit to play polo and would, with gentle exercise only, take at least six months to recover, if ever. I was lucky enough to play fairly often on borrowed mounts, but after a few weeks it became clear I would have either to give up polo, or acquire another horse. It was an irony that as the Assam Valley Light Horse was to be disbanded, we could keep our horses without paying for them. I was very fond of Conker, but to keep him and buy another horse looked difficult, more so because the allowance paid by the AVLH for horse care and maintenance was terminated. It happened therefore, when a horse came up for sale by a planter who was leaving to settle in Kenya, Foyle took me to see it: a tall, dark gelding which had been a Calcutta racehorse. It had not played polo, and needed to be trained into play gradually. It was nervous, but when I rode up and down the empty field it felt good, and when I decided to canter, touching gently with my heels, he shot into a gallop like an arrow from a bow. I had to turn him away from the lists and put plenty of pressure on the snaffle to slow him down, but thought the speed was marvellous. Foyle, who was much heavier than I, also tried him out, and although he did not try a gallop, he said it was a bonny handful, and young enough to learn about polo. The seller advised I should not take it into a game for some time, and train him well with stick and ball for a month or two. The horse was for sale at six hundred rupees. Foyle told me it was a bargain, and helped me work out how I could finance it. The sum was a little less than two months' pay, and I was just about finished with paying Nicky for rifle and camera. We were talking in a group, and to everyone's amazement, a tough and parsimonious Yorkshireman called Ted Pately said he would lend me six hundred rupees if I promised to pay him a hundred rupees monthly and no interest which, knowing how tough and tight he was with his money, Foyle said was an unbelievable benevolence.

Thus it was that I came to a decision to become a vegetarian for six months; after all, Gandhi managed extremely well on it, walking long distances at his age, and no doubt practised in the business of fasting. Dr Pal said it would be quite safe for me to make an experiment, and gave me much good advice. Fortunately there were always bananas and papayas, and I was able to buy whole wheat flour, village home-pounded rice, and plenty of various lentils and spinaches; as eggs were cheap and plentiful I kept them in my diet. With this and other small economies I was able to save at least a hundred rupees a month. My servants were not at all convinced I should subsist on vegetable food, and the Telfords' head bearer was brought to advise me against it, making a strong case for plenty of meat being necessary for the exercise of a pukka sahib's authority and admirable stamina. I thanked him and said I would remember his advice.

I decided to call my new horse Jet, as he was jet black, and very fast. When our squadron made a trial switch from Spitfires to Meteors we all had to admit jet aircraft had superior speed, and were easier to fly than the beautiful Spitfire; but before long it was proved that the Meteors had far too short a range for our needs, and we were happy to continue with our sleek and sensitive beauties as before. I hoped Jet would not turn out to fail as a polo pony. It was not long before I discovered he was indeed of what appeared to be unstable temperament, and often without warning would begin bucking and twisting, sometimes at speed, sometimes at the walk or trot. I managed to cope with this, but came off three times, about two miles or more from the stables, having to roll quickly away from his flailing rear hooves. Villagers and estate workers were terrified of what they called the *pagla* (mad) new horse. It was then I discovered none of the experienced riders, not even Foyle, would take Jet for what I called a 'test flight'. Ramjan and the other syces would never dare to ride him, and I took him in to polo one day, a month after finding he was reasonably manageable with gentle stick and ball practice. It was suggested I ride without a stick, not too close to the players, but near enough for Jet to become accustomed to the other horses, and the roared expletives of the riders. It worked for about ten minutes and then, turning quickly to canter into position when the play reversed direction, it was clear Jet heard the thunder of hooves behind us and began to gallop strongly, following his racehorse instincts. I managed to hold his head down for a bit, but when the ball bounced close alongside us and went ahead, converging with our path, Jet went berserk. Being in the line of the players pursuing the ball I tried to steer Jet away to the right, and he bucked at the gallop. He had slowed enough for two or three horses to overtake us on the left, but where the others were I had no time to see. Twice I managed to land square in the saddle, but with my rein against his neck to keep him diverging right he bucked with a nasty twist, sending me into the air off balance, and I sensed I was not going to come down square into the saddle again. There came the familiar lightning strike of cold, split-second calculation that without a parachute I was in danger of falling in the path of several horses, bunched somewhere close behind, galloping all out, and gaining fast. The simple horror of being trampled switched my brain to remember, as a small boy, seeing the Royal Scots Greys roughriders leaving the saddle at the gallop, holding the pommel, hitting the ground with feet together like a gymnast, and being thus thrown up again into the saddle. If it failed it would have been a good try, and the hooves would win. Being in trim with gymnastic agility probably gave me a wild, if desperate confidence, and I managed to hook my fingers in the side of the pommel as I came down clapping my boots together. I hit the ground so hard I thought I was being thrown in a somersault, but I landed back in the saddle, and almost whooped with joy. I had no hope of finding the stirrups, and kept my knees clamped on the saddle, with Jet's tremendous reach and rhythm taking me in a large circle away from the game. I felt almost disappointed that the game had not faltered, and the ball was still in play, back in the other direction again. For some reason Jet did not buck again, but responded to a touch of rein on his neck, and swung tightly to gallop much too fast past the tea table where the ladies flocked like startled chickens to the other end. He frightened the other horses and syces by coming to a sliding halt exactly at his tether post, rearing on his hind legs. I slid off and moved out of range of his hind feet, but he stood quivering and whickering, so I went round to his head and ran my hand down his nose, which he seemed to appreciate.

There was another time about a fortnight later, when he threw me more or less bucking on the spot, with only one other practiser on the field, before play had started. I had my leg pulled by most of the other riders, but there were still no volunteers to show me how to deal with the problems of Jet's strange behaviour. The man who sold me this horse was by this time probably halfway to Kenya, and the general opinion of the good horsemen was that there must be some history which would explain what was now seen to be a dangerous tendency. I felt cheated that only Colley had seen my Scots Grey vault, being well behind the cluster as full back, and being a dour Scot he gave the trace of a grin and said, 'Showing off a wee bit, eh! Ye'll surely get a job with a circus though.'

I tried hard with Jet, but early one September morning after several days without rain I galloped him along an earth road leading out towards a village near the river. On both sides of the roads in Assam there are borrow pits from which the earth was taken to raise the roads above flood level. Reeds and wild shrubs grew in profusion around these pits, and from a clump of shrubs on the edge of the water a marabou stork suddenly rose into the air on its immense and creaking wings. I had quite a shock, but to Jet it was clearly a terrible trauma. He skidded to a halt with hind quarters down and ears up, then gave vent to a frenzied spasm of bucking, throwing me off after about fifteen seconds. He seemed mad with fear, and I managed to escape his flailing hooves by rolling down, almost into the pit, fearing I had damaged my knee. I had to lie there until he turned and galloped back to Medeloabam. I followed limping, with one boot filled with water, feeling beaten. All along the way back people were saying one day the black horse would kill me; they had all had to run and take the children away from the track, and said it was no good, sahib, no good.

That afternoon I stood with Foyle discussing Jet as we stroked his neck, felt his legs, looked at his teeth, and shook our heads. It was bright sunshine, and Foyle and I kept waving our hands to keep the large horse flies off his head. Foyle suddenly said 'Look!' and with his hand close to the right eye he flicked finger and thumb, and Jet blinked. He did the same to the left eye, and there was no reaction. Foyle said perhaps the eye had been damaged, and it had led to the eye becoming blind if the sun was bright. We eventually managed to bring the local vet, who examined the eye, and confirmed it was exactly what Foyle had guessed. That was the end of Jet, and it hurt, less from a financial point of view than from the loss of a horse which could move beautifully and fast, with a gentle temperament and a rare friendliness. We wondered how it had happened but was never found out. Foyle offered to put Jet down for me, but I thanked him and said I would take him to a vast area of scrub near the river where I had seen vultures frequently on tiger kills, and put him to sleep as he reached down for a small bag of oats. It was a long walk back in the heat, and when I had taken a cup of tea I took Conker for his long walk exercise, approaching near enough to see the vultures descending into the eupatorium scrub, half a mile away. In late September we had news that Telford was on his way from Britain to Assam with a new Auster aircraft, accompanied by a professional pilot. In mid-October they arrived in Assam.

Just as the fifteenth of June was widely accepted as the arrival of the monsoon in Upper Assam, the fifteenth of October was accepted as the arrival of the cold weather. By the beginning of September everyone in Assam had reached the stage where life was threatening to become intolerable. The heat and humidity were slowly degrading the way of life, shortening peoples' tempers, and spoiling every kind of enjoyment. One slept always with brief cotton shorts, and a flap of sheet protecting the belly. Many used fans to keep them cool; under a thin sheet it worked for most, but for me the fans led to aches and pains and feelings of frustration instead of peaceful sleep. Bedclothes smelt mouldy, and felt damp. Wardrobes smelt mouldy, and leather shoes would grow a kind of penicillin within a week of polishing. The psychological effects of being sweaty, pale except for red noses and elbow joints, and crowned with lank, wet hair, were remarkable. It was the time for people to hand in resignations; for squalid rows between colleagues; for labour and staff quarrels; for breakdowns of generating engines and factory machinery, with leaf still growing almost belligerently to the point where one would curse the whole confounded idea of trying to make a living out of so awkward a crop; and sick lists were long, people were tired, and life had no lustre. The great steamy air mass still came from somewhere in Polynesia and Australia, travelling west to the Indian Ocean, where the rotation of the earth swung it northwards across the equator and sent it from the south-west across eastern India up to Assam. There came the night when the heat and the sweat delayed sleep until late, but somewhere around three in the morning one reached myopically for the whole sheet to cover a body now dry and feeling a distinct chill. Before dawn came the call of domestic cocks as well as the slightly more shrill and distant calls of the wild jungle cocks. Riding out towards the river at dawn I could feel a distinct, fresh breeze in my face, and see a beautiful clear sky, with the distant Himalayas bright cobalt blue in the rising sun. The golden sunshine cast blue shadows; dogs and cattle moved into the sun; flocks of white egrets flew down the banks of the Brahmaputra in gleaming white echelons and vee formations; mynahs of several kinds bounced and swarmed around houses and cattle, screeching with busy delight. Returning to the estate I greeted the pluckers with cane baskets on their heads, smiling and laughing, some with a scarlet hibiscus in their hair. It was a world changed overnight with such dramatic suddenness in light and sound that one enjoyed a kind of religious thrill, a rebirth of spirit. People sang; the roads and paths dried; the vast stretches of tea lost the vivid, raw green, and within a week became a pastel shade of lighter colour, reflecting kindlier light on the faces of us all; and the sun began again to bronze the skins of the palefaces, and the darker skins of the women and children, mahogany, honey and caramel, lost the sweaty shine and became like peach. I found it was cold enough to wear a sweater until after breakfast, when I would change into shorts. The estate workers began wearing blankets when they went to work, discarding them when the sun and the exertions of work warmed them enough. Foyle told me temperatures seldom went below 42° Fahrenheit, but the mists which were now forming overnight would become thicker, and take longer to clear in the mornings, when it was often colder after sunrise as the sun evaporated the top of the mist, which tended to persist until about nine-thirty. On the North Bank it was colder, as there was always a cold breeze coming down from the mountains, beginning after sunset and stopping only when the mountains were heated by the sun. The miracle of the climate change in October was straight away to my mind the reason even the worst British immigrants never seemed to take the final step of resignation. It was the nearest thing to a magic spell one could imagine.

George Fraser came to tell us that part of the area where old tea had been uprooted for replanting with new young tea, was to be converted as an airstrip for Telford. He had managed to convince the Home Board, who gave instructions to the Calcutta office for the strip to be allowed for the purpose of an experiment in using an aeroplane to improve the company's

205

communications in Assam, where there were no regular air services, and no really adequate ambulance services to bring serious cases to the company's central hospitals. 'Did you know all about this, MacStorm?' I said I had suggested months ago such an air service might be feasible and desirable, but had no idea it was to be taken up officially. George said he thought it was a splendid idea, but couldn't understand why Telford hadn't spoken with him on the subject. 'He does play his cards very close to his chest, you know. No idea of going through the chain of command, either. Had you no idea of what he was thinking, MacStorm?' to which I could but say it was only when Fraser himself had told me Telford was learning to fly that I thought my notes on the possibility of a company air scheme had begun to move him at least to learn to fly. George then produced a letter from which he read to me that he should ask if I would be willing to fly the aeroplane Telford was bringing out, in order to evaluate the possibility of developing a company scheme in due course. He quoted duties such as flying visiting directors around the Assam estates, making weekly visits to the North Bank to collect serious medical cases, and bringing senior planters to the South Bank for important conferences etc. I asked if it would be possible for me to see the intended organisation of the air scheme before I made up my mind. I said I would be very happy to fly at any time, but would not be able, even as an officer on the reserve, to fly for hire or reward. George said the whole thing was bound to be experimental initially, but he would take it that I would be prepared to help. 'Constable tells me you are an excellent pilot, MacStorm. Coming from such a hypercritical man who knows something about flying that means a lot to me.' We all drove over to the uprooted area, and I realised how Telford must have been thinking far ahead when he had one side of the thirty-acre rectangle, running along the side of the main estate road not far from the centre, levelled and cambered slightly. The huge albizzia lebbek tree which had stood in a patch of fallow twenty-five yards from the strip, a magnificent tree, had been uprooted and felled by Telford's own orders and under his own supervision, oblivious to my pleas to let it remain. Now it was clear he had as long ago as that been carrying out his plans under another programme, perhaps covertly and in such a way that failure to win permission would simply mean the replanting programme would go ahead as normal. I told Fraser and Foyle there were other shade trees at the other end which would have to be uprooted, and others progressively pollarded to ensure safe approach and landing paths, and I was told to organise for this to be done.

In the days that followed I became enthusiastic at the prospect of an aeroplane taking up residence at Medeloabam, and spent time trying to work out where to make a hangar for its protection. Supervising the work on the reduction of trees on the approaches to the strip, I found some of the men apparently taking a long time to remove what turned out to be a smaller and younger lebbek tree. They told me it was very tough wood, hard to cut, and would have to be uprooted whole. I thought they were somehow going slow on their chopping, and asked for an axe. I told them to stand back, and took up my position over one of the buttressed roots which had been cut through the pale outer wood to the dark red heartwood. I was determined to demonstrate my prowess to the full, and raising the axe well above my head, brought it down with all my strength upon the notched root. As I hit, it seemed there was something like a severe electric shock to my hands and forearms, and the axe flew out of my hands, humming like a swarm of hornets as it spun in an arc towards a cluster of men drinking their tea on the road. They scattered with whoops of feigned panic, with all the others at their various trees in the tea laughing heartily at my air of astonishment. I laughed once I was sure no-one was hurt, and borrowing a sharp *dao* (bushknife) found by careful strokes just how tough that red heartwood really was. Once the landing strip was in my opinion fit to be used, with Foyle's permission I asked Constable if we could try it out with his Piper Cub, but he was quite emphatic in declining. 'You don't really know Telford yet. I'll wait to be invited. He'll arrive before long. The best thing you can do is to load a couple of lorries with wet sand, and run them up and down the strip leaving nothing untracked by the wheels. You'll soon see if there's any need for filling in any depressions, but you'll need to do it quickly, and bring good, friable sub-soil to be rolled level as soon as possible.'

Eventually a telegram was brought over by Fraser, giving us a date on which to expect the Auster at Mohunbari, the wartime tarmac landing field once used by the Air Force. Just before the end of October they flew over Medeloabam one afternoon, and went on to land at Mohunbari. We drove with speed to greet and congratulate them: Telford on having taken his licence, and both of them on their long flight from England. We brought them to Medeloabam, where Telford and the professional pilot inspected the strip. Captain Norton thought the length at a hundred and fifty yards was rather short for Telford, who looked at me with his piercing stare and asked what I thought. I said I had done a few trips in Austers during the War, but I wouldn't give an opinion without doing a few landings myself. Norton was not ex-air force, but had plenty of experience in light civil flying. It was decided he and I would be driven to Mohunbari next day, and we would fly the Auster to Medeloabam, where I would do a few landings. Norton said, after my first landing, that he hoped I would not let Telford follow my style of low circuits and Spitfire-style curving approaches, and taking his point I did the next two landings flying school-style. Having flown the Piper Cub so much on rather short landing spaces, I had acquired the habit of touching down within about ten yards of the beginning of the strip, and in the Auster, which had landing flaps, we were able to turn without brakes well within a hundred yards. Norton was impeccably careful, and said he would fulfil his promise to instruct Telford until he was confident he would be able to cope safely. When Telford spoke to us after my landings he said he was delighted to see there was plenty of room, and Norton repeated what he had said to me, and I backed his words. At tea Telford made a sketch which he gave to me, showing an extension of twenty-five yards into the fallow at the westerly end, which he wanted me to start next morning. Foyle said he hoped too many men wouldn't be required, as the leaf was roaring away, and we needed every man jack on plucking. Telford said I should put twenty of our permanent men on, and call in another twenty villagers to help.

Norton stayed another two weeks. Before he left he had a quiet talk with me, saying he hoped I would be in a position to help Telford to develop his flying skills, and I said I would be very happy to do so. Within a week of Telford's arrival the Foyles left for Panitola, where they were to live in a senior assistant's bungalow at Panitola, where he was to work alongside Nicky MacFortune. Foyle and I were taken aback by the criticisms of Telford on the state of affairs he found on his fief. I found it insensitive and inconsiderate the way he criticised Foyle in front of me, and twice I was called back when I felt it was correct for me to withdraw: once when Telford said he was furious to find from the staff and the *sirdars* that Foyle had been forcing people to pluck smaller leaf, which was something he had warned should not be done. Foyle pointed out the crop was well up on the previous year, and the tea liquors seem to have earned good reports, but this seemed to anger Telford. There were many criticisms, and I was accustomed to accept such from a senior officer, but I sensed there was some deliberate aim to denigrate, and was disappointed to hear no approval for anything we had done. It was sad to have faced a most unexpected accusation that Foyle and I had run down the maize and paddy grown on the estate for horse fodder. Foyle said we had the impression that we were to use it, and we bought the extra bran and other fodder to replace what we had used of that. Afterwards Foyle said he found it strange that estate-produced fodder was the property of Telford alone, despite what he had led us to believe before he left; but Foyle said one had to swallow these things, because to argue back could mean an adverse report, and delayed promotion. This led me to speak to Telford, frankly but politely, after Foyle had left, explaining we had understood from what he told us before he left that we were to do what we had done on his recommendation. I said it was not reckoned previously that I would have to buy a second horse, and I would pay him for that extravagance; but I assured him that Foyle and I respected his rank and position completely, and would not have dreamed of abusing the fodder arrangements in the way he accused us. To my amazement he said he was not worried about payments for anything; he simply could not stand sloppiness, fuzzy organisation, lack of positive control. 'You ex-service officers, I know you, I met plenty of you in the War. The government paid you all, provided your food, your transport, your aeroplanes, your supplies; but there was no discipline, no real discipline! You knew whom to salute, and when to salute, but you didn't know what you ought to have been doing. I run this place, these people, with positive control. I am responsible for making this place pay, and I won't let anyone get in my way. You'd better understand that.' He was staring with his leopard eyes, and they were watering with the intensity of his passion. I said as gently as I could that he seemed to believe in fear as an instrument. I told him I wanted to do well at this job, if it lasted, but my developed instinct to fear was the same as any free, wild animal: to fight bare-fanged against it. He looked at the horses in the stable for a while.

'As I understand it, they let you buy a pony which was blind in one eye. This is the sort of thing I mean. If I had been there it wouldn't have happened. They were all fuzzed with you being bucked off, weren't they?'

We seemed to get on well after that, but I began to tire of his repeated assertions of remembering exactly what he had told me he wanted me to do, when discovering I had either forgotten or deliberately ignored. 'You must trust me,' he would say, time after time, 'I'm always right, and people don't like it.' Early in November Captain Norton left for Calcutta, to return to England. About the same time the person mentioned by George Fraser as B.P. Kentwell arrived at Hiloibhanga by road from Calcutta, and George called a meeting of his senior managers, including Telford. I had found it very odd, and so had Foyle, not only that Telford had no questions on what had happened over Independence in Assam, or at Medeloabam in particular, but told us he had heard all about it. This provoked Foyle to say to me he would have been very curious to know how he would have dealt with the situation had he been here, and I wondered.

I had been briefed on clearing an area between Telford's bungalow and the new airstrip, and there to build a hangar, mainly from bamboos with iron pillars and truss at the front, and when Telford came to see progress he told me about the man who was generally known by the British planters as 'BP'. He had been in the Indian Civil Service since leaving the Navy after the First World War, and had become a junior magistrate, living with his young wife mostly in Bengal, where he had achieved brilliant ability to speak and write Bengali. In the 1930s he worked in an area where there was an outbreak of active resistance to British rule. Most of the trouble was controlled by police and army, except for several assassinations, publicly committed by young Bengalis prepared to die by hanging for their part in the fight against foreign occupation. In BP's area, the senior magistrate was shot whilst playing in a football match, watched by hundreds of local people. His successor was shot whilst refereeing a football match some weeks later. The third senior magistrate was shot by a girl student in her teens who, with another girl presented a petition to the magistrate on his verandah steps. He had been having breakfast with his wife and children on the verandah, and came to the steps to take and read the petition.

The girl had a revolver under the petition, and having been taught how to aim it, shot the magistrate, who fell dead. The girl was imprisoned for life. The ICS found it extremely difficult to deal with the filling of the vacancy, but when BP volunteered to fill the post if granted appropriate promotion, they found it a welcome solution to their problem. On his first day in the new position BP walked around the local bazaar, speaking with the people. Like the Britishers, the local people thought BP was amazingly brave or rather mad; but when his colleagues expressed admiration for his fearlessness, he told them he was indeed afraid, but he needed the money, because his wife was expecting their first child. 'When you see him,' said Telford, 'you will wonder at this story even more. He is small, intense, and he is a wonderful speaker. He was once a British member of the Legislative Assembly, on which many Indians also served, and he made a speech which horrified his British colleagues by its trenchant criticism of what the Indians on this occasion wanted to be done. At the end of his speech his countrymen were astonished to see the Indian members queuing up to shake his hand, congratulating him for making such a wise speech.' BP was the man who people said had been discussing the future of British commercial interests in India, particularly the tea industry, and Telford said he hoped for great things from him that evening.

Next morning when I arrived at the stable at about five-thirty, a servant from Telford's bungalow handed me a note which said, 'I want to talk to you before you disappear on your lame Conker.' When I climbed the verandah steps he was sitting before a trolley laden with tea things, and he bade me sit and take tea with him. He came straight to the point. He said George had asked if MacStorm could fly B.P. Kentwell to selected planters' clubs in Assam where he wanted to speak to every single British planter about what was going to happen to the tea industry. Telford said he had agreed straight away, and hoped I would find it an interesting diversion. When I indicated keen pleasure he produced some large maps, which he told me he had purchased in Kingsway, London, on someone's advice. They were copies of military maps of Assam, and with the one most suitable he had marked destinations and tracks to the various clubs required. He said it was thought best to return to Mohunbari each afternoon. There would be his speech and questions from about eleven-thirty, lunch, and then return. It would probably last a week all told. I studied the maps closely, noted the scale, and said I would like to take the one I needed to study more closely the general topography. Telford handed it to me, asking for care in handling it. I was fascinated to note that north of Bogahilonia and other estates which were at the frilled edge of the Himalayan skirts, there were considerable white patches, in which the word 'unsurveyed' was printed, and I asked

Telford about them. He said there had been very little survey of the whole area. People had seen birds which had still not been identified, langurs, strange animals, unidentified sounds: it was a fascinating wilderness. I told him by January I understood I would have two weeks annual leave, and would like nothing better than to trek for that time on the North Bank, if possible. He said he would see.

Two days later he swung the propeller of the Auster, and I took off with full tank to pick up BP at Mohunbari. He had thought I would not be keen to take off, even at nine-fifteen, with visibility only about 150 yards, but I showed him the mist was not very deep as we could see the blue sky overhead. Mohunbari being unused by other aircraft meant I could locate the runway from about 800 feet, and fly a pattern which would bring me down onto the long and broad tarmac strip with plenty of room to spare. This would help us to be airborne without delay in reaching Tezpur, some 264 miles down on the north bank of the Brahmaputra. When I landed as planned, there was no sign of a vehicle on the control tower apron, and so I switched off the engine, took the wheel chocks from the rear seat floor and kicked them gently against the wheels. It was cold, even in sweater and slacks, and I began exercising to warm myself up, amused that it was such a short while since I had been bathed in sweat round the clock. Twenty minutes later Fraser's Riley sports saloon arrived. George introduced me to the slight, small figure of B.P. Kentwell, whose sparkling grey-blue eyes and firm, warm handshake impressed me.

'I'm very lucky to be meeting you, and this aeroplane. It is going to make my task so much easier, so much quicker, giving me more time for other things which are coming to the boil. You must have landed when the mist was rather thick; was it quite safe?' I told him what I had explained to Telford, and said there would be no mist down at Tezpur, where the dry katabatic winds came down from the cold mountains and kept it clear. BP frowned at me, with finger on the side of his nose, then smiled and said, 'Anabatic winds will soon begin and blow up the mountain slopes as the sun heats them. Right!' I complimented him on this demonstration either of a long memory, or an interest in meteorology. He nodded and turned to Fraser. 'I think we should take off then. I look forward to seeing you this afternoon at . . .' he looked at me, and not being sure of when it would be I said I would fly over Hiloibhanga at about 300 feet before landing at

212

Mohunbari. I helped him into the right-hand seat and fixed his safety belt comfortably. Respecting his standing as a first war aviator, I went to the other side, and called out the prestart check: brakes on, petrol on, switches off, throttle set, then switched on the ignition, and swung the prop. On the second swing she started sweetly. I took the chocks away, put them in the back, and strapped myself in. There was no radio, and no control tower contact. The visibility was now about 500 yards, and I taxied down to the western end of the runway, spoke out the crosswind check, lined up and opened the throttle. Within a few minutes we left the mist and climbed on course in the brilliant sunshine, with the sharp cobalt ridges of the Himalayas to our north above the gilded forested hills, rising steeply below them. We climbed across the Brahmaputra, marvelling at the way the monsoon water level was falling, leaving the great islands of graven ivory, carved in beautiful curves and sweeps by the greenish blue snow waters coming from the snows above the Tsang Po, flowing from west to east through the tortuous chasms of Tibetan ranges for many miles before turning south as the Dihang, then west into the great Assam Valley, becoming the Brahmaputra for the next 800 miles to Calcutta, on its way to the Indian Ocean. We map-read our west-south-westerly course along the North Bank, crossing the many rivers coming out of Tibet now like lambs, diverging into several sinuous courses which rejoined and diverged again between slim islands of forest, boulders, and pale sands, with white plumes in rapids and tailing huge dark boulders. It was a great contrast with the turbid and violent floods carrying the vast volume of water coming from the 200 inches or more (it had never been properly measured) of monsoon rain like a violent Noah's flood.

When we were at 3,000 feet the brilliant snow ranges of the high Himalayas stretched north and westwards in breathtaking beauty. It was cold, and we decided to fly lower for comfort. I pointed out the altimeter, the airspeed indicator, the directional gyro and the compass, and invited him to fly, which he did with obvious pleasure, taking little time to become accustomed to the feel of a modern light aeroplane. We arrived at the Tezpur club polo ground to see many men standing beside the clubhouse in the warm sun. There was little wind, and after a smooth landing taxied to where I saw a man beckoning with both hands raised; clearly someone who knew about aircraft.

Thus began a week which was one of the most significant learning periods of my life. At Tezpur the speech was begun without delay, and although I was to hear basically the same speech many times at other places, all made without notes, I was each time captivated by this man who, without any trace of the histrionic oratory of those like George Fraser, gripped the closest attention of all his listeners without pause or digression. The first time was for me the most memorable: be began by saying that there was much detail still to be worked out for many of the things which had been agreed upon in principle; but he was able to say the Indian government had made it clear they wanted the Indian tea industry in south India, Bengal Dooars, Darjeeling and Assam to carry on earning money, and to invest in expansion and improvement of estates and factories, providing work for as many people as were needed to support it. 'Yes, yes,' we all thought, 'but what about us?' He went on to say that the tax revenue from tea was vitally important to India, and Nehru and Vallabhai Patel wanted nothing to disturb or distort the tea industry's efforts for the country in which the tea was produced. Then it came, loud and clear: the Indian government hopes the British companies will honour what can only be called a gentlemen's agreement to carry on as they now do; but realising tea planters require years of experience in order to excel at their work, they would leave it to the tea companies to recruit suitable young Indians so that when the experienced British planters retired at the usual age of fifty-five, there would be experienced Indian managers to carry on with the work. It was as if BP had waved a magic wand over the gathering. There was a soft sighing, and an almost palpable feeling that a dark net had been lifted from us, something like waking from a miserable dream. Someone began to clap, and BP held up his hand, continuing to talk, quoting statistics of the British government's financial support for the industry, and the need for planters to regard development and expansion as their best security for staying in the career they loved. He went on to suggest it was worth thinking of the splendid way the Indians of the Indian Army had fought with the British and Commonwealth forces during the recent war, and to regard it as showing appreciation for such support by giving one's best in the far less lethal business of producing the excellent beverage which without a doubt also helped us to win the War, and would without a doubt help India to deal with the problems of financing its future. His speeches were longer than I have indicated by these few points, remembered from forty-eight years ago. His delivery was almost hypnotic, clearly enunciated, and in tones which were strong, even incisive, but courteous and totally credible. He stifled the applause and began asking for questions, of which there were few. The senior planter made a speech of thanks and congratulations, and invited everyone to have beer and lunch without delay, as BP had to fly back to Dibrugarh before sunset. 'And please, gentlemen, no drinks for the pilot!'

Throughout these few days BP had time to talk to me, elaborating on what lay behind his talks. One of the things he said was any young man wanting to enjoy a career in Assam tea should without delay begin to learn, not only to speak, but to read and write Assamese. He was impressed to learn of my efforts, and I assured him I would accelerate progress with even greater enthusiasm than before. He said the British government had agreed to send a team of experts to help India to organise trade unions, and labour legislation. He had already advised the Indian Tea Association to draft employment and disciplinary procedures of its own, which the Indian government would surely appreciate if they found it had been well done. He made the point that trade unions would only become powerful if bad employers gave them grounds for just criticism; this was a deeply seeded principle which grew in my own personal working philosophy in the years to come.

When I arrived back at Medeloabam early, Telford was always at the end of the strip, and insisted on getting in for an hour or so of practice. I began to show him curved approaches, not at all steep, but useful for landing on short strips or surfaces. One could shorten or lengthen the radius of the turn in order to arrive accurately, but it was clear he would have to practise the art of being able to watch the strip and the airspeed indicator in the continuous turn without power. We agreed if he did not touch down by the white bar he would immediately open throttle and go round again, without thinking of the extra fuel it took. One afternoon we flew low over his beloved fishing camp, but I refused to try a landing, as there had been high floods during the monsoon, and we would have to inspect it on foot first. I told him the Auster was not only heavier than the Piper Cub, but the Piper Cub had larger tyres, less likely to sink into sand or mud, and he took the point. He had left his wife to come back by sea, and she was due to arrive soon with their son and two daughters. The daughters were keen on riding, and at tea after flying one day he said Conker was ideal for his younger daughter, aged thirteen. He said he would swap Conker, who would never play polo again in his opinion, for Rani, an Australian Waler mare which could play well. I was very grateful for this deal, as I felt badly about turning up at polo hoping for the loan of a pony, and once I had established some mutual understanding with Rani I felt on top of the world.

Pruning operations began in November, and I missed out on the start because of my interlude of flying BP about. I asked Telford for some detailed lessons on the various kinds of pruning. He told me to draw a set of the four sizes of knife from the stores, have them well sharpened, and then begin slowly to follow what I saw in the field, asking staff and *sirdars* for hints. It was difficult to have the knives sharpened to the degree I wanted, but I persisted, and enjoyed trying to swing and cut, except for the fact that my hands being soft from the tender handling of aircraft controls led to the forming of large blisters. The pruning men said that always happened, but one had to carry on as if one depended, as they did, on earning their food from the pruning. It was not as easy as it sounded, and when I went to seek relief from the pain of torn blisters, Dr Pal was horrified, and told me I must wear bandages until they had healed, and then only do a little each day until the hands hardened. Telford told me there was little hope of a European being able to compete with Indian peasants, whose hands were like rhino skin, and said I shouldn't try. Because of that I became determined I would by sheer practice and perseverance harden my hands to the point when I would be able to complete a man's task of slashing or medium prune. It was not to be easy: slashing was like trimming a hedge which had been allowed to grow more than a foot, about 720 feet long and four feet wide. Medium prune tasks depended on the thickness of the branches low in the frame. If they were about an inch thick the task would be thirty-two bushes, to be cut with a sharp, thick, hooked knife, the blade being nine inches long. It was essential that all pruning was to be cut as nearly level as possible. The chopping was physically hard, and the establishment of a level surface, all bushes the same height, was not only hard work but difficult to align. I became obsessed with the latter, and sometimes cycled back to the area being pruned after tea to try different methods of swinging the knife, and eyeing the place to cut. It took a long time to make any progress. The remedies for blistered hands recommended by some of the older women were ghastly, leading me to believe they were pulling my leg.

Chapter XII

The visit of BP to Assam brought about a remarkable change in the attitudes of the planting community of the area where I lived. People said there was still no real certainty they would be able or to permitted to complete their careers, but the fact that the new India wanted them to carry on was enough to encourage them to do so. Many said, however, it would not be easy; as time went on we would soon find out what the difficulties would be: already congress party officials had made their visits, and with the management chose whom the managers had classified as reliable and intelligent workers and staff members as their union committees, told them they would be receiving copies of labour laws and regulations, and told them they would receive visits from district union officials who would take up their complaints with the management; and union meetings for the workers would be organised which all workers could attend etc. etc. I have to say Telford was firm but polite in requesting the union headquarters to consider his belief that managers should be allowed to deal with complaints from their workers, and only when the workers were unsatisfied with the manager's settlement would they take their grievance to the district headquarters through their own estate representatives. The union official was an Assamese of obvious education, who made a note of what Telford had suggested, saying he understood it well, but it was essential for the Congress party to establish confidence amongst the estate workers, because other parties were also beginning to emerge who would spend their time trying to influence the workers to follow their brand of politics, which the British planters would certainly not welcome. We were to find out soon what he had meant. As he was about to leave Telford invited him to come round to see the hospital, the staff quarters and the new labourers' houses he had been building over

217

the past six years, but Sri Debeswar Saikia said he needed to move on, as there was so much to do, and he would gladly come later, when he would have more time. He shook hands with us, saying he had heard Medeloabam was one of the better estates, with a hospital and good water supply. The Assamese third clerk told him as he was about to leave in a very battered ex-army jeep, that I could speak Assamese, and he asked me in Assamese how long I had been in Assam. Fortunately his diction was excellent: I was able to understand, and to enunciate 'nearly ten months', upon which he complimented me, and said he would like to speak with me on his next visit.

There were fair numbers of planters who despite the prospect of continuing decided to leave. They were mostly those who were more than halfway through their careers, and I heard them in the club say it would not be possible to make a go of it once the 'babus' destroyed the respect of the workers for the 'sahibs'. They held it would not be possible to sack people for corruption, as the unions would without doubt grow fat from the bribes the corrupt would give them to protect their rackets. They quoted rumours of the unions making a signal demonstration for wages to be raised, and said the industry would be run into the ground within a few years. They went to places like Kenya, Tanganyika and South Africa. Some, with Australian and New Zealand wives, went to their wive's homelands, doubtful of getting of job. It took time for those of us who stayed to be rid of the idea it would slowly become intolerable when the novelty wore off. Like so much in life, like lung cancer from smoking, 'if it happens gradually, its not happening to me', it was something to be filed away in the non-urgent files on survival. Many of the changes which actually took place, had they been collected and put down in some sage's book of prognostication to be read by damfools and other planters, would very likely have led to a prompt decision to cut adrift, to seek a new livelihood.

Telford was curious about my progress with the various languages, especially Assamese. 'You seem to be a very good mimic,' he said. 'I've heard you are learning Munda and Koya tongues, as well as Assamese. I think I should tell you one of the most disruptive problems in dealing with Indians of any kind is jealousy. One learns never to show favouritism for any person or any caste, tribe, gotra, clan, province or whatever. They all want to be favourites, and if you keep them guessing they keep trying to earn your favour. It's probably better not to develop your proficiency in only three or four languages, you know. There must be at least a dozen different languages on this estate alone, and if you spend your time learning all of them you won't be much good at learning all the things you need to know about tea, and the people who work for us. I speak a little Assamese, enough to speak with the villagers, Gerella, contractors, but I don't use it with the staff. It shows already that our Bengali office staff are just a little disapproving about your Assamese. Don't speak anything but English to the office staff. They actually prefer English.' Instinct stopped me from telling him of BP's advice on the subject; but I saw his point about using English in the office.

The weather continued to be wonderful, far better than it would be by the end of January. Gerella came to see Telford, and I spoke with him in Telford's office. He told us the season for deer had opened, and he had delivered a haunch of venison to Telford's bungalow. He said I should go down to the forest reserve, where the sambar would often come out on to the peninsulas now forming as the Brahamputra's level dropped, where they could drink just after sunset. If one hid in the driftwood well down the river, where tracks would show the best place to hide, there was a good chance of dropping a deer; there were many, many sambar now. Telford looked slightly stern, and told me he would take me into the forest office in town on Wednesday, where I would ask for a royalty to the forest department if I shot a sambar, or a barking deer (muntjac), but it was as well to keep on the right side of the foresters. I had his permission to spend Friday and Saturday nights down the river, but as he was not going to be at home he could not offer me a lift over the very little used track for six or more miles down to the reserve, so he suggested I should see if I could make another arrangement. Eventually I managed to hit on something I had been wanting to do. The Miri villagers, belonging to a tribe of ruggedly independent and clannish people who Telford said were related to tribes living in the mountains of the North Bank – Sino-Tibetans who spoke a tonal language reminiscent of Chinese – they always chose to live as far away from other people as possible. They were expert fishermen, good hunters, and skilful watermen in their well-formed dugout canoes. They spoke some Assamese, and I rode a long way one afternoon after work, which finished in the cold season about two-thirty to three, to a small Miri village where I knew there were small, slender boats of about fourteen feet, which I had seen them ply with a single slim oar which in the shallows was used as a punt pole. I managed to arrange for some practice the following day, and they said they would lend me the dugout for the coming weekend, refusing payment, but if I managed to shoot a deer they would gladly accept a haunch.

I borrowed a lorry tarpaulin from the factory, took a hurricane lamp, matches, a kettle, tea leaf, powdered milk mixed with sugar, some wholemeal flour, a tin of cheese, my Mauser rifle, and a sharp kukri which Nicky had given me from his big collection. Maneklal, Nunoo, and Ramlal, one of my gardeners, helped to carry all this to the Miri village, and displayed concern at my intention to go alone in a Miri dugout. The Miris helped me to place the load well aft, giving me plenty of room to stand and steer. They warned me coming back would be much more difficult than going downriver with the current, and I should not go too far down. I had warm slacks and a sweater, with a horse blanket for the nights. Seeing my rifle one of the older Miris, who never spoke a word, signed I should tie a 24-foot length of fishing line round the neck of the rifle butt, and tie the other end to a piece of bamboo tube enclosing an air compartment. If the rifle fell overboard the bamboo float would be very useful, but I began to wonder if my first dugout expedition of a few miles was going to be more hazardous than I had imagined. I made good progress, and as the first part of the trip was parallel to a gentle sandy beach, I practised using the oar as a pole, and seemed to find it fairly easy. After a mile or so I reached the forest, where the giant trees grew right up to the river bank which was mostly vertical, rising about eight feet above the water. The current was strong, and I decided to turn so as to test my propulsion against the current in the homeward direction. I found I was able to make slow headway, but became sure I would have to find soon one of the peninsulas Gerella had mentioned. Taking an optimistic view, I thought, with the carcass of a large deer it was going to take a long time to make my way back. As I floated along I saw how the bank curved gradually to the north. The current was cutting the bank at water level, and there were occasional plops as a large dollop dropped into the water. I could see beyond the headland something which could be the point of a peninsula, and thought all was going to work out well. With about 200 yards to go to the headland, I heard a great splash behind, and turned to see a tall, slender tree had collapsed, crown first, into the river, its riverside roots having been eroded away. It remained attached to the bank, and the trunk, pushed by the current at an angle downstream, presented an ominous obstacle for an inexperienced dugout traveller. The speed of the current where the trunk met the water was shown by a high 'bow wave', telling me that unless I could manage to hack through the thick branches blocking the course along the bank, I was going to have a big problem. I rounded the headland to find what Gerella had described, and with great relief steered into the shallows where the current was hardly noticeable, finding a bay where there was a lot of huge driftwood, some of it coniferous above 5,000 feet. I beached the dugout and pulled it well clear of the water, surprised at its weight. It was about four-thirty, and I hurriedly rigged the tarpaulin, camouflaged it on the forest side, lit a small fire, and made tea. It was beginning to be cool, and I put on a green 'pig's bristle' sweater. Sitting on a gnarled log of driftwood which gleamed in the westering sun, stripped of its bark and polished by the Himalayan torrents, I savoured the wild solitude as I sipped the tea.

A greenshank swooped and sped across the gilded sand, putting up several sandpipers with its soprano peals of alarm as it saw me. I heard what I thought must be a barking deer, deep inside the great wall of forest. I saw an undulating formation of eight hornbills silhouetted against the sky over the huge trees, the first I had seen since Africa. Flying over the forest with tails to the sun and moving up the river, were continuous echelons and vee formations of white egrets, some over the peninsula, but mostly on a track taking them over the near edge of the forest, clearing the trees by fifty to a hundred feet. Five teal shot past me at incredible speed, making me spill tea down my chin as they took evasive action to swerve and dive behind the driftwood. As the sun touched the distant horizon downriver, I decided not to change into slacks, but stay in jungle green shorts and dark brown plimsolls, a dress recommended by Gerella, who said the sound of long trouserlegs brushing against each other, and hard shoes squeaking was easily picked up by any wild quarry. I found three long branches of driftwood about four inches in diameter, and set their ends in the glowing embers of my fire, boy scout style, so that they would be glowing still when I returned, making it easy to build a good campfire. I took my loaded rifle and a kukri, where I could see three places where the bank had collapsed in a kind of vee, the only places where men or animals could reach the peninsula from the forest. There were plenty of tracks of all sorts of creatures, including tiger and Himalayan bear, wild pig, barking deer, monkeys, and some small tracks I couldn't recognise.

By the time the sun set I had placed myself up on the bank about fifty yards from the middle path, which seemed to be the most used, leading to the closest water. The twilight doesn't last long in those latitudes, and when I saw a young sambar hind plunge down the cleft about 200 yards away to the north-east, I cursed my luck. Within seconds of her appearance I heard the call of a sambar stag, and saw the hind put her head down, and with curious jerky motions of her legs climb slowly back up the way she had come. Then I realised the dark stump past which the hind disappeared was in fact the head and shoulders of a large stag, motionless as the hind passed him, but even in the gloaming I was sure he was gazing not in my direction, but upstream. He disappeared, and I decided to try a fast but quiet walk along the bank, within sight of the open peninsula. I reached the spot near where I had last seen him, sweating with exertion and excitement, but could see no sign of any living thing. Moving slowly on the forest floor to where the tracks diverged from the cleft in the bank, I chose to follow the most used one. I moved quietly for about ten yards, still able to see in patches of dim light from the afterglow penetrating the small gaps in the forest roof. I heard a branch swish, and froze. There was a sudden crash and a thump, and I saw movement in the undergrowth ahead, heard the soft swish through low branches, then another thump. It seemed clearer beyond the curtain of leaves, and I took time to move in a small arc, finding a position to see into the tiny area of dim light. He was there, motionless and staring at me. I raised the rifle and fired into the base of his neck. He fell heavily, kicked spasmodically with his hind legs, and then lay still. Darkness was falling fast. With the kukri I managed to take out a lobe of his liver, an atavistic urge having thrust my pious and parsimonious vegetarian diet suddenly into the background. I decided some grilled liver with a large chupatti would make a marvellous supper; but whichever gods had favoured me as an eater of fruit and grains, they must have decided at that point to abandon me. In the time taken to extract the liver it had become dark.

I could not have been more than twenty yards from the river bank where I had entered. In the gloom where the stag lay I could not be sure which way I entered the small clearing, and almost having to feel my way to a likely exit, I realised I had earlier found it by moving in an arc. I struggled to remember roughly how many degrees I had turned after leaving the vague track I had chosen. I waited, trying to form a calm plan of action. Looking up I saw but the slightest glint of a star through the black canopy. Remembering advice on wandering the hills in Scotland, that when the mist fell, or it became dark, stay where you are, keep warm, but don't try to move when you can't see where you go. I decided to try a reverse arc out of the clearing, and to keep turning until I could feel the vague track. I did this, and decided to measure twenty-five paces, and if I found nothing, nowhere near the edge of the forest, where I was sure the starlight on the pale sand would surely show from about ten yards. I settled on a tree root, and told myself sunrise was only about seven, perhaps eight hours away. It was fortunately warm under the dense trees, and I eventually felt hungry enough to try to eat some raw liver, which I still clutched in one hand of the arm crooked round the rifle. After chewing and swallowing about five cubic inches of liver I felt it was as much as I could eat. It had a strong flavour, and I threw it above five yards away, the smell being nowhere as pleasant as grilled liver. I listened, hoping there might be some sound giving a clue to the direction of the river. Had there been a moon there might have been the call of geese, ruddy sheldrake, or duck, seeing a backwater on the peninsula, but there was nothing. Later I heard what was definitely a small owl, crying slowly up a scale, then ending with a hysterical clashing. There were two or three insects calling at long intervals, a pleasant mellow call sounding like 'up, the navy'.

It must have been after two or three hours that I came suddenly to my senses when there was a snuffle and a scurrying, then a strange choking call, only about five yards or so away. There were two small creatures, probably quarrelling over the piece or liver I had discarded. Later I found out from Gerella they were, according to my description, possibly civet cats, whose night vision was phenomenal. It suddenly occurred to me that the scent of blood would carry far in the forest, and remembering the tiger and bear tracks I had seen, I began to fear one of these carnivores might well home in, either on me with my gory hands, or on the dead sambhar, which couldn't be very far away. I decided to change my seat, and counted another forty paces on what seemed like a game track before finding another comfortable root to sit on. In sheer concern for my safety in this strange

223

environment I voided my bladder in a rough circle round the tree which was my home for the night, hoping what I had read about the way wolves, dogs, and tigers marked their territory would work for me.

It was until then one of the longest nights of my life. I dosed off several times, heard a few strange but distant calls, and began whilst I was awake to fall under the presbyterian inclination to feel guilty when misfortune began to overshadow one's life. Being lost, and blind and dumb, I began to think such things as the agony of shooting Jet, leaving his splendidly muscled body to be ravaged by vultures and jackals. At Medeloabam I had grown used to hearing jackals after dark, a sound I had heard first in Palestine, shaken at the sound of tortured souls in hell, and extremely worried until a sentry laughingly told me: 'They was jackals.' In the forest there was no sound of jackals which meant, people said, there were tigers, or leopards about. I wondered if I should sing, but the idea was ridiculous enough to make me smile, in spite of my feelings of undignified uncertainty. For that read fear, fear of the unknown. I was awake when I formed the idea that dawn was close. The calling of jungle cocks had wakened me, and my depression cleared immediately with the silvery clarion calls, and even the wingbeating of these ancestors of the British barnyard chicken; I could have cheered. Soon the sun would rise in the east, and I would be back to the river within half an hour at the most. What a lesson! What a story!

It was not long until I realised something unusual and unexpected had happened. Watching for the sky I eventually saw mist, or low cloud, in amongst the treetops, and looking at my watch reckoned I would have to wait three hours or a little more until the sun shone brightly on my world. I was thirsty, and hungry, and well in control of my patience. After returning to my camp I would have a dip and rub down, have some tea and chupattis, return to find the sambar carcass which, being a mature stag, would still be fresh and certainly be tender by the time I quartered it and got it back to the Miri village. I would size up the fallen tree, and if it was going to be too difficult I would take a haunch and walk the few miles along the forest edge to the village, where the women, and the girls with the honey-peach bare shoulders would cook a meal for us when we returned with two dugouts and plenty of venison. The mist lifted a little, but I saw there was a thick sheet of cloud, which by ten o'clock had so solidified that my weather instinct told me it was going to remain so all day. It was warm, it was light.

I thought out a plan of action. I knew, and had seen from the air two or three times on my flights, that the forest reserve was 90 per cent dead flat, and in the longest dimension was nearly twenty miles, the shortest about seven. There was hardly any wind. I made up my mind I would do what the Air Force called a 'square search', and cut blazes on three trunks, on every ten or so yards on the first three sides, two on the second, longer sides, and three on the third, still longer sides. It sounded sane, and I began with the idea of pacing thirty steps on the first three sides, sixty on the second, and so forth. The trouble was that to pace out a straight line was quite reasonable, but on the very second line I began, meant to be at right angles to the first, I ran into a brake of vicious thorny cane, with long cruel tendrils, and in avoiding it went about seventy yards off course. I had to be content with beginning a new set of squares designed to keep me clear of the thorn thickets, having faith that the nature of the enlarging squares would be bound to bring me closer to the river bank. Time passed quickly. I found small jewels of dew in the centre of large leaves, and drank a fair amount. Finding leaves browsed by deer I tried chewing the tender ones, but it was not a success. Leeches began to attach themselves to my legs, arms and neck. Large elephant flies and furry clegs became an irritating nuisance. I stopped and began swiping at those settling on my bare legs, attracted by the blood smeared by leeches I picked off, and I cursed out loud, slapping in anger and frustration. I kept telling myself what a navigation teacher in the Air Force had made us remember: 'In the Air Force, competent pilots or navigators are never lost, only temporarily unaware of their position', but it began to pall. I moved on suddenly, to be brought up in my tracks by a hoarse, rasping cough. A large wild boar stood not more than twenty feet away, huge tusks gleaming, ears aimed at me, and bristles vibrating on his back. I pushed off the safety catch and raised the rifle, less in self-defence but, I was amazed to realise, I was ready to eat raw jungle pork. In a moment he turned and started like a scrum half to stampede a sounder of goodness knows how many wild pig, far into the distance.

It was about three in the afternoon when I came to a relatively thin canopied area, where there was something like wild ginger growing, and I wondered if it was safe to eat it uncooked. I strode forward and bent to use the kukri to spade out a root, when there was a strange grunt from somewhere not far away. I straightened my back, and looked directly at a large black

Himalayan bear. Again I pushed the safety catch forward, but waited, confident I could stop him if he tried to cover the six or seven yards between us. He moved his muzzle to and fro like an old black labrador seeking a scent. I remained still, sure he could hear my heart thudding. Slowly he dropped to his forefeet, turned away, went slowly for about another ten yards and then cantered noisily off. Within an hour, when I was admitting to myself my expanding squares were a failure, my heart leapt with joy when I saw a blaze on a tree ahead: three blazes. The blazes were my own: I was lost. The cloud was still thick, and the light was dull, with no sign of the sun breaking through. I felt suddenly tired, hungry and ashamed. Finding a comfortable-looking root I sat, put the rifle beside me, and leant back, looking at the grey cloud. I heard a quiet kind of crooning, and watching the thin undergrowth in front I saw a cock kalij pheasant with three hens, feeding like chickens, and I wondered if I could kill a hen with the Mauser rifle. A 10.75cm bullet would make a mess of it, but there would be something to eat. I began to reach for the rifle, and when I began to raise it to my shoulder the pheasants exploded, leaping into the air on frenzied wings, disappearing before I could swing and aim. I wished them well, and sat disconsolately, trying to convince myself the cloud would surely clear by dawn tomorrow; but there came the memory of Foyle saying there would certainly be a brief period of rain in the cold weather. People called it the Christmas rain, but it could come any time between late November and early January, and lasted about three days. Now was late November, and I couldn't hope to steer a straight course through this great forest. There were no rivers in it, only one small one on the northern boundary, and one large one on the southern. Tomorrow I would have to eat something, and have strength enough to follow game tracks all day, come what may. I would shoot anything, just to drink its blood or chew its flesh: I would not give in. I was tempted to pray, but I remember my father telling his small sons: don't pray for anything you want for yourself, pray for others. I sat and raised my eyes to the cloud again, and across the small clear path of grey cloud I saw, bless them, small echelons of white egrets flying, gracefully and straight, on a course I knew and to be both within a hundred yards of the river, and aiming north-east. More came, and I quickly cut small saplings, and laid out a line at right angles to their course. I would do this and hold to the line if I had to hack my way through cane brakes, bamboos, creepers at a hundred yards an hour. I began laying the line, and before it became dark had moved about fifty yards. I was undaunted: tomorrow I would make it to the river. I found some tares where I decided to spend the night. There were pig rootings amongst wild ginger, and I tried munching the ginger roots. It was coarse on the tongue. The villagers and the tea estate people ate tare roots which they roasted, and I skinned one root to try it raw. I was careful only to take a small morsel, but it burned my tongue and cheek, raising blisters which frightened me. Fortunately I swallowed none of it.

I slept deeply and awoke feeling very stiff, very thirsty, and wet! It was raining gently, and was too dark to see the time. I found a place close by where I was more sheltered, and waited for dawn like a lonely human for a lover. Dawn came. Stiff and weak, I began to extend the sight line, checking and rechecking, not meeting much resistance, and soon came to a single blaze on a tree, which gave me strong hope. Within half an hour I staggered into the light of the drizzling day on the high bank of the river, and raised my rifle, my kukri, and my heart in sheer joy. What a fool I had been! I found the middle cleft, and stumbled down to walk to my camp, only about 150 yards away. As I approached the driftwood camouflage my heart leapt to see smoke, and I praised the spirits that had kept my fire burning, hurrying round to see my camp. There was a whoop, and two figures rose from the fire. Two of the Miri villagers greeted me with laughter, asking in baby Assamese where I had been, what had I done? We soon made tea, which I needed desperately, and made some chupattis which we all ate as if we had all been marooned. I told them what had happened, and said we must try to find the sambar straight away. They said perhaps other creatures would have found it, civets, jungle cats, or insects, but we would soon find out. They found their way easily to the carcass, and I was amazed how close it was to the river. They virtually repeated the old highland rule of not moving in the mist or the dark, even if the land was dead level, and laughed heartily at my first lesson in real jungle craft. Quickly they took off the antlered head for me, cut the unspoiled bulks of flesh which they said would be good to eat, and soon they had brought it all down to the boats, eager to break camp and move. The drizzle stopped. I told them I wanted to bathe in the river and change my shorts, and they said I should go ahead whilst they dismantled the tarpaulin. I had a towel, and drying myself by the fire had to let them count the number of leech bites – small dark red blots about four

227

or five millimetres wide, all over my body. They found 132 blots, like dark red tattoo marks, where blood had been sucked, and never stopped laughing, repeating the number. When I told them about the boar and the bear they nodded, saying I had done well to let them live, and would enjoy their respect in the wilderness. I asked if they didn't kill these creatures. They said only if wild boar ravaged their crops or if a bear killed one of their people, they would kill; but they would only eat the boar, not the bear, from which they would make ointments and pouches. One of them came in my dugout, and it was quite clear I had been allowed to pilot a dugout without proper training or experience. He showed me what I should have done had I been on my own, pointing at the peninsula headland, and the fast water running near the forest bank. He amazed me by steering out into the main stream, something they had warned me not to do. We steered across about 200 yards of fast water, and reached shallow water against an island on the other side, where we turned upstream to regain the distance we had lost by crossing, and carried on for about another two miles, diverging further and further from the bank, but gaining on the other dugout which had, in the hands of an expert, negotiated the obstructive tree easily, using oar and hand grips on the upstream side of the tree. Beyond the forest the current was in the middle of the main stream, and we crossed with about forty-five degrees of drift, closing with the other side about 300 yards behind the other dugout.

When we ultimately arrived, the villagers were delighted to find the venison, and wanted to give me some rice beer, but I declined, saying I had to return to Medeloabam straight away. They gave me two young Miris, with strong calf muscles, who tied four parcels of my gear with bands of creeper, and suspending them from seasoned bamboo shoulder yokes, set off with a kind of bouncing trot, the yokes acting like the leaf springs of a car. Carrying the head of the stag in one hand, and the rifle on my shoulder, I tried to keep up with them, which was difficult, as they wasted no time following beaten tracks, but wended narrowly on a straighter line where there was no mud, over the countryside to Medeloabam. The antlered head attracted dogs from various homesteads as we went, and I found it difficult to carry; but one of the village casual labourers came out and took it from me, saying he would carry it. For that welcome service I told Sitaram the cook to let him have the tongue, but noted the glum looks of the other servants, and told them to be patient. Sitaram nodded his grizzled head when he smelled the venison close to his broad nostrils, and I sent a large sirloin to Telford's bungalow, with a brief note saying it was from a sambar stag. The rest I divided amongst all the servants, with a basket of chopped pieces, amounting to about ten pounds weight, to the hospital, with a note to Dr Pal asking him to take some for his family, and have the rest cooked for patients able to eat it, emphasising it should all be cooked without delay. Maneklal and Sitaram remonstrated vigorously when it was obvious I had kept none for myself, saying a *shikari* must eat something of what he kills; but I told them, with a twinkle in my eye, that the spirit of the sky was pleased I had been eating no killed creatures, and had been so angry when I shot this stag that I was led into the darkness of the forest, lost for two days and two nights as a punishment. I saw their remonstrative expressions change, and they nodded with what showed like sympathy, making me feel mean for having told them such a story; but later that night, well blanketed in bed, there was a persistent return of the mood when, lost in the forests of the night I had been as depressed and superstitious as a prehistoric hunter, whose thoughts were in pictures and images, and imagined occult powers, with no language yet created to compete with the instinct of survival.

Next morning when I returned from a most enjoyable ride on Rani, who was proving to be a lively and well-disposed horse, Telford met me at the stable and thanked me for the venison. He asked me to tell him how the trip went, and I said, looking at my watch, it would take time. He smiled, almost as if he knew all that had happened, and said I should join him for breakfast, over which he could tell me of plans to fly to the North Bank, and I could recount my experiences of the weekend. At the office I was called to Telford's room, where two families and the welfare officer stood on the verandah, all looking distressed. Telford kept me standing at the end of his desk, and told me in his quiet drawl these two families had been given work during the rains at my insistence. Bhose babu had said he made it clear these people had been sacked two years ago for brewing and selling rice beer, something which was forbidden by law, and forbidden on Medeloabam, where nothing was said if people made rice beer for their own family consumption and gave no trouble from disorderly behaviour. I said it was true I was told they had been sacked, but I did not remember hearing what they had been sacked for. At this point Bhose babu put his hands together and came forward to say I was correct, he did not tell me why they were sacked because I had been shocked that the people were so thin and badly clothed, and having learned a lesson they would surely behave in future. Telford read from the well-thumbed recorded book in which notes were kept on all that happened at morning office: 'Because of late planting of the rice this year, many of the casual workers are not available for work on the estate. In view of this shortage we shall give the families of Manjit and Jivrai temporary work as pluckers and weeders on promise of good behaviour.' He looked at me, with a patient type of smile, and said it was the only mistake he had found in the register of any importance, but the lesson to be learned was vital: we all learn to be compassionate when we are young, because children soon develop a vested interest in compassion, learning how to recognise and exploit it in their parents, their teachers. Remembering the appearance of destitution and malnutrition, the latter confirmed by Dr Pal, to whom I sent them, I found my blood rising fast, and instinctively tried to suppress my emotions. He saw this with his panther eyes, and nodded, turning to the welfare babu. He asked him why he had allowed both families to occupy one vacant estate house in the Old Line, and had failed to terminate their employment when casual pluckers were no longer necessary, and all other casual labour had been paid off two weeks before. Bhose became grey, and protested it was forgetfulness, for which he was most sorry. Telford called the two family heads forward, and to my distaste asked them if they were paying rent for their quarters and their employment. Both men remained silent and with eyes slightly widened, looking at the welfare babu, who waved both hands at them saying shrilly they should answer the *burra sahib*. 'Don't tell any lies! Tell the truth! Are you paying money to someone? Tell the sahib!' He was sweating and his hands quivered slightly. The men showed their palms upturned, and with sickly smiles mumbled they paid for their rations, bought food and clothes, and didn't have anything left for anybody. Bhose waved a frenzied finger at them and shouted at them saying they were '*badmashes*' (rascals or rogues) for whom, the *chota sahib* had shown mercy, and now look at the trouble they were causing. Telford interrupted him, telling him to wait. He looked at him with tilted head, staring as if to penetrate his mind. After several seconds he told him to take these people away, pay them off, see that they vacate the house, and warn them never to appear on Medeloabam again.

When they had all gone he asked me to sit down, and said one had to learn to detect who spoke the truth by setting up such traps. He said the men would never tell the truth, but he was sure there was a strong scent of corruption. Bhose babu was as good a man as one would ever find for the job he was doing; but there was little doubt about what he had been up to, knowing the history of those men. I asked what would happen to him, and Telford explained how with the coming of Independence we would have to be very careful never to sack a man without following the legal procedures which would ensure a manager would never lose a case. 'These men would never talk, and their refusal to talk would be a good investment for them, by which they could reverse the progress and milk Bhose for a long time. Bhose knows I know he extorted money from these people, and he knows I am prepared to let this carry on so long as I don't catch him in the act, backed by witnesses.' He said I had to learn two things: to beware of destitute, ill-fed people, because in this part of the world people have to look after themselves, unless they are caught up with working for tea estates or mines, or all the drudgery of towns. Anyone who can't grow his own food and look after his own family is not worth having; nature lays down the law of the survival of the fittest. That is why animals, birds, ants and so on, mostly have stable populations: only those for whom the natural resources are sufficient will survive. That's why human beings keep on killing each other in bigger and bigger wars as time goes on. He said even when he joined tea twenty years before, India's population was a hundred million less than now. The British stopped them from fighting each other, put in huge irrigation projects in the Punjab, started sugar, coffee and tea plantations, taught modern medicine, and now we were going to conquer malaria. He said that it must sound dreadful to me, and to most people living in relative comfort in the West, when he warned that interference with the natural balance in places like India and China would ultimately lead to terrible disasters and suffering, with more and more violent power and corruption, growing as fast as or faster than what people call improvements. He looked at his watch and said we should go and have breakfast.

As we walked past the stables he was telling me our system of justice in tea was derived from the wise systems of ancient history, improved only by the prevention of corruption. He explained how the coming of the bureaucratic system of law, beginning with the Mughals and modified by the British, was one of the dreadful shackles of India. Litigation was so rife, so profligate and impoverishing. He said the law was believed by most Indians to be a system of circumventing natural justice; if one had enough money one's lawyer could put a case before the court which would turn the law in one's favour, whatever the facts of natural justice. He said it was rather the same in too many cases in Britain. The judiciary in India was much admired, and one prayed for it to be able to remain incorruptible and independent, but even the judges could not control what happened in the corrupt process of preparing cases, beginning with the extortions of lawyers; the recommended bribery of the clerks of court for acceleration of production of papers in the long list of cases awaiting a hearing; the induced bending of junior police evidence; the production of good capons for fair round bellies etc. The law fertilised a contempt for justice, and that, he said more than once, was why he would always have to be ready to give our own people justice in a way that could never land anyone in a legal duel which would impoverish him; and that would take me a lot of time to learn.

We sat at the breakfast table which was set on the lawn, with sunshine enough to warm us. We had pomelo, like a giant grapefruit, pink and pleasantly brisk in flavour. This was followed by small bananas, and cream from the Telfords' herd. I found I was very hungry, and when the next course was brought, being two fried eggs with several rashers of New Zealand bacon, I swallowed my saliva and wiped my lips whilst duelling with my earnest intention to remain vegetarian. Telford, applying salt to the deep orange yolks of the eggs, said casually he had heard the servants discussing my humble diet, some saying it was because I was paying off huge debts, having borrowed money to buy the *pagla* (mad) horse which I had to kill. I said it was really the debt, and he told me to enjoy my breakfast and spare my host embarrassment, immediately changing the subject to my trip to the forest reserve. I told him the story fairly briefly but sparing no facts. He watched me closely. At the end of it he said in case I had any ideas of fasting for religious reasons, it was not a bad idea. He said Indians believed, provided one eschewed onions and garlic, a vegetarian diet helped one to cope with the problem of controlling too strong a sexual desire. It was not a bad idea for a young bachelor like me, who would have to wait three or more years before he could marry. Placing his knife and fork together on his cleaned plate he stared straight at me and said 'Rupni, Kumari, Belmoti, Jaoni, Belamdina, Pingli, Reshmi, and a few others. Everyone has noticed your glances of poorly hidden admiration. They are very attractive young ladies, and perhaps your vegetarian diet would help to prevent what could end up by being indiscreet refusal to follow the advice of your senior manager, which is: remain celibate until you marry. Never risk indulging in an affair which you believe can be kept secret on the estate. Out here even the little lizards on the wall, the snakes in the garden, they all listen and tell tales.' He smiled like a poker player showing winning cards. 'If it comes out you will want to disappear to escape the squalid embarrassment and financial discomfort you have invited. You need a lot of moral fibre, but I have an idea you have plenty of that.'

I think I blushed, partly from the truth of what he said, but also from anger that my natural and innocent (so far) attraction to feminine beauty had become the widespread subject of comment throughout Medeloabam. It was true I had somehow evolved a frequent circuit on horseback in the evenings which included passing three wells where these particular young ladies seemed regularly to be completing their second bathe at whatever time I happened to pass, some along with several other ladies, one on her own. Horseback was the way to approach closely such otherwise shy creatures as pheasants, jungle fowl, civets and jungle cats without them suspecting danger. So it was that even in remote villages where young women were near where I rode, there was always happy laughter for me, and bubbling conversation, but never anywhere on the estate when I was on foot. 'I think Foyle must have educated you well as to the attitudes of Indians in general to the strong currents of sexual attraction in this climate and way of life. He has earned the reputation of being quite an authority on that sort of thing; but that's his business. We Christians have all been born into a rigid society where moral forces have been controlled so strictly that you and I take it simply as the permanent way of life. These people in the vast country life that has been going on for centuries, even before the Mughals invaded, have a down-to-earth system of morals, but there is no pretence of trust being able to deal with the raw forces of nature in this fertile environment. As far as you are concerned you need to be selfish, to protect yourself from false steps that nature tries to make you take. All nature wants is to have males and females unite to produce young. All I want is to avoid the damned nuisance of having to straighten out sordid labour trouble, and having an assistant posted elsewhere to lick his wounds.'

Changing the subject with his now typical suddenness, he said he was astonished I had not taken a compass with me on my trip, and could not understand why I had entered the reserve without one. He said I was very lucky to have come out alive, because many people disappeared in that reserve, mostly local hunters who went alone. I refrained from claiming I had bad luck with the sudden advent of cloud, and had at least followed a sensible plan, made intelligent observations. His critical scepticism did not encourage debate. Finally he said Fraser had discussed a letter from Calcutta which said: with a view to examining the possibilities of clearing airstrips on the more remote estates in the companies of Assam Lothian group, it was required that MacStorm should visit first of all the North Bank estates, and thereafter those estates on the South Bank which were more than two hours drive, or had more than one monsoon-susceptible bridge on roads to the nearest hospital. There was no need to have strips for people within easy reach of the Dikom or Dinjan wartime airfields. He said clearly that morning he had written some notes which the head clerk was typing confidentially, which he would discuss with me at his bungalow in the afternoon at three. I must have beamed when I heard this, and said I looked forward to be there, with the maps.

When we settled at three at a table in the sun, Telford handed me three foolscap pages, typed on both sides, with two sketch maps showing locations of estates: seven on the North Bank, and I think eighteen on the South Bank. I was surprised to see the numbers, and the wide spread of estates, especially on the South Bank. I read the sheets of typescript, and was amazed at the detail on so many points. I thought the brief from Calcutta had been fairly simple, and that I had first to visit all the appropriate places first, then make recommendations as required. Telford seemed to have written a conclusive report, either in anticipation of what I would find, or to instruct me in the business of planning the various airfields. He had laid down minima for lengths and breadths, and positions of windsocks, landing tees and parking areas, and I said he had got most of these basically right, intending to compliment him, but he said with an air scheme in view he had taken time to consult experts in England, to make sure there were no mistakes. I looked at him for some kind of smile or expression to give me a clue to how

I should respond, but he was showing only a kind of fierce concentration, and began to read from another sheet a programme of visits which he would make with me, by jeep on the South Bank, and by air to the North Bank. He told me he had been on the North Bank as an assistant at Mirijuli estate, and knew all the other estates well. He said he had heard me speak of landing the Piper Cub at Bogahilonia, and we would fly there tomorrow as soon as the mist lifted, and make contact with the manager, a huge Cumbrian called Jonson, and try to establish contact with the other estates by car or bicycle, for us to visit each or them later in the week, staying perhaps one night at Mirijuli, and one night at Bogahilonia. He told me it would take over a week if we were to drive to Tezpur and cross by the vehicle ferry, and travel the 150 and more miles back eastwards to the estates we wanted to visit. There were three or four other rivers which might not have had their cold weather bridges made from timber and bamboo, in which case we would have to be taken across each one by man-powered ferry: a tiresome business with much delay and uncertainty, depending on the number of vehicles waiting to cross. It showed how poor communications were over there, and gave weight to the idea of using an aircraft. That cooled my professional resentment quite a bit, as I had to acknowledge Telford was more motivated by experience than I was in theory. Tea was brought, and Telford said he was becoming concerned at having no news of the whereabouts of his wife and family. They were due to arrive within seven days, but there had been neither letter nor telegram to confirm which train they would be on.

I asked if he had a copy of the pilots' notes for the Auster I might borrow, and without a word he went into the bungalow, returning with the small book which he gave to me saying he wondered why I had not asked for it before. At that moment the head bearer appeared, saying the estate postman (*dakwalla*) had arrived with the mail. He said there was a telegram, and handed it to Telford.

'Look at the bloody date!' he rasped. 'Five days ago! They're arriving tomorrow at two-thirty in the morning.'

He became involved with the head bearer, who exhibited much concern, and carried on an anxious conference for so long that I rose and suggested I should retire; but Telford said I must wait, as we would have to change plans.

'Be ready to fly tomorrow. Fill up with petrol, through the chamois leather, straight away. I'll send you a letter for Jonson. I'll ask Fraser to send letters to all managers explaining you will be coming, and what for. It'll be good for you to see them all. A very mixed bunch. You won't be welcome everywhere; probably be put with assistants for the night. Not a bad idea for you to go alone. Keep reporting to me as often as you can.' I thanked him and descended to the lawn, my thoughts dancing around in unfamiliar areas. 'Oh, MacStorm!' he called me as I was striding over the lawn, 'do you mind if we use Rani if all three ladies want to ride out together? They probably won't, my wife will be very busy.' I said since it seemed I would be busy too I would be happy for Rani to have the exercise. Telford raised the papers in his hand and said, 'I'll be there to swing the prop for you about nine-thirty tomorrow. We must train someone reliable to do this sort of thing, you know.' I waved and carried on. The thought of visiting the North Bank filled me with a fierce keenness. I would be able to spend the night with MacDonald, and talk about flying again. That night I wrote to Bobby Constable explaining what was about to happen, excusing my non-availability for flying practice. Since Telford had returned Bobby had definitely been less communicative. I was happy to be flying to the North Bank by myself as recommended by the board in London. It would be good to meet Steve MacDonald, and to congratulate ourselves that we had been successful in recommending a company air service for the North Bank which would save lives, and make life easier for wives of our generation – once we found them. But we hoped there would not be too many intruders who would ruin the quiet wilderness. Steve and I met and talked well into the night about how fate had struck down what we had thought was a Damfool Career. We now had a future here, and were raring to continue with what promised to be a real and absorbing vocation. We lay in the sun after an invigorating swim in the Subansiri, where snow water had swirled amongst the warmer currents of the foothill streams, and we gazed at the splendid forested islands which hid the mountainous gorge to our north. We thought they should be called 'the Sentinel Isles of Subansiri', where the only tracks beyond were those of wild animals.